CASES, READINGS, AND REVIEW GUIDE FOR PRINCIPLES OF MANAGEMENT

Cases, Readings, and Review Guide for Principles of Management

FRED LUTHANS

University of Nebraska
Lincoln, Nebraska

JOHN WILEY & SONS, INC.

NEW YORK · LONDON · SYDNEY · TORONTO

10   9   8   7   6   5   4   3   2   1

Library of Congress Catalog Card Number: 69-19929
SBN 471 55658 0
Printed in the United States of America

Preface

THE PURPOSE OF this book of concepts, cases, readings, and self-tests is to serve as a study aid and supplement for the beginning student in management. The book is designed to correlate with Henry H. Albers' *Principles of Management: A Modern Approach,* Third Edition. It could also be effectively adapted to any of the other leading management textbooks.

The field of management has become increasingly broad and complex. The beginning student is often overwhelmed by the lecture-textbook material that he is expected to comprehend. Thus, there seemed to be a definite need for an accompanying book that would serve the student in two ways:

1. As a *study aid*—a chapter-by-chapter study guide, with a brief summary, a listing of major concepts, and a self-test—leading to better understanding of the textbook material.

2. As a *supplement*—illustrative, real-world cases, outside journal articles by leading management authorities, and management simulation games—making the lecture-textbook material more meaningful for the student. Case analysis, questions on readings, and playing a very simple or a complex management game would help the student relate back to the more theoretical, abstract lectures and textbook.

Cases, Readings, and Review Guide for Principles of Management fulfills the study aid and supplemental needs of the management student. The book is unique in that it takes an eclectic approach. The casebook, the readings book, and the workbook approaches are all incorporated into this relatively short volume. It bridges the gap between the workbook concept and the readings and/or casebook concept.

Each chapter begins with a brief summary, which is followed by three sections. Section I lists the major management concepts relevant to that chapter. Section II is a self-test consisting of five true-false, ten multiple-choice, and three essay-discussion questions. The major emphasis is given to Section III, which has three to five short, illustrative cases, followed by suggested questions for analysis. These eighty-five cases were developed from actual situations that I thought would be very interesting and stimulating to the beginning management student. A sampling of case titles—"Napalm Manufacturer," "Marry the Company," "Swiss-Cheese Bats and Peekers," and "The Flying Edsel"—indicates the nature of these cases. They will provoke much class discussion and illustrate key concepts from the lectures and text material.

Each major part of the book contains outside readings, followed by essay-discussion questions. The seven journal articles were selected for two reasons. First, the selections are significant papers written by authors well known in the management field. Second, the articles give a good overview of the textbook chapters that they cover. In addition to the reprinted journal articles, the last part of the book on executive development contains two unique articles written specially for this book. The first article is an elementary explanation of management gaming, which includes a practical exercise for the student. This hand-scored management game is very simple to play and was designed to minimize the time and effort required to play. The second article deals with computerized management gaming. A more advanced computer game is included. If time and facilities are available, these games should prove very fruitful. Instructions for either the noncomputer or computer game are available upon request. It is hoped that the instructor will be able to utilize the games, but if they are not actually played, the student will nevertheless benefit from a reading of the two articles.

The preparation of this book required the cooperation of many people. I owe a debt of gratitude to Dr. Henry H. Albers, Chairman of the Department of Management at the University of Nebraska. Although I take full responsibility for any defects this book may have, much of the positive credit belongs to Dr. Albers. It was under his intellectual guidance and moral encouragement, first in a student-teacher relationship and now as a colleague, that this book was made possible. He also directly contributed many of the summaries, some questions, and seven cases. Special thanks go to Dr. Richard M. Hodgetts of the University of Nebraska and Lester A. Digman of the University of Iowa for their management games. I would also like to recognize and thank the scholars whose contributions are reprinted and the publishers who granted their permissions. Specific acknowledgment of authors and publishers is noted at the beginning of each article, and each case reference is footnoted. My thanks go to Dr. Charles S. Miller, Dean of the College of Business Administration, University of Nebraska, for his encouragement and support. Finally, I thank my typist, Phyllis Verzola, and my wife, Kay, for her expert editing assistance and continual understanding and support.

Fred Luthans

Lincoln, Nebraska
January 1969

A Guide for the Student

IN TODAY'S INDUSTRIALIZED, organized world, management is becoming increasingly important. Moreover, its body of knowledge is expanding at a very rapid rate and becoming more and more complex. This book is designed to help you better understand this important, growing, and complex field of study.

To ensure your optimum utilization of the book, I have the following comments and suggestions.

Summaries, Major Concepts, and Self-Tests. These sections of each chapter are to help you better understand your textbook material. You can use them in combination with your text in several ways. I suggest that you first make a quick overall survey of the textbook chapter. Next, carefully read the summary and major concepts found in this book. Then return to the textbook and read the chapter very carefully. Finally, reread the chapter summary and make sure you completely understand the major concepts. You should now be ready to take the self-test. All the questions are taken from your textbook. If you are not sure of an answer, go back to the text and find it. Your instructor will give you the correct answers. If you follow this suggested approach, you should obtain the maximum degree of comprehension with a minimum amount of time and effort.

Illustrative Cases. These short cases have a twofold purpose: first, they should stimulate your interest in class discussion, and second, they illustrate some of the key concepts under consideration. I suggest that you take time to carefully read, and often reread, each case. There are many subtleties and between-the-lines implications in these cases. How you will specifically use the cases depends on your instructor. The analysis questions found at the end of each case do not generally have a right or wrong answer. Some questions relate only to the case under discussion, but most often the questions should be interpreted in light of relevant managerial concepts found in your book or presented in lecture. Hopefully, many other questions besides those suggested will be brought out during your readings and/or discussion. I have made a determined effort to select cases or incidents that I thought would be relevant and stimulating to your interests. I hope you respond by speaking up if your instructor chooses to discuss a case in class. Moreover, I think you will enjoy reading these cases, and they should make the theories presented in your lectures and textbook reading more realistic.

Outside Readings. The purpose of the journal articles at the end of each major part of the book is to give you some degree of depth in management. The authors are generally recognized experts on the subject matter the article covers. These articles occasionally give you a somewhat different, but usually comprehensive, viewpoint. How the questions at the end of each article are utilized will depend on your instructor. The first three essay-discussion questions relate directly to the article under consideration. The last question is a more general one, requiring an answer that incorporates your lectures, textbook, and previous readings. In Part VII on executive development you have the opportunity to play a management game. If you do, read the instructions carefully and enter the game with an enthusiastic attitude. As with the rest of this book, you only get out of the game what you put into it.

Once again, let me remind you that this is *your* book, designed to *help you* better understand the important, growing, and complex field of management.   F. L.

Contents

PART I: THE MANAGEMENT PROBLEM: PAST AND PRESENT   1

1   PRELIMINARY PERSPECTIVES   3

    Section 1   MAJOR CONCEPTS   3
          2   SELF-TEST   3
          3   ILLUSTRATIVE CASES   5
            Of the Division of Labour   5
            Bicycle Regulations   6
            A Thinking Sputnik?   6
            "Lament for a Mongrel"   6
            DaVinci versus the Computer   7

2   TOWARD SCIENTIFIC MANAGEMENT   8

    Section 1   MAJOR CONCEPTS   8
          2   SELF-TEST   8
          3   ILLUSTRATIVE CASES   10
            Scientific Management in Manufacturing Typewriter   10
            Field System   10
            The Mislaid Check   11

3   THE EMERGING PATTERN   13

    Section 1   MAJOR CONCEPTS   13
          2   SELF-TEST   13
          3   ILLUSTRATIVE CASES   15
            "Fat Cats"   15
            C.L.U.   15
            "Fringe Benefits"   16

4   ORGANIZATIONAL SYSTEMS: THE DECISIONAL AND
INFORMATIONAL PROCESS   17

    Section 1   MAJOR CONCEPTS   17
          2   SELF-TEST   18
          3   ILLUSTRATIVE CASES   19
            Jumping Off the Bandwagon   19
            The Edsel Story   19
            A Typewriter Decision   20
            What's the Verdict?   21

Reading: THE MANAGEMENT THEORY JUNGLE
by Harold Koontz   22

PART II: ORGANIZATION FOR MANAGEMENT   35

5 THE ORGANIZATIONAL STRUCTURE   37

   Section 1 MAJOR CONCEPTS   37
           2 SELF-TEST   37
           3 ILLUSTRATIVE CASES   39
              Not Squares   39
              Organizational Breakdown   39
              All Work and No Play   40

6 DEPARTMENTATION   41

   Section 1 MAJOR CONCEPTS   41
           2 SELF-TEST   41
           3 ILLUSTRATIVE CASES   43
              Geographic versus Product   43
              International Product Departmentation   43
              Microwaves Plus Jets   44

7 LINE-STAFF-FUNCTIONAL RELATIONSHIPS   45

   Section 1 MAJOR CONCEPTS   45
           2 SELF-TEST   45
           3 ILLUSTRATIVE CASES   47
              Staff Power   47
              "Me"   47
              Global Staff   48

8 CENTRALIZATION AND DECENTRALIZATION   49

   Section 1 MAJOR CONCEPTS   49
           2 SELF-TEST   49
           3 ILLUSTRATIVE CASES   51
              Conglomerate   51
              Central Control of Faculty Promotions   51
              Decentralization: Philosophy of GE Chairman of the Board 52

9 COMMITTEE ORGANIZATION   53

   Section 1 MAJOR CONCEPTS   53
           2 SELF-TEST   53
           3 ILLUSTRATIVE CASES   55
              "Quadrumvirate"   55
              Organization for Standards   55
              Mathematical Formulation of Committees   55

10 BOARD OF DIRECTORS AND OTHER COMMITTEES   57

   Section 1 MAJOR CONCEPTS   57
           2 SELF-TEST   57
           3 ILLUSTRATIVE CASES   59
              President's Views of the Board   59
              Task Force   59
              "A" Committee   60

Reading: ORGANIZATION THEORY: AN OVERVIEW AND
AN APPRAISAL *by William G. Scott*   61

**PART III: MANAGERIAL ORGANIZATION: BEHAVIORAL
ASPECT**   77

11 AUTHORITY, STATUS, AND POWER   79

Section 1 Major Concepts   79
        2 Self-Test   79
        3 Illustrative Cases   81
           Starting Them Young   81
           Down with Executive Washroom Keys   81
           "Corporate Symbology"   81

12 ORGANIZATIONAL DYNAMICS   82

Section 1 Major Concepts   82
        2 Self-Test   82
        3 Illustrative Cases   84
           Tailor-Made Organization   84
           "A Behavioral Science Laboratory"   84
           "Clean House"   85

13 FROM ORGANIZATION TO PROCESS   86

Section 1 Major Concepts   86
        2 Self-Test   86
        3 Illustrative Cases   88
           Supplementary Channels   88
           "Smoke in the Filament"   88
           Delegation, Facts, and Common Sense   89

Reading: CHANGING ORGANIZATIONS *by Warren G. Bennis*   90

PART IV: DECISION-MAKING: PLANNING STRATEGIES   97

14 SURVEYING THE ENVIRONMENT   99

Section 1 Major Concepts   99
        2 Self-Test   99
        3 Illustrative Cases   101
           Everybody Talks about It   101
           "QE2"   101
           "Swiss-Cheese Bats and Peekers"   102

15 THE DEVELOPMENT OF PLANNING STRATEGIES   103

Section 1 Major Concepts   103
        2 Self-Test   103
        3 Illustrative Cases   105
           "Progress: The Most Important Product"   105
           The House Craps Out   105
           Hasn't Made a Nickel   105
           Modern Champagne   106

16 DYNAMIC PLANNING I   107

    Section 1 MAJOR CONCEPTS   107
            2 SELF-TEST   107
            3 ILLUSTRATIVE CASES   109
               Dynamic Hardware   109
               "The Flying Edsel"?   109
               Instant Creativity   109

17 DYNAMIC PLANNING II   111

    Section 1 MAJOR CONCEPTS   111
            2 SELF-TEST   111
            3 ILLUSTRATIVE CASES   113
               Don't Call on Me, I'll Call on You   113
               "The Great Debate"   113
               A Piggyback Ride   113

Reading: SHAPING THE MASTER STRATEGY OF YOUR FIRM
            by William H. Newman   115

PART V: COMMUNICATION AND CONTROL   129

18 INFORMATION AND COMMUNICATION   131

    Section 1 MAJOR CONCEPTS   131
            2 SELF-TEST   131
            3 ILLUSTRATIVE CASES   133
               "Stalag 18"   133
               "Semantic Walls"   133
               History is Bunk   133

19 COMMUNICATION MEDIA: MESSAGE CONSTRUCTION
    AND RECEPTION   135

    Section 1 MAJOR CONCEPTS   135
            2 SELF-TEST   135
            3 ILLUSTRATIVE CASES   137
               "An Avalanche"   137
               Executive Vocabulary   137
               "Read Your Way Out of a Paper Bag"   137

20 SPECIALIZED INFORMATIONAL SYSTEMS   139

    Section 1 MAJOR CONCEPTS   139
            2 SELF-TEST   139
            3 ILLUSTRATIVE CASES   141
               Accountancy of Oil Drilling   141
               In the "Red," But Doing Well   141
               Real "FIFO"   142

21 COMPUTERIZED INFORMATIONAL SYSTEMS   143

    Section 1 MAJOR CONCEPTS   143
            2 SELF-TEST   143

3   ILLUSTRATIVE CASES   145
     Computer Hysteria   145
     Automated Hamburgers   145
     Talking Computer   145
     Computerized Football   146

Readings: COMMUNICATION IN ORGANIZATIONS:
           SOME PROBLEMS AND MISCONCEPTIONS
           by William H. Read   147

           AN APPROACH TO COMPUTER-BASED
           MANAGEMENT CONTROL SYSTEMS
           by D. G. Malcolm and A. J. Rowe   152

PART VI: LEADERSHIP AND MOTIVATION   163

22   THE PROBLEM OF MOTIVATION   165

     Section 1   MAJOR CONCEPTS   165
             2   SELF-TEST   165
             3   ILLUSTRATIVE CASES   167
                 "Poor Richard's" Incentives   167
                 "Playboy of the Year"   167
                 Young Mavericks   167

23   DYNAMIC LEADERSHIP   169

     Section 1   MAJOR CONCEPTS   169
             2   SELF-TEST   169
             3   ILLUSTRATIVE CASES   171
                 A Happy Birthday   171
                 The Death Penalty   171
                 Long-Distance Participation   171

24   THE RESPONSIBILITY OF MANAGEMENT   173

     Section 1   MAJOR CONCEPTS   173
             2   SELF-TEST   173
             3   ILLUSTRATIVE CASES   175
                 It Beats a Box Lunch   175
                 Discriminatory Aptitude Tests   175
                 "A Fair Day's Wage for a Fair Day's Work"   176
                 Napalm Manufacturer   176

Reading: THE ANATOMY OF LEADERSHIP by Eugene E. Jennings   177

PART VII: EXECUTIVE DEVELOPMENT   189

25   EXECUTIVE QUALITIES AND EXECUTIVE EDUCATION   191

     Section 1   MAJOR CONCEPTS   191
             2   SELF-TEST   191
             3   ILLUSTRATIVE CASES   193
                 "Marry the Company"   193
                 The Generation Gap   193
                 "The M.B.A."   194

26 COMPANY EXECUTIVE DEVELOPMENT PROGRAMS   195
    Section 1 MAJOR CONCEPTS   195
            2 SELF-TEST   195
            3 ILLUSTRATIVE CASES   197
               Recruiting "Bonus-Babies"   197
               "Insult Training"   197
               "Charm School"   197
               "Seminarmania"   198

Readings: MANAGEMENT GAMING: A PRACTICAL EXERCISE
        by Richard M. Hodgetts   199

        COMPUTERIZED MANAGEMENT GAMING
        by Lester A. Digman   203

CASES, READINGS, AND REVIEW GUIDE FOR
PRINCIPLES OF MANAGEMENT

PART I

THE MANAGEMENT PROBLEM: PAST AND PRESENT

Chapter One

Preliminary Perspectives

THIS CHAPTER PROVIDES various points of departure for the study of organization and management principles. Initial attention is given to the part played by organizations in modern society. The advantages that can be derived from formal and informal cooperation are then discussed. Consideration is given to the relationship between cooperation and technology and the problem of balancing the requirements of technology and the human side of industry. The fact that management is as old as human society is illustrated by a number of examples from early and more recent history. The manner in which the development of the factory system, the rise of the managerial class, the organization of trade unions, and the philosophy of laissez faire relate to modern management is emphasized. The last section of the chapter deals with the second industrial revolution. The development of electronic computers is traced, and their ability to think is analyzed.

Section I MAJOR CONCEPTS

Organizational society
Cooperation
Industrial revolution
Factory system
Managerial revolution

Unionism
Government regulation
Second industrial revolution
Thinking machines

Section II SELF-TEST

True-False

_____ 1. The "ideal of competition" has become an important basis for government intervention in the affairs of the businessman.

_____ 2. The modern business corporations, unlike the quilting bee of early America, do not have informal social interaction.

_____ 3. Wide dispersion of stock ownership contributes to managerial control of corporations.

_____ 4. The basic theories on which modern computers are based were developed after World War II.

_____ 5. The flush box of a toilet could be said to have a logical ability.

Multiple Choice

_____ 1. In collective bargaining, contract negotiations usually result in important decisions about
   a. production standards
   b. plant layout
   c. conditions of employment
   d. a, b, and c

_____ 2. Which of the following is a distinguishing characteristic of the factory system?
   a. Production performed in the home
   b. Production controlled by the worker
   c. Merchant furnishes the raw materials
   d. Workers concentrated under one roof

_____ 3. Which of the following was the *first* to utilize the line production concept?
   a. Henry Ford
   b. Boulton and Watt Company
   c. Arsenal of Venice
   d. The American quilting bee

_____ 4. What is true of the quilting bee of early America?
   a. It is an example of informal cooperation being a cause of social living.
   b. It is an example of informal cooperation being an effect of social living.
   c. Both a and b
   d. Neither a nor b

_____ 5. Which of the following is *not* true?
   a. The Clayton Act prohibits interlocking directorates.
   b. The Sherman Act was designed to promote trusts.

   c. The Wagner Act gives the right to collectively bargain a contract if a majority of the employees so desire.
   d. The Fair Labor Standards Act set a minimum wage.

_____ 6. Which of the following best defines the origin of organization?
   a. Product specialization
   b. The division of labor
   c. Standardization of methods
   d. Scientific management

_____ 7. Which of the following statements is in accord with historical fact?
   a. The systematic study of management principles is as old as human history.
   b. Many management principles were practiced long before systematic study was begun.
   c. The practice of successful management and the development of a field of management represent the same phenomena.
   d. There are no good examples of effective management before the industrial revolution.

_____ 8. Which of the following differentiates formal organization from informal modes of cooperation?
   a. There exists an informal social system.
   b. The will to cooperate is not necessary in informal modes of cooperation.
   c. Human behavior is far less important in formal organizations than in informal modes of cooperation.
   d. Formal organizations are consciously directed and designed for the achievement of predetermined objectives.

_____ 9. What is the best statement concerning the "second industrial revolution"?
   a. It will have the largest impact on blue-collar workers.
   b. Machines will replace man as a source of power.

    c. Electronic computers will play a minor role.

    d. Machines may be used to perform mental operations.

_____ 10. Which of the following elements of computer functioning is most closely related to the idea of "thinking machines"?

    a. Magnetic tape

    b. Printing speeds

    c. Logical capacities

    d. Arithmetical capacities

Essay-Discussion

1. What is some evidence that the United States has become an organizational society?

2. What is the relationship between cooperation and technology?

3. Analyze and discuss the idea that a computer can think.

Section III   ILLUSTRATIVE CASES

OF THE DIVISION OF LABOUR[1]

The greatest improvement in the productive powers of labour, and the greater part of the skill, dexterity, and judgment with which it is anywhere directed, or applied, seem to have been the effects of the division of labour. . . . To take an example from a very trifling manufacture, but one in which the division of labour has been very often taken notice of, the trade of the pin-maker; a workman not educated to this business (which the division of labour has rendered a distinct trade), nor acquainted with the use of the machinery employed in it (to the invention of which the same division of labour has probably given occasion), could scarce, perhaps, with his utmost industry, make one pin a day, and certainly could not make twenty. But in the way in which this business is now carried on, not only the whole work is a peculiar trade, but it is divided into a number of branches, of which the greater part are likewise peculiar trades. One man draws out the wire, another straights it, a third cuts it, a fourth points it, a fifth grinds it at the top for receiving the head; to make the head requires two or three distinct operations: to put it on, is a peculiar business, to whiten the pins is another; it is even a trade by itself to put them into the paper; and the important business of making a pin is, in this manner, divided into about eighteen distinct operations, which in some manufactories, are all performed by distinct hands, though in others the same man will sometimes perform two or three of them. I have seen a small manufactory of this kind where ten men only were employed, and where some of them consequently performed two or three distinct operations. But though they were very poor, and therefore but indifferently accommodated with the necessary machinery, they could, when they exerted themselves, make among them about twelve pounds of pins in a day. There are in a pound upwards of four thousand pins of a middling size. Those ten persons, therefore, could make among them upwards of forty-eight thousand pins in a day. Each person, therefore, making a tenth part of forty-eight thousand pins, might be considered as making four thousand eight hundred pins in a day. But if they had all wrought separately and independently, and without any of them having been educated to this peculiar business, they certainly could not each of them have made twenty, perhaps not one pin a day; that is, certainly, not the two hundred and fortieth, perhaps not the four thousand eight hundredth part of what they are at present capable of performing, in consequence of a proper division and combination of their different operations.

Analysis

1. Adam Smith wrote this in 1776. Does his reasoning apply to the modern manufacturing organization? How?

---

[1] From *The Wealth of Nations*, by Adam Smith, 1776.

2. Are there any problems associated with high degrees of specialization? What?

3. Has Adam Smith had any other impact on modern business organizations?

BICYCLE REGULATIONS[1]

A major bicycle company thought that it had the right to restrict independent wholesalers' and distributors' selling activities for bicycles purchased from them. The Supreme Court ruled 5 to 2 against the bicycle company. The Court did provide for "reasonable" restrictions on dealers who received the company's bicycles on consignment.

The two dissenting Justices argued that the bicycle manufacturer had the right to restrict the selling activities of bicycles sold, as well as consigned, to the "middleman." They stated: "Centuries ago, it could perhaps be assumed that a manufacturer had no legitimate interest in what happened to his products, once he had sold them to a middleman. . . . But this assumption no longer holds true in a day of sophisticated marketing policies, mass advertising and vertically integrated manufacturers' distributors."[2]

Analysis

1. Do you agree with the majority or the dissenting opinion? Why?

2. Who is restricting or promoting competition? The bicycle company? The Court? The middleman?

A THINKING SPUTNIK?[1]

Dr. Nicholai M. Amosov, a Russian engineer and medical surgeon, recently reported at the annual meeting of the American Society for

Cybernetics that artificial intelligence can be created. The Russians have built a model of purposive behavior. Dr. Amosov does not claim that his system has complete similarity with the brain, but it can be carried out in models which he defined at the cybernetics meeting.

The key to the Russian's model is the concept of SRI, which is a system of reinforcement and inhibition. The function of SRI is to select and reinforce only one model (circuit) at any given moment—the most active one. All the other models automatically become inhibited. After a time, the connection with the model becomes "tired," and reinforcement turns to the next model having the highest activity. This functioning of SRI is the Russian's explanation of conscious and subconscious, of thinking and thought. Consciousness is a program providing, at any given moment, the domination of activity of one model over the others. The model reinforced at a given moment is a thought.

Analysis

1. In your opinion, is there any substance to this report, or is it just another Russian claim?

2. What impact would this have on the argument that machines are capable of thinking?

"LAMENT FOR A MONGREL"

There is much discussion on the creative capacities of electronic computers. R. M. Worthy and his staff at the Advanced Research Department of General Precision, Inc., Glendale, California, have categorized thousands of words and set up sentence patterns and rhyming rules that "generate" verses. The following is a product of this venture.

Lament for a Mongrel

To belch yet not to boast, that is the hug,
The high lullaby's bay discreetly crushes the bug.
Your science was so minute and hilly,
Yes, I am not the jade organ's leather programmer's recipe.

---

[1] This case is reported in an editorial in *Industrial Distribution*, August 1967, p. 8.
[2] *Ibid.*

---

[1] This case is reported in "Russian Cybernetics Expert States Artificial Intelligence Can Be Created," *Journal of Data Management*, January 1968, p. 48.

As she is squealing above the cheroot, these obscure toilets shall squat.
Moreover, on account of hunger, the room was
hot.[1]

Analysis

1. Do you consider this poem creative?
Why?

2. Compare and contrast the creative capacities of a computer with the creative capacities of humans.

DA VINCI VERSUS THE COMPUTER[1]

A computer manufacturer recently displayed
computer art. The works of art are a result of
taking a photograph of a desired scene or
person. The photograph's design elements are
plotted on graph paper and translated into
Fortran computer language which is processed
on a Univac 1107 and recorded on a 2400-
foot reel of magnetic tape. The tape serves as

input, and the output is a plotter that turns
out one finished piece of "art" every 75
minutes.

What about the quality of this art? A
woman at the exhibit observed, "I don't understand a bit of it, but it's just fascinating."[2]
A more expert opinion came from the head of
a university art department. The professor
declared that computers have "definite potential as an art medium" and praised computer
art for its "orderliness and precision."[3] He said
that computers may be a new medium, especially in abstract art.

The computer programmer for the paintings
stated that his purpose is to persuade non-
scientific disciplines to adapt computers. The
computer company's president was quoted as
saying, "The computer comes close to representing the world of machines in the way
Leonardo da Vinci represented the world of
man."

Analysis

1. Do you think that this computer is
creating artwork? Why?

2. Analyze the company president's statement quoted above. In your opinion, would
da Vinci agree or disagree with this analogy?

[1] Reprinted with permission of the publisher.
Gilbert Burck, "Will the Computer Outwit Man,"
Fortune, October 1964, p. 166.

[1] Reported in "Computers, Artists of Future?,"
Lincoln Journal and Star, August 11, 1968, p. 14F.

[2] *Ibid.*
[3] *Ibid.*

Chapter Two

Toward Scientific Management

THIS CHAPTER CONCENTRATES on the contributions of pioneers in the development of management knowledge. It begins with the famous pig iron and shoveling experiments at the Bethlehem Steel Company and evaluates the work of Frederick W. Taylor and his lieutenants. Attention is then directed to Henri Fayol, Max Weber, Alfred P. Sloan, Jr., and others concerned with the development of management organization. The final section gives comprehensive consideration to the famous experiments conducted at the Hawthorne Plant of the Western Electric Company.

Section I MAJOR CONCEPTS

Scientific management
Managerial organization
Management functions

Bureaucracy
Human behavior in organizations

Section II SELF-TEST

True-False

_____ 1. Henri Fayol was concerned with a systematic study of the functions of management.

_____ 2. The illumination experiments at Hawthorne failed to support the original assumptions of the researchers.

_____ 3. The output norms of the Hawthorne wire bank group were what workers thought output should be.

_____ 4. As a result of his pig iron handling experiment, Frederick W. Taylor made large reductions in the amount of rest time.

_____ 5. Frederick W. Taylor would probably take a negative attitude toward individualizing the worker.

Multiple Choice

____ 1. The development of scientific management in the United States is generally considered to have begun with the experiments
   a. at the Arsenal of Venice
   b. of F. W. Taylor at Midvale Steel Company
   c. at Boulton and Watt Company
   d. of Wilfred Lewis at the Tabor Company

____ 2. What is *not* true of the pig iron handling experiments?
   a. They were performed at Bethlehem Steel Company.
   b. About a 25 per cent increase in output was achieved.
   c. Schmidt did not seem to be an exception.
   d. Increased wages resulted.

____ 3. Frederick W. Taylor would probably take a negative attitude toward
   a. high wages through higher output
   b. individualizing the worker
   c. group pressures against workers
   d. planning by management

____ 4. "Scientific management" became a household term as a direct result of
   a. a famous golf match
   b. the discovery of high-speed steel
   c. a railroad rate hearing
   d. the shoveling experiments

____ 5. Which of the following best describes the contribution of Max Weber to the management field?
   a. Scientific management
   b. The management process
   c. Technological innovation
   d. Managerial organization

____ 6. Henri Fayol divided the management function into five parts:
   a. planning, organization, inspection, supervision, and control
   b. planning, organization, supervision, coordination, and command
   c. planning, organization, command, coordination, and control
   d. planning, organization, command, supervision, and inspection

____ 7. Which of the following represents an important difference between Henri Fayol and Frederick Taylor?
   a. Fayol was a Frenchman and, for that reason, his ideas conflicted with the ideas of the American, Taylor.
   b. Taylor was a practicing engineer and executive; Fayol was an "armchair theorist."
   c. Fayol was concerned with the managerial level; Taylor was more concerned with the operating level.
   d. None of the above.

____ 8. Which of the following was not an aspect of the Hawthorne Study?
   a. Empirical study of the primary group
   b. Elaborate interviewing program
   c. A sociological perspective
   d. Union-management committees to improve productivity

____ 9. The actual output of the Wirebank Group of the Hawthorne Study
   a. generally attained but rarely exceeded the company norm
   b. had every individual produce the amount stipulated by group norms
   c. was considered to be "about right" by the foreman
   d. was closely related to the productive capacity of the individual worker

____ 10. All of the following were norms of the Hawthorne Bank Wiring Room Group EXCEPT:
   a. You should be anxious to perform the leadership function.
   b. You should not turn out too much work.
   c. You should not turn out too little work.
   d. You should not be a "squealer."

Essay-Discussion

1. How did scientific management change the way in which planning is performed?

2. What was the significance of the illumination experiments at the Hawthorne Plant?

3. Compare and contrast Frederick W. Taylor with Henri Fayol in regard to their contributions to management knowledge.

Section III   ILLUSTRATIVE CASES

SCIENTIFIC MANAGEMENT IN MANUFACTURING TYPEWRITERS

After leaving the Bethlehem Steel Company in 1901, Henri L. Gantt worked as a consultant for more than fifty concerns. He considered his work at the Remington Typewriter Company as the most successful of his career. He studied the whole range of company operations over a period of some seven years.[1] The first undertaking was a thorough study of operating procedures of the factories. A study was then made of the flow of material throughout all the manufacturing operations. After completing his study of the operating procedures and material flow, Gantt first corrected bottleneck situations. Some workers had to work overtime to keep up with the flow of production. He improved these operations and made a careful study of machine stoppage. His over-all analysis of the work of the organization was followed with time study and a bonus system. He initiated and improved the planning department by charts showing the capacity of machines and the production departments. The charts indicated the amount of productive capacity that was available for additional work assignment.

The results at Remington were impressive in spite of the fact that the company had excellent tools, well-developed methods, and high-grade personnel when Gantt began his work. Gantt succeeded in cutting down the quantity of raw and finished material in storage and the material needed for work-in-process. This

change reduced the amount of inventory required for a given volume of production. Factory production increased some 64 per cent; working hours per week were reduced from 59 to 50. In addition, a ten minute rest period during each half day was introduced. Wages rose approximately 23 per cent and average labor cost was reduced 20 per cent. A steady improvement also occurred in the quality of the finished product. The duties of both the employees and management were carefully defined, and a planned promotion program was initiated. Factory executives were relieved from the supervision of routine affairs, which gave them time for exceptional matters.

Analysis

1. Compare and contrast Gantt's work at Remington with Frederick W. Taylor's work at Bethlehem Steel.

2. Compare and contrast Gantt's approach to managerial problems at Remington with Alfred P. Sloan's approach to problems at General Motors.

FIELD SYSTEM

Frank B. Gilbreth began his work in the building construction industry. He learned the bricklaying trade and a few years later organized his own contracting firm. His early contributions to scientific management evolved from his experiences in construction. His first

---

[1] L. P. Alford, *Henry Laurence Gantt* (New York: The American Society of Mechanical Engineers, 1934), pp. 149-165.

major contribution, published in 1908 under the title *Field System,* was an elaborate system of control for the contracting business.[1] This system played an important role in the phenomenal success of the Gilbreth organization. It enabled the organization to build three complete industrial towns (Sprague's Falls, Me., Piercefield, N. J., and Canton, N. C.), each in a record time of a few months. Before its publication, the Gilbreth "field system" was available only to people employed by the firm. The success of the system is indicated by the frequent attempts of some competing contractors to obtain copies of the manual. "Office boys were bribed, certain pages were photographed, and discharged superintendents in one or two instances carried the book with them."[2]

The Gilbreth "field system" applied scientific management to the construction industry. It set forth standard practices and procedures for every aspect of construction. These practices and procedures were carefully preplanned, and all supervisors and employees were required to "follow these rules to the letter unless they received written permission to suspend certain rules."[3] A copy of *Field System* was kept in the office of each of the construction projects of the Gilbreth organization.

The *Field System* gave superintendents, foremen, and employees information about the use of forms, such as purchase requisitions, payroll orders, time sheets, and cost reports. These forms were designed to give the local and the home office detailed information about the progress, efficiency, and cost of the project. In addition to the forms designed for a particular purpose, a "Daily Letter" form had to be completed by the timekeeper and countersigned by the superintendent. Photographs were used for a number of purposes: (1) to keep the home office in touch with conditions on each project; (2) for advertising; (3) to provide a record in case of lawsuits or other misunderstandings; and (4) to record conditions at the time of an accident. Detailed information on the use of the camera was provided in *Field System.* Gilbreth gave much attention to the care of tools and machinery.

The Gilbreth system shifted a great deal of responsibility from the worker to management. The *Field System* enabled management to enforce uniform work methods, procedures, and standards on all projects. Like the Taylor system, these standards, methods, and procedures were determined by scientific study and measurement rather than by the "rule of thumb" of workers and supervisors on the job. What is the best way to mix mortar? What kind of scaffolding should be used? What is the best method for constructing tall chimneys? The answer to these and similar questions was provided by *Field System.*

Analysis

1. Compare Gilbreth's approach to managerial problems with those of Henri Fayol and Max Weber.

2. Would *Field System* be useful in the modern construction industry? Why? Why not?

THE MISLAID CHECK

Morris L. Cooke was the Director of Public Works of Philadelphia from 1912 to 1916.[1] The department employed more than 4,000 men and women and had the following major responsibilities: (1) the building and maintenance of roads, streets, sewers, and bridges; (2) the filtering and distribution of the water supply; (3) the construction and maintenance of public buildings; and (4) the administration of the public lighting system. Cooke believed that Taylor's principles could be applied to city work, as they have been applied to industrial work. "Government work (federal, state, and municipal)," wrote Cooke, "is still almost exclusively in the unsystematized stage."[2] The application of the principles and techniques of scientific management to city administration will, thought Cooke, open up "a field of endeavor which staggers the imagination."[3]

---

[1] Frank B. Gilbreth, *Field System* (New York: The Myron C. Clark Publishing Company, 1908).
[2] *Ibid.,* p. 5.
[3] *Ibid.,* p. 14.

[1] Morris L. Cooke, *Our Cities Awake* (Garden City, N. Y.: Doubleday, Page and Co., 1918).
[2] *Ibid.,* p. 82.
[3] *Ibid.,* p. 84.

The Department of Public Works saved more than $1 million a year during Cooke's tenure. The annual cost of collecting and disposing of the city's garbage was cut by a quarter of a million dollars. The handling of coal at one pumping station was reduced from 40 cents a ton to 10 cents. These accomplishments can be credited to both major changes and thousands of minor economies in many phases of the department's work. One major change was a better functional division of work. For example, the employment of all labor, skilled and unskilled, for the various bureaus in the department was concentrated in a central Labor Bureau in the director's office. The paying of wages was placed under the direction of one head paymaster. The function of purchasing was centralized.

The physical layout of the central offices of the department was rearranged. Flat-top desks replaced the old pigeonhole dust catchers in which papers were often lost or held up. An interbureau messenger service was initiated with a predetermined route every hour between twelve regular stations. Filing and record-keeping procedures were improved. During the housecleaning in the offices, a six-year-old certified check for $9,700 was found tucked away with some unimportant papers.

Analysis

1. Does Cooke's analysis of municipal administration imply universal applicability of scientific management? How about military, hospital, and university applications?

2. What are the implications of the title of this illustrative case? Could such a thing happen today?

Chapter Three

The Emerging Pattern

THIS CHAPTER BUILDS a bridge between the pioneering contributions considered in Chapter 2 and more recent developments. Brief attention is given to the manner in which people in such subjects as sociology, psychology, economics, statistics, and mathematics have advanced the field of management. The importance of a conceptual framework for management knowledge and the part played by the management process in this respect are discussed in depth. The present state or organization theory is then reviewed, and the parts of the management process (such as planning and communicating) are brought into focus. The next section indicates future prospects for a more comprehensive science of management. It points to the problem of uncertainty and the way it limits the development of knowledge. The final section deals with the development of a profession of management.

Section I MAJOR CONCEPTS

Management process
Organization theory
Planning methodology
Game theory

Communication and control
Motivation and leadership
Science
Profession

Section II SELF-TEST

True-False

____ 1. The functions that make up the management process have become a basis for specialization in the field of management.

____ 2. Frederick W. Taylor can be credited with a modern conceptual framework for management knowledge.

____ 3. A hypothesis can be thought of as a tentative theory about the nature of the phenomenon that is to be studied.

_____ 4. According to Chester I. Barnard, the first task of the organizer is created by the need for a definite system of communication.

_____ 5. The opportunity to earn a sufficient salary to enable a person to live at a proper social level is used to differentiate a profession from an ordinary vocation.

Multiple Choice

_____ 1. The relationship between the social sciences and the field of management is similar to the relationship between
    a. sociology and psychology
    b. biological and physical sciences
    c. political and economic theory
    d. basic sciences and medicine

_____ 2. Which of the following does *not* describe the management process?
    a. Conceptual framework for management knowledge
    b. Management functions
    c. Statistically derived sequences
    d. Interrelationship among activities

_____ 3. Which of the following best describes the emphasis given in the early management literature to communication problems and processes?
    a. Little attention given to these matters
    b. No attention given to communication
    c. A great deal of attention given to them
    d. Completely ignored such subjects

_____ 4. The "game theory" developed by Morgenstern and von Neumann
    a. was used by Taylor in his study of golf
    b. assumed that there would soon be a marked reduction in the workweek
    c. takes into account the strategies developed by others

    d. is not related to the problems of management

_____ 5. The following statements about science are valid EXCEPT:
    a. Hypotheses are necessary to make sense out of the facts.
    b. Facts and only facts are involved in scientific conclusions.
    c. The scientist must be willing to change his mind in conducting his research.
    d. The scientific method can be used in studying society.

_____ 6. Which of the following would conclude that "there can be no science of cooperation"?
    a. Oliver Sheldon
    b. Lillian Gilbreth
    c. Henry L. Gantt
    d. Frederick W. Taylor

_____ 7. What are usually considered to be the three "learned professions"?
    a. teaching, law, medicine
    b. theology, law, medicine
    c. management, teaching, medicine
    d. teaching, management, acting

_____ 8. What is the most accurate statement about the concept of management?
    a. It is only a theoretical concept.
    b. It is an applied field.
    c. It is based solely on two disciplines—economics and psychology.
    d. As yet, it has no body of knowledge.

_____ 9. What is the best statement concerning sequence of the management functions in the process concept?
    a. Planning always precedes organizing.
    b. Planning always precedes directing.
    c. The process cycle will always be completed.
    d. Staffing may lead to planning.

_____ 10. Which of the following is generally *not* considered to be a criterion for a profession?

a. Learning of a systematic body of knowledge
b. Existence of an association
c. Conformance to personal values rather than an established set of standards
d. Legal or other restrictions to entry

Essay-Discussion

1. What part has the management process played in the development of management knowledge?
2. To what extent can management become scientific?
3. Does management measure up to the criteria of a profession?

Section III ILLUSTRATIVE CASES

"FAT CATS"[1]

No one doubts that spectacular technological advances have been made in American industry. Some executives, however, are beginning to discover major flaws in this glowing portrayal. One executive candidly speaks of "a collection of fat cats." "They are so blown up with success," he warns, "they are forgetting that new techniques superimpose brand new problems on the ones they haven't solved yet."[2]

Recurring and neglected problem areas, such as maintenance, mismanaged quality control, misuse of new highly productive equipment, ill-advised policies on capital outlays, and operating managements' failure to think systems, are realities of the supposedly infallible supertechnological productive process. As a vice president stated, "The real gaps in production are more conceptual than physical. They can be found in everything from management attitudes to vendor-buyer communications."[3]

Analysis

1. Do you think that this is unfair criticism? Why?
2. What does this say for the "science of management"?
3. Does this suggest that a "gap" exists between productive processes and the concept of the management process? Why or why not?

C.L.U.

The letters C.L.U. stand for Chartered Life Underwriter. This designation is an attempt of the insurance industry to have its sales force become professionalized. The American Society of Chartered Life Underwriters puts out an attractive pamphlet titled *The Meaning of C.L.U.* The booklet states that the designation is given to life insurance men and women "on the basis of stringent intellectual, ethical, and experience requirements."[1] The golden-rule professional pledge of the C.L.U. is as follows:

I shall, in the light of all circumstances surrounding my client, which I shall make every conscientious effort to ascertain and to understand, give him that service which, had I been in the same circumstances, I would have applied to myself.[2]

The pamphlet goes on to state that the objective of C.L.U. is to gain subject knowledge, serve clients well, and instill a professional attitude of placing the client's interests above his own.

Analysis

1. Why do they want to be recognized as a profession?
2. How many of the life insurance salesmen that you have come in contact with would meet the professional code described? How

[1] Based on "New Factories and Old Flaws," *Dun's Review*, March 1968, pp. 71–76.
[2] *Ibid.*, p. 71.
[3] *Ibid.*

[1] *The Meaning of C.L.U.* (Bryn Mawr, Pa.: The American Society of Chartered Life Underwriters).
[2] *Ibid.*

many do you think had the C.L.U. designation?

3. What are some other professional designations in the business community?

"FRINGE BENEFITS"[1]

A magazine article recently estimated some startling statistics. Embezzlement by employees is believed to cost United States companies a staggering $3 billion per year. When another estimated $1 billion in theft is added, the total is twice the size of the nation's antipoverty budget. The article goes on to say that about 30 per cent of small businesses fail because of employee dishonesty, and known employee crime is increasing at the rate of 15 per cent a year. Most of this loss is, surprisingly, attributed to the managerial class. One investigator who uncovered more than $60 million worth of fraud in companies said that 62 per cent was committed on supervisory level or higher.

---

[1] Reported in "The Case of the Disloyal Executive," *Dun's Review,* December 1967, pp. 35-37, 79-81.

How do they get by with it? An example is the undated order used by dishonest sales managers. The manager writes up an order for $100,000 worth of goods at a price of $1 per item but leaves the order undated. When the price per item goes up a few cents, he dates the order, the billing goes out with the higher price, and the manager pockets the difference.

Why do they steal? The dean of a college of criminal justice commented: "A sociological schism has risen between management and owners. Up to a certain level, managers are frustrated by their inability to rise faster and make more money. So out of frustration and resentment, they regard the ability to steal as one of the fringe benefits of their position."[2]

Analysis

1. Why do you think there is an apparent increase in executive dishonesty?

2. How does this case illustration tie in with the separation between ownership and control in today's large corporation?

3. Can the concept of a profession play any future role?

---

[2] *Ibid.,* p. 36.

Chapter Four

Organizational Systems: The Decisional and Informational Process

THE FIRST PART of this chapter is concerned with the system concept. System is defined and related to the process and problems of management. The next section discusses management decision making in light of organizational objectives and the means that are used to achieve them. Problems of ethics and uncertainty are shown to place limits on decisional rationality. Types of decisions are classified, and a discussion of the decisional problem in a business organization is presented. The final portion of the chapter is concerned with the managerial functions and the manner in which they interrelate in the management process. This last part serves as the conceptual framework for the remaining chapters in the book.

Section I MAJOR CONCEPTS

System

Models

Cybernetics

Black box

Decision making

Rationality

Means-ends chain

Ethics

Certainty

Risk

Uncertainty

Probability

Static

Dynamic

Management process

Universality

Section II   SELF-TEST

True-False

_____ 1. There are very few systems known to man.

_____ 2. The primary ingredient of systems control is feedback information.

_____ 3. The decisional problem in the static theory of the firm is essentially mathematical.

_____ 4. Statistical probability techniques would be very accurate for forecasting the sales potential of an entirely new product.

_____ 5. The universality of the management process means that executives can move from one organization to another with no real problems.

Multiple Choice

_____ 1. It is not true that the cybernetic concept
  a. can utilize the "black box" concept of control
  b. can only be applied to the physical sciences
  c. can be associated with feedback control mechanisms
  d. can be thought of as a systems model

_____ 2. Which of the following statements best describes management decision making?
  a. A scientific solution can generally be found.
  b. Mathematical probability has created certainty for a majority of decisions.
  c. There is generally a definite solution to decisional problems.
  d. There often appear to be several equally good alternatives.

_____ 3. Assume that a person's sole objective is to quench his thirst. What would be a rational decision?
  a. Eat an ounce of salt

  b. Drink some whiskey
  c. Drink some water
  d. Smoke a cigarette

_____ 4. Which of the following is *not* true about statistical probability theory?
  a. It is based on the idea of large numbers.
  b. The assumption of homogeneity is important.
  c. It is highly useful in solving some decisional problems.
  d. It provides a solution to the problem of true uncertainty.

_____ 5. Which of the following describes a situation in which statistical probability assignment would be most beneficial?
  a. Uncertainty
  b. Risk
  c. Abstraction
  d. Certainty

_____ 6. Katona's classification of routine decisions would be similar to Simon's
  a. unprogrammed decisions
  b. programmed decisions
  c. genuine decisions
  d. risk decisions

_____ 7. Which of the following is the best statement concerning the static theory of the firm?
  a. It was developed by sociologists.
  b. The decisional problem is essentially mathematical.
  c. It incorporates change.
  d. The objective is an acceptable profit.

_____ 8. What is the best statement concerning policy making?
  a. It is clearly a separable function.
  b. It is similar to decision making.
  c. It is mainly concerned with governmental problems.
  d. It is a term rarely used by executives.

___ 9. All of the following describe the management process EXCEPT:
   a. It is made up of management functions.
   b. It is a product of the Taylor school of scientific management.
   c. It is often used as a conceptual framework for the study of management.
   d. It is generally assumed to be a universal attribute of organized endeavor.

___ 10. What is *not* true of control?
   a. It can be viewed as an aspect of the problem of motivation.
   b. It involves a comparison of planning and performance.
   c. A thermostat is a good example.
   d. It makes the rules for the organization.

Essay-Discussion

1. How does management relate to the systems concept?

2. What functions make up the management process?

3. In the traditional economic theory of the firm, how do the problems of the executive differ from those of the entrepreneur?

Section III   ILLUSTRATIVE CASES

JUMPING OFF THE BANDWAGON[1]

A company that processed 30,000 to 40,000 invoices a year saw its annual sales volume of several million dollars surge to a 22 percent increase in six months, while the number of orders jumped 30 percent. The president expressed his company's order-processing problems as follows:

> Obviously we needed a system that would enable us to handle this growth, make the paperwork less costly and less complex, and our operations more efficient. We could have gone in either of two directions—ultrasophisticated methods and EDP equipment, or ultrasimplicity.[2]

The company chose a simple, manual system of handwritten master invoice copies; an electrostatic copier, for duplicating original orders; and two systems duplicators, for making copies from masters. This simple manual system realized about $15,000 annual savings in labor costs, plus $3000 in cost of forms, and cut the processing time in half.

Analysis

1. Was the president an exception in choosing a simplified system over a sophisticated EDP system?

2. Could better results have possibly been obtained from a more complex EDP system?

3. What implications does this case have for systems analysis?

THE EDSEL STORY

Late in 1957 the Ford Motor Company launched a new automobile called the Edsel. The actual arrival of the Edsel was preceded by a year of intensive advertising to whet the public's appetite for the new product. According to a top Ford executive, the plan was to produce 200,000 cars during the first year.[1] Almost exactly two years later, after producing a total of 110,000 Edsels, the Ford Motor Company reluctantly announced that it had made a most expensive mistake.[2] After costing

---

[1] "We Streamlined Our Paperwork without EDP," *Industrial Distribution,* September 1967, p. 46.
[2] *Ibid.*

[1] *Business Week,* November 24, 1956, p. 31.
[2] *Business Week,* November 28, 1959, p. 27.

some $250 million to bring to the market, the Edsel lost an estimated $200 million more during the two years of its life-span.

The strategy of Ford was to use the Edsel (in several models) to match General Motors and Chrysler in the medium-priced field. General Motors in particular had been highly successful in building a line of automobiles that were differentiated to fit the various socio-economic levels that make up the American society.[3] Ford lost a large percentage of its customers to both General Motors and Chrysler when they decided to move from the basic Ford to a more expensive automobile.

Many reasons have been given for the failure of the Edsel to get a foothold in the automobile market. One was that the Edsel came out during a recession which reduced the size of the medium-priced market. Another was that the small economy car from abroad was beginning to gain large consumer acceptance. Still another was that Edsel styling and performance did not come up to the standards set by other medium-priced automobiles.

Edsel headquarters pulled out all stops in an effort to avert complete failure.[4] They gave sales bonuses to dealers to provide a means for discounting Edsels and organized a system of dealer exchanges with respect to model, color, sizes, and so on. The national advertising budget was upped a reported $20 million. Edsels were offered at a discount to state highway officials to get the car on the road so that it could be seen. A huge demonstration-ride program in which 500,000 prospects drove the car was launched to entice customers.

Analysis

1. Was the Edsel a "rational" managerial decision on the part of Ford Motor Company?

2. Was this a risk- or an uncertainty-type decision? Why?

3. How could the Edsel disaster have been avoided?

[3] Alfred P. Sloan, Jr., *My Years with General Motors* (Garden City, N.Y.: Doubleday and Co., Inc., 1964).

[4] *Consumer Reports,* April, 1958, p. 217.

A TYPEWRITER DECISION[1]

In a series of case studies conducted by Survey Research Center of the University of Michigan, commissioned by *Time* magazine, it was found that the following was involved in the purchase of an electric typewriter. "The secretary to a company's director of public relations used an electric typewriter for typing letters and masters of financial and stockholder reports for reproduction. At one point, the machine required repairs extensive enough to make replacement more economical. The defect was first noticed by the offset duplicating department supervisor who called it to the attention of the office services manager.

"The office services manager discussed the problem with the woman using the typewriter, then called in a supply representative for a repair estimate. Deciding that a new machine was preferable, the office services manager sent a purchase requisition to his superior, the data processing manager. The requisition had already been signed by an officer in the public relations department.

"Having approved the recommendation, the data processing manager then sent it to the executive vice-president. With his OK on the requisition, it was forwarded to the budget manager who approved the expenditure and passed it along to the president. When the president affixed his signature, the document was returned to the purchasing department. A buyer then contacted the supplier who sold him the original typewriter and ordered a new one."

Analysis

1. Would you consider this to be a routine or genuine decision? Why?

2. Briefly sketch the path of this typewriter decision on an organization chart basis. How many people did it take to replace one electric typewriter?

3. In this case, what improvements, if any, would you make in the decision process?

[1] Reprinted with permission of the publisher. "Decisions to Purchase Office Equipment," *The Office,* May 1968, p. 59.

WHAT'S THE VERDICT?

A few years ago, a number of electrical company executives were convicted of violating the Sherman Act by conspiring to fix prices, rig bids, and divide markets on electrical equipment valued at one and three-quarters billion annual sales. Some of the accused executives, while on trial, were quoted as follows: "It is the only way a business can be run. It is free enterprise." "Sure collusion was illegal, but it wasn't unethical."

After a vice-president was found guilty and fined $4000 and sentenced to thirty days in Pennsylvania's Montgomery County Prison, he declared: "There goes my whole life. Who's going to want to hire a jailbird? What am I going to tell my children?"

The judge in the case stated; "This court . . . is not at all unmindful that the real blame is to be laid at the doorstep of the corporate defendants and those who guide and direct their policy . . . for one would be almost naive indeed to believe that these violations of the law . . . involving so many millions upon millions of dollars, were facts unknown to those responsible for the corporation and its conduct."

Analysis

1. What is your verdict? Why?

2. Would you have made the same decisions if you were in the electrical executive's shoes? Why?

3. Discuss this case with reference to ethics in decision making.

READING: THE MANAGEMENT THEORY JUNGLE

HAROLD KOONTZ

Although students of management would readily agree that there have been problems of management since the dawn of organized life, most would also agree that systematic examination of management, with few exceptions, is the product of the present century and more especially of the past two decades. Moreover, until recent years almost all of those who have attempted to analyze the management process and look for some theoretical underpinnings to help improve research, teaching, and practice were alert and perceptive practitioners of the art who reflected on many years of experience. Thus, at least in looking at *general* management as an intellectually based art, the earliest meaningful writing came from such experienced practitioners as Fayol, Mooney, Alvin Brown, Sheldon, Barnard, and Urwick. Certainly not even the most academic worshipper of empirical research can overlook the empiricism involved in distilling fundamentals from decades of experience by such discerning practitioners as these. Admittedly done without questionnaires, controlled interviews, or mathematics, observations by such men can hardly be accurately regarded as *a priori* or "armchair."

The noteworthy absence of academic writing and research in the formative years of modern management theory is now more than atoned for by a deluge of research and writing from the academic halls. What is interesting and perhaps nothing more than a sign of the unsophisticated adolescence of management theory is how the current flood has brought with it a wave of great differences and apparent con-

Reprinted from *Academy of Management Journal,* Vol. 4, No. 3, December 1961, pp. 174–188, with permission of the publisher. Harold Koontz is Mead Johnson Professor of Management, Graduate School of Business Administration, University of California, Los Angeles.

fusion. From the orderly analysis of management at the shop-room level by Frederick Taylor and the reflective distillation of experience from the general management point of view by Henri Fayol, we now see these and other early beginnings overgrown and entangled by a jungle of approaches and approachers to management theory.

There are the behavioralists, born of the Hawthorne experiments and the awakened interest in human relations during the 1930's and 1940's, who see management as a complex of interpersonal relationships and the basis of management theory the tentative tenets of the new and undeveloped science of psychology. There are also those who see management theory as simply a manifestation of the institutional and cultural aspects of sociology. Still others, observing that the central core of management is decision-making, branch in all directions from this core to encompass everything in organization life. Then, there are mathematicians who think of management primarily as an exercise in logical relationships expressed in symbols and the omnipresent and ever revered model. But the entanglement of growth reaches its ultimate when the study of management is regarded as a study of one of a number of systems and subsystems, with an understandable tendency for the researcher to be dissatisfied until he has encompassed the entire physical and cultural universe as a management system.

With the recent discovery of an ages-old problem area by social, physical, and biological scientists, and with the supersonic increase in interest by all types of enterprise managers, the apparent impenetrability of the present thicket which we call management theory is not difficult to comprehend. One can hardly be surprised that psychologists, sociologists, anthropologists, sociometricists, economists, mathematicians, physicists, biologists, political scientists, business administration scholars, and even practicing managers, should hop on this interesting, challenging, and profitable band wagon.

This welling of interest from every academic and practicing corner should not upset anyone concerned with seeing the frontiers of knowledge pushed back and the intellectual base of practice broadened. But what is rather upsetting to the practitioner and the observer, who sees great social potential from improved management, is that the variety of approaches to management theory has led to a kind of confused and destructive jungle warfare. Particularly among academic disciplines and their disciples, the primary interests of many would-be cult leaders seem to be to carve out a distinct (and hence "original") approach to management. And to defend this originality, and thereby gain a place in posterity (or at least to gain a publication which will justify academic status or promotion), it seems to have become too much the current style to downgrade, and sometimes misrepresent, what anyone else has said, or thought, or done.

In order to cut through this jungle and bring to light some of the issues and problems involved in the present management theory area so that the tremendous interest, intelligence, and research results may become more meaningful, it is my purpose here to classify the various "schools" of management theory, to identify briefly what I believe to be the major source of differences, and to offer some suggestions for disentangling the jungle. It is hoped that a movement for clarification can be started so at least we in the field will not be a group of blind men identifying the same elephant with our widely varying and sometimes viciously argumentative theses.

THE MAJOR "SCHOOLS" OF MANAGEMENT THEORY

In attempting to classify the major schools of management theory into six main groups, I am aware that I may overlook certain approaches and cannot deal with all the nuances of each approach. But it does seem that most of the approaches to management theory can be classified in one of these so-called "schools."

The Management Process School

This approach to management theory perceives management as a process of getting things done through and with people operating in organized groups. It aims to analyze the process, to establish a conceptual framework for it, to identify principles underlying it, and to build up a theory of management from them. It regards management as a universal process, regardless of the type of enterprise, or the level in a given enterprise, although recognizing, obviously, that the environment of management differs widely between enterprises and levels. It looks upon management theory as a way of organizing experience so that practice can be improved through research, empirical testing of principles, and teaching of fundamentals involved in the management process.[1]

Often referred to, especially by its critics, as the "traditional" or "universalist" school, this school can be said to have been fathered by Henri Fayol, although many of his offspring did not know of their parent, since Fayol's work was eclipsed by the bright light of his contemporary, Frederick Taylor, and clouded by the lack of a widely available English translation until 1949. Other than Fayol, most of the early contributors to this school dealt only with the organization portion of the management process, largely because of their greater experience with this facet of management and the simple fact that planning and control, as well as the function of staffing,

---

[1] It is interesting that one of the scholars strongly oriented to human relations and behavioral approaches to management has recently noted that "theory can be viewed as a way of organizing experience" and that "once initial sense is made out of experienced environment, the way is cleared for an even more adequate organization of this experience." See Robert Dubin in "Psyche, Sensitivity, and Social Structure," critical comment in Robert Tannenbaum, I. R. Weschler, and Fred Massarik, *Leadership and Organization: A Behavioral Science Approach* (New York: McGraw-Hill Book Co., 1961), p. 401.

were given little attention by managers before 1940.

This school bases its approach to management theory on several fundamental beliefs:

(1) that managing is a process and can best be dissected intellectually by analyzing the functions of the manager;

(2) that long experience with management in a variety of enterprise situations can be grounds for distillation of certain fundamental truths or generalizations—usually referred to as principles—which have a clarifying and predictive value in the understanding and improvement of managing;

(3) that these fundamental truths can become focal points for useful research both to ascertain their validity and to improve their meaning and applicability in practice;

(4) that such truths can furnish elements, at least until disproved, and certainly until sharpened, of a useful theory of management;

(5) that managing is an art, but one like medicine or engineering, which can be improved by reliance on the light and understanding of principles;

(6) that principles in management, like principles in the biological and physical sciences, are nonetheless true even if a prescribed treatment or design by a practitioner in a given case situation chooses to ignore a principle and the costs involved, or attempts to do something else to offset the costs incurred (this is, of course, not new in medicine, engineering, or any other art, for art is the creative task of compromising fundamentals to attain a desired result); and

(7) that, while the totality of culture and of the physical and biological universe has varying effects on the manager's environment and subjects, as indeed they do in every other field of science and art, the theory of management does not need to encompass the field of all knowledge in order for it to serve as a scientific or theoretical foundation.

The basic approach of this school, then, is to look, first, to the functions of managers. As a second step in this approach, many of us have taken the functions of managers and further dissected them by distilling what we see as fundamental truths in the understandably complicated practice of management. I have found it useful to classify my analysis of these functions around the essentials involved in the following questions:

(1) What is the nature of the function?

(2) What is the purpose of the function?

(3) What explains the structure of the function?

(4) What explains the process of the function?

Perhaps there are other more useful approaches, but I have found that I can place everything pertaining to management (even some of the rather remote research and concepts) in this framework.

Also, purely to make the area of management theory intellectually manageable, those who subscribe to this school do not usually attempt to include in the theory the entire areas of sociology, economics, biology, psychology, physics, chemistry, or others. This is done not because these other areas of knowledge are unimportant and have no bearing on management, but merely because no real progress has ever been made in science or art without significant partitioning of knowledge. Yet, anyone would be foolish not to realize that a function which deals with people in their various activities of producing and marketing anything from money to religion and education is completely independent of the physical, biological, and cultural universe in which we live. And, are there not such relationships in other "compartments" of knowledge and theory?

The Empirical School

A second approach to management I refer to as the "empirical" school. In this, I include those scholars who identify management as a study of experience, sometimes with intent to draw generalizations but usually merely as a means of teaching experience and transferring it to the practitioner or student. Typical of this school are those who see management or "policy" as the study and analysis of cases and those with such approaches as Ernest Dale's "comparative approach."[2]

This approach seems to be based upon the premise that, if we study the experience of successful managers, or the mistakes made in management, or if we attempt to solve management problems, we will somehow understand and learn to apply the most effective kinds of management techniques. This approach, as often applied, assumes that, by finding out what worked or did not work in individual circumstances, the student or the practitioner will be able to do the same in comparable situations.

No one can deny the importance of studying experience through such study, or of analyzing the "how-it-was-done" of management. But management, unlike law, is not a science based on precedent, and situations in the future exactly comparable to the past are exceedingly unlikely to occur. Indeed, there is a positive danger of relying too much on past experience and on undistilled history of managerial problem-solving for the simple reason that a technique or approach found "right" in the past may not fit a situation of the future.

Those advocating the empirical approach are likely to say that what they really do in analyzing cases or history is to draw from certain generalizations which can be applied as useful guides to thought or action in future case situations. As a matter of fact, Ernest Dale, after claiming to find "so little practical value" from the principles enunciated by the "universalists," curiously drew certain "generalizations" or "criteria" from his valuable study of a number of great practitioners of management.[3] There is some question as to whether Dale's "comparative" approach is not really the same as the "universalist" approach he decries, except with a different distiller of basic truths.

By the emphasis of the empirical school on study of experience, it does appear that the research and thought so engendered may assist in hastening the day for verification of principles. It is also possible that the proponents of this school may come up with a more useful framework of principles than that of the management process school. But, to the extent that the empirical school draws generalizations from its research, and it would seem to be a necessity to do so unless its members are satisfied to exchange meaningless and structureless experience, this approach tends to be and do the same as the management process school.

The Human Behavior School

This approach to the analysis of management is based on the central thesis that, since managing involves getting things done with and through people, the study of management must be centered on interpersonal relations. Variously called the "human relations," "leadership," or "behavioral sciences" approach, this school brings to bear "existing and newly developed theories, methods, and techniques of the relevant social sciences upon the study of inter- and intrapersonal phenomena, ranging fully from the personality dynamics of individuals at one extreme to the relations of cultures at the other."[4] In other words, this school concentrates on the "people" part of management and rests on the principle that, where people work together as groups in order to accomplish objectives, "people should understand people."

The scholars in this school have a heavy orientation to psychology and social psychology. Their primary focus is the individual as a socio-psychological being and what motivates him. The members of this school vary from those who see it as a portion of the manager's job, a tool to help him understand and get the best from people by meeting their needs and responding to their motivations, to those who see the psychological behavior of individuals and groups as the total of management.

[2] *The Great Organizers* (New York: McGraw-Hill Book Co., 1960), pp. 11–28.
[3] *Ibid.*, pp. 11, 26–28, 62–68.

[4] R. Tannenbaum, I. R. Weschler, and F. Massarik, *Leadership and Organization* (New York: McGraw-Hill Book Co., 1961), p. 9.

In this school are those who emphasize human relations as an art that the manager should advantageously understand and practice. There are those who focus attention on the manager as a leader and sometimes equate management to leadership, thus, in effect, tending to treat all group activities as "managed" situations. There are those who see the study of group dynamics and interpersonal relationships as simply a study of sociopsychological relationships and seem, therefore, merely to be attaching the term "management" to the field of social psychology.

That management must deal with human behavior can hardly be denied. That the study of human interactions, whether in the environment of management or in unmanaged situations, is important and useful one could not dispute. And it would be a serious mistake to regard good leadership as unimportant to good managership. But whether the field of human behavior is the equivalent of the field of management is quite another thing. Perhaps it is like calling the study of the human body the field of cardiology.

The Social System School

Closely related to the human behavior school and often confused or intertwined with it is one which might be labeled the social system school. This includes those researchers who look upon management as a social system, that is, a system of cultural interrelationships. Sometimes, as in the case of March and Simon,[5] the system is limited to formal organizations, using the term "organization" as equivalent to enterprise, rather than the authority-activity concept used most often in management. In other cases, the approach is not to distinguish the formal organization, but rather to encompass any kind of system of human relationships.

Heavily sociological in flavor, this approach to management does essentially what any study of sociology does. It identifies the nature of the cultural relationships of various social groups and attempts to show these as a related, and usually an integrated, system.

Perhaps the spiritual father of this ardent and vocal school of management theorists is Chester Barnard.[6] In searching for an answer to fundamental explanations underlying the managing process, this thoughtful business executive developed a theory of cooperation grounded in the needs of the individual to solve, through cooperation, the biological, physical, and social limitations of himself and his environment. Barnard then carved from the total of cooperative systems so engendered one set of interrelationships which he defines as "formal organization." His formal organization concept, quite unlike that usually held by management practitioners, is any cooperative system in which there are persons able to communicate with each other and who are willing to contribute action toward a conscious common purpose.

The Barnard concept of cooperative systems pervades the work of many contributors to the social system school of management. For example, Herbert Simon at one time defined the subject of organization theory and the nature of human organizations as "systems of interdependent activity, encompassing at least several primary groups and usually characterized, at the level of consciousness of participants, by a high degree of rational direction of behavior toward ends that are objects of common knowledge."[7] Simon and others have subsequently seemed to have expanded this concept of social systems to include any cooperative and purposeful group interrelationship or behavior.

This school has made many noteworthy contributions to management. The recognition of organized enterprise as a social organism, subject to all the pressures and conflicts of the cultural environment, has been helpful to the management theorist and the practitioner alike. Among some of the more helpful aspects are the awareness of the institutional foundations

---

[5] *Organizations* (New York: John Wiley & Sons, Inc., 1958).

[6] *The Functions of the Executive* (Cambridge, Mass.: Harvard University Press, 1938).

[7] "Comments on the Theory of Organizations," 46 *American Political Science Review*, No. 4 (December, 1952), p. 1130.

of organization authority, the influence of informal organization, and such social factors as those Wight Bakke has called the "bonds of organization."[8] Likewise, many of Barnard's helpful insights, such as his economy of incentives and his theory of opportunism, have brought the power of sociological understanding into the realm of management practice.

Basic sociology, analysis of concepts of social behavior, and the study of group behavior in the framework of social systems do have great value in the field of management. But one may well ask the question whether this *is* management. Is the field of management coterminous with the field of sociology? Or is sociology an important underpinning like language, psychology, physiology, mathematics, and other fields of knowledge? Must management be defined in terms of the universe of knowledge?

The Decision Theory School

Another approach to management theory, undertaken by a growing and scholarly group, might be referred to as the decision theory school. This group concentrates on rational approach to decision—the selection from among possible alternatives of a course of action or of an idea. The approach of this school may be to deal with the decision itself, or to the persons or organizational group making the decision, or to an analysis of the decision process. Some limit themselves fairly much to the economic rationale of the decision, while others regard anything which happens in an enterprise the subject of their analysis, and still others expand decision theory to cover the psychological and sociological aspect and environment of decisions and decision-makers.

---

[8] *Bonds of Organization* (New York: Harper & Brothers, 1950). These "bonds" or "devices" of organization are identified by Bakke as (1) the functional specifications system (a system of teamwork arising from job specifications and arrangements for association) (2) the status system (a vertical hierarchy of authority); (3) the communications system; (4) the reward and penalty system; and (5) the organization charter (ideas and means which give character and individuality to the organization, or enterprise).

The decision-making school is apparently an outgrowth of the theory of consumer's choice with which economists have been concerned since the days of Jeremy Bentham early in the nineteenth century. It has arisen out of such economic problems and analyses as utility maximization, indifference curves, marginal utility, and economic behavior under risks and uncertainties. It is, therefore, no surprise that one finds most of the members of this school to be economic theorists. It is likewise no surprise to find the content of this school to be heavily oriented to model construction and mathematics.

The decision theory school has tended to expand its horizon considerably beyond the process of evaluating alternatives. That point has become for many only a springboard for examination of the entire sphere of human activity, including the nature of the organization structure, psychological and social reactions of individuals and groups, the development of basic information for decisions, an analysis of values and particularly value considerations with respect to goals, communications networks, and incentives. As one would expect, when the decision theorists study the small, but central, area of decision *making,* they are led by this keyhole look at management to consider the entire field of enterprise operation and its environment. The result is that decision theory becomes no longer a neat and narrow concentration on decision, but rather a broad view of the enterprise as a social system.

There are those who believe that, since management is characterized by its concentration on decisions, the future development of management theory will tend to use the decision as its central focus and the rest of management theory will be hung on this structural center. This may occur and certainly the study of the decision, the decision process, and the decision maker can be extended to cover the entire field of management as anyone might conceive it. Nevertheless, one wonders whether this focus cannot also be used to build around it the entire area of human knowledge. For, as most decision theorists recognize, the problem of choice is individual, as well as organizational, and most of what has been said that is pure decision theory can be applied to the existence and thinking of a Robinson Crusoe.

The Mathematical School

Although mathematical methods can be used by any school of management theory, and have been, I have chosen to group under a school those theorists who see management as a system of mathematical models and processes. Perhaps the most widely known group I arbitrarily so lump are the operations researchers or operations analysts, who have sometimes anointed themselves with the rather pretentious name of "management scientists." The abiding belief of this group is that, if management, or organization, or planning, or decision making is a logical process, it can be expressed in terms of mathematical symbols and relationships. The central approach of this school is the model, for it is through these devices that the problem is expressed in its basic relationships and in terms of selected goals or objectives.

There can be no doubt of the great usefulness of mathematical approaches to any field of inquiry. It forces upon the researcher the definition of a problem or problem area, it conveniently allows the insertion of symbols for unknown data, and its logical methodology, developed by years of scientific application and abstraction, furnishes a powerful tool for solving or simplifying complex phenomena.

But it is hard to see mathematics as a truly separate school of management theory, any more than it is a separate "school" in physics, chemistry, engineering, or medicine. I only deal with it here as such because there has appeared to have developed a kind of cult around mathematical analysts who have subsumed to themselves the area of management.

In pointing out that mathematics is a tool, rather than a school, it is not my intention to underestimate the impact of mathematics on the science and practice of management. By bringing to this immensely important and complex field the tools and techniques of the physical sciences, the mathematicians have already made an immense contribution to orderly thinking. They have forced on people in management the means and desirability of seeing many problems more clearly, they have pressed on scholars and practitioners the need for establishing goals and measures of effectiveness, they have been extremely helpful in getting the management area seen as a logical system of relationships, and they have caused people in management to review and occasionally reorganize information sources and systems so that mathematics can be given sensible quantitative meaning. But with all this meaningful contribution and the greater sharpness and sophistication of planning which is resulting, I cannot see that mathematics is management theory any more than it is astronomy.

THE MAJOR SOURCES OF MENTAL ENTANGLEMENT IN THE JUNGLE

In outlining the various schools, or approaches, of management theory, it becomes clear that these intellectual cults are not drawing greatly different inferences from the physical and cultural environment surrounding us. Why, then, have there been so many differences between them and why such a struggle, particularly among our academic brethren to obtain a place in the sun by denying the approaches of others? Like the widely differing and often contentious denominations of the Christian religion, all have essentially the same goals and deal with essentially the same world.

While there are many sources of the mental entanglement in the management theory jungle, the major ones are the following.

The Semantics Jungle

As is so often true when intelligent men argue about basic problems, some of the trouble lies in the meaning of key words. The semantics problem is particularly severe in the field of management. There is even a difference in the meaning of the word "management." Most people would agree that it means getting things done through and with people, but is it people in formal organizations, or in all group activities? Is it governing, leading, or teaching?

Perhaps the greatest single semantics confusion lies in the word "organization." Most members of the management process school use it to define the activity-authority structure of an enterprise and certainly most practitioners believe that they are "organizing" when they establish a framework of activity groupings and authority relationships. In this case, organization represents the formal framework within an enterprise that furnishes the environment in which people perform. Yet a large number of "organization" theorists conceive of organization as the sum total of human relationships in any group activity; they thus seem to make it equivalent to *social* structure. And some use "organization" to mean "enterprise."

If the meaning of organization cannot be clarified and a standard use of the term adopted by management theorists, understanding and criticism should not be based on this difference. It hardly seems to me to be accurate for March and Simon, for example, to criticize the organization theories of the management process, or "universalist," school for not considering the management planning function as part of organizing, when they have chosen to treat it separately. Nor should those who choose to treat the training, selecting, guiding or leading of people under staffing and direction be criticised for a tendency to "view the employee as an inert instrument" or a "given rather than a variable."[9] Such accusations, proceeding from false premises, are clearly erroneous.

Other semantic entanglements might be mentioned. By some, decision-making is regarded as a process of choosing from among alternatives; by others, the total managerial task and environment. Leadership is often made synonymous with managership and is analytically separated by others. Communications may mean everything from a written or oral report to a vast network of formal and informal relationships. Human relations to some implies a psychiatric manipulation of people, but to others the study and art of understanding people and interpersonal relationships.

Differences in Definition of Management as a Body of Knowledge

As was indicated in the discussion of semantics, "management" has far from a standard meaning, although most agree that it at least involves getting things done through and with people. But, does it mean the dealing with all human relationships? Is a street peddler a manager? Is a parent a manager? Is a leader of a disorganized mob a manager? Does the field of management equal the fields of sociology and social psychology combined? Is it the equivalent of the entire system of social relationships?

While I recognize that sharp lines cannot be drawn in management any more than they are in medicine or engineering, there surely can be a sharper distinction drawn than at present. With the plethora of management writing and experts, calling almost everything under the sun "management," can one expect management theory to be regarded as very useful or scientific to the practitioner?

The a priori Assumption

Confusion in management theory has also been heightened by the tendency for many newcomers in the field to cast aside significant observations and analyses of the past on the grounds that they are *a priori* in nature. This is an often-met accusation made by those who wish to cast aside the work of Fayol, Mooney, Brown, Urwick, Gulick, and others who are branded as "universalists." To make the assumption that the distilled experiences of men such as these represent *a priori* reasoning is to forget that experience in and with managing *is* empirical. While the conclusions that perceptive and experienced practitioners of the art of management are not infallible, they represent an experience which is certainly real and not "armchair." No one could deny, I feel sure, that the ultimate test of accuracy of

---

[9] J. G. March and H. A. Simon, *Organizations* (New York: John Wiley & Sons, Inc., 1958), pp. 29–33.

management theory must be practice and management theory and science must be developed from reality.

The Misunderstanding of Principles

Those who feel that they gain caste or a clean slate for advancing a particular notion or approach often delight in casting away anything which smacks of management principles. Some have referred to them as platitudes, forgetting that a platitude is still a truism and a truth does not become worthless because it is familiar. (As Robert Frost has written, "Most of the changes we think we see in life are merely truths going in or out of favor.") Others cast away principles of Fayol and other practitioners, only to draw apparently different generalizations from their study of management; but many of the generalizations so discovered are often the same fundamental truths in different words that certain criticized "universalists" have discovered.

One of the favorite tricks of the managerial theory trade is to disprove a whole framework of principles by reference to one principle which the observer sees disregarded in practice. Thus, many critics of the universalists point to the well-known cases of dual subordination in organized enterprise, coming to the erroneous conclusion that there is no substance to the principle of unity of command. But this does not prove that there is no cost to the enterprise by designing around, or disregarding, the principle of unity of command; nor does it prove that there were not other advantages which offset the costs, as there often are in cases of establishing functional authorities in organization.

Perhaps the almost hackneyed stand-by for those who would disprove the validity of all principles by referring to a single one is the misunderstanding around the principle of span of management (or span of control). The usual source of authority quoted by those who criticize is Sir Ian Hamilton, who never intended to state a universal principle, but rather to make a personal observation in a book of reflections on his Army experience, and who did say, offhand, that he found it wise to limit his span to 3 to 6 subordinates. No modern universalist relies on this single observation, and, indeed, few can or will state an absolute or universal numerical ceiling. Since Sir Ian was not a management theorist and did not intend to be, let us hope that the ghost of his innocent remark may be laid to deserved rest!

What concerns those who feel that a recognition of fundamental truths, or generalizations, may help in the diagnosis and study of management, and who know from managerial experience that such truths or principles do serve an extremely valuable use, is the tendency for some researchers to prove the wrong things through either misstatement or misapplication of principles. A classic case of such misunderstanding and misapplication is in Chris Argyris' interesting book on *Personality and Organization*.[10] This author, who in this book and his other works has made many noteworthy contributions to management, concludes that "formal organization principles make demands on relatively healthy individuals that are incongruent with their needs," and that "frustration, conflict, failure, and short-time perspective are predicted as results of this basic incongruency."[11] This startling conclusion—the exact opposite of what "good" formal organization based on "sound" organization principles should cause, is explained when one notes that, of four "principles" Argyris quotes, one is not an organization principle at all but the economic principle of specialization and three other "principles" are quoted incorrectly.[12] With such a postulate, and with no attempt to recognize, correctly or incorrectly, any other organization and management principles, Argyris has simply proved that wrong principles badly applied will lead to frustration; and every management practitioner knows this to be true!

The Inability or Unwillingness of Management Theorists to Understand Each Other

What has been said above leads one to the conclusion that much of the management theory jungle is caused by the unwillingness or inability of the management theorists to under-

---

10 New York: Harper & Brothers, 1957.
11 *Ibid.,* p. 74.
12 *Ibid.,* pp. 58–66.

stand each other. Doubting that it is inability, because one must assume that a person interested in management theory is able to comprehend, at least in concept and framework, the approaches of the various "schools," I can only come to the conclusion that the roadblock to understanding is unwillingness.

Perhaps this unwillingness comes from the professional "walls" developed by learned disciplines. Perhaps the unwillingness stems from a fear that someone or some new discovery will encroach on professional and academic status. Perhaps it is fear of professional or intellectual obsolescence. But whatever the cause, it seems that these walls will not be torn down until it is realized that they exist, until all cultists are willing to look at the approach and content of other schools, and until, through exchange and understanding of ideas some order may be brought from the present chaos.

DISENTANGLING THE MANAGEMENT THEORY JUNGLE

It is important that steps be taken to disentangle the management theory jungle. Perhaps, it is too soon and we must expect more years of wandering through a thicket of approaches, semantics, thrusts, and counter-thrusts. But in any field as important to society where the many blunders of an unscientifically based managerial art can be so costly, I hope that this will not be long.

There do appear to be some things that can be done. Clearly, meeting what I see to be the major sources of the entanglement should remove much of it. The following considerations are important:

1. THE NEED FOR DEFINITION OF A BODY OF KNOWLEDGE. Certainly, if a field of knowledge is not to get bogged down in a quagmire of misunderstandings, the first need is for definition of the field. Not that it need be defined in sharp, detailed, and inflexible lines, but rather along lines which will give it fairly specific content. Because management is reality, life, practice, my suggestion would be that it be defined in the light of the able and discerning practitioner's frame of reference. A science unrelated to the art for which it is to serve is not likely to be a very productive one.

Although the study of managements in various enterprises, in various countries, and at various levels made by many persons, including myself, may neither be representative nor adequate. I have come to the conclusion that management is the art of getting things done through and with people in *formally organized groups,* the art of creating an environment in such an organized group where people can perform as individuals and yet cooperate toward attainment of group goals, the art of removing blocks to such performance, the art of optimizing efficiency in effectively reaching goals. If this kind of definition of the field is unsatisfactory, I suggest at least an agreement that the area should be defined to reflect the field of the practitioner and that further research and study of practice be done to this end.

In defining the field, too, it seems to me imperative to draw some limits for purposes of analysis and research. If we are to call the entire cultural, biological, and physical universe the field of management, we can no more make progress than could have been done if chemistry or geology had not carved out a fairly specific area and had, instead, studied all knowledge.

In defining the body of knowledge, too, care must be taken to distinguish between tools and content. Thus mathematics, operations research, accounting, economic theory, sociometry, and psychology, to mention a few, are significant *tools* of management but are not, in themselves, a part of the *content* of the field. This is not to mean that they are unimportant or that the practicing manager should not have them available to him, nor does it mean that they may not be the means of pushing back the frontiers of knowledge of management. But they should not be confused with the basic content of the field.

This is not to say that fruitful study should not continue on the underlying disciplines affecting management. Certainly knowledge of sociology, social systems, psychology, economics, political science, mathematics, and other areas, pointed toward contributing to the field of management, should be continued and encouraged. And significant findings in these and other fields of knowledge might well cast important light on, or change concepts in, the field of management. This has certainly happened in other sciences and in every other art based upon significant science.

2. INTEGRATION OF MANAGEMENT AND OTHER DISCIPLINES. If recognition of the proper content of the field were made, I believe that the present crossfire of misunderstanding might tend to disappear. Management would be regarded as a specific discipline and other disciplines would be looked upon as important bases of the field. Under these circumstances, the allied and underlying disciplines would be welcomed by the business and public administration schools, as well as by practitioners, as loyal and helpful associates. Integration of management and other disciplines would then not be difficult.

3. THE CLARIFICATION OF MANAGEMENT SEMANTICS. While I would expect the need for clarification and uniformity of management semantics would largely be satisfied by definition of the field as a body of knowledge, semantics problems might require more special attention. There are not too many places where semantics are important enough to cause difficulty. Here again, I would suggest the adoption of the semantics of the intelligent practitioners, unless words are used by them so inexactly as to require special clarification. At least, we should not complicate an already complex field by developing a scientific or academic jargon which would build a language barrier between the theorist and the practitioner.

Perhaps the most expeditious way out of this problem is to establish a commission representing acedemic societies immediately concerned and associations of practicing managers. This would not seem to be difficult to do. And even if it were, the results would be worth the efforts.

4. WILLINGNESS TO DISTILL AND TEST FUNDAMENTALS. Certainly, the test of maturity and usefulness of a science is the sharpness and validity of the principles underlying it. No

science, now regarded as mature, started out with a complete statement of incontrovertibly valid principles. Even the oldest sciences, such as physics, keep revising their underlying laws and discovering new principles. Yet any science has proceeded, and more than that has been useful, for centuries on the basis of generalizations, some laws, some principles, and some hypotheses.

One of the understandable sources of inferiority of the social sciences is the recognition that they are inexact sciences. On the other hand, even the so-called exact sciences are subject to a great deal of inexactness, have principles which are not completely proved, and use art in the design of practical systems and components. The often-encountered defeatist attitude of the social sciences, of which management is one, overlooks the fact that management may be explained, practice may be improved, and the goals of research may be more meaningful if we encourage attempts at perceptive distillation of experience by stating principles (or generalizations) and placing them in a logical framework. As two scientists recently said on this subject:

> The reason for this defeatist point of view regarding the social sciences may be traceable to a basic misunderstanding of the nature of scientific endeavor. What matters is not whether or to what extent inexactitudes in procedures and predictive capability can eventually be removed . . . : rather it is *objectivity*, i.e., the intersubjectivity of findings independent of any one person's intuitive judgment, which distinguishes science from intuitive guesswork however brilliant. . . . But once a new fact or a new idea has been conjectured, no matter how intuitive a foundation, it must be capable of objective test and confirmation by anyone. And it is this crucial standard of scientific objectivity rather than any purported criterion of exactitude to which the social sciences must conform.[13]

In approaching the clarification of management theory, then, we should not forget a few criteria:

---

[13] O. Helmer and N. Rescher, "On the Epistemology of the Inexact Sciences" (Santa Monica, Calif.: The Rand Corporation, P-1513, 1958), pp. 4–5.

(1) The theory should deal with an area of knowledge and inquiry that is "manageable"; no great advances in knowledge were made so long as man contemplated the whole universe.

(2) The theory should be *useful* in improving practice and the task and person of the practitioner should not be overlooked.

(3) The theory should not be lost in semantics, especially useless jargon not understandable to the practitioner.

(4) The theory should give direction and efficiency to research and teaching.

(5) The theory must recognize that it is a part of a larger universe of knowledge and theory.

Outside Reading: Essay-Discussion Questions

1. What are the six major schools of management theory? Briefly define and comment on each of them.

2. Under what school of management theory would Frederick W. Taylor's scientific management fall? Why?

3. What steps does Koontz recommend to disentangle the management theory jungle?

4. If you were to develop an eclectic theory of management (take the best parts of the various theories), what would it be? Defend your eclectic theory against anticipated attacks from the other schools of management theory.

PART II

ORGANIZATION FOR MANAGEMENT

Chapter Five

The Organizational Structure

THIS CHAPTER DIRECTS attention to the organizational structure and some of the factors that determine its shape and size. It begins with a brief description of the hierarchical relationships involved in managerial organization. The span of management concept is then considered, with data about actual spans in government and industry. Internal and external forces that influence the size of the span are analyzed. Fatigue, knowledge, executive personality, social factors, spatial dispersion, and the kind of activity are important in this respect. The advantages and disadvantages of flat and tall structures are also presented. The final section analyzes the impact that information technology and the computer have had and will have on organization structure.

Section I MAJOR CONCEPTS

Hierarchy
Span of management
Flat structure

Tall structure
Hourglass structure

Section II SELF-TEST

True-False

____ 1. The management hierarchy represents both a centralization and a decentralization of decision making.

____ 2. According to the Biblical account of the Exodus, Moses experienced a span of management problem.

____ 3. Sir Ian Hamilton, a British general, concluded that span of management should increase as you approach the head of the organization.

____ 4. A flat structure has more administrative distance than a tall structure.

____ 5. Empirical research and experience do not substantiate many of the Leavitt and Whisler predictions of "Management in the 1980's."

Multiple Choice

_____ 1. Which of the following is *not* a characteristic of the management hierarchy in its pure form?
  a. Work division
  b. Centralization
  c. Decentralization
  d. Anarchy

_____ 2. Which of the following best defines "span of management"?
  a. Number of subordinates under a supervisor
  b. The size of the board of directors
  c. The number of levels in a hierarchy
  d. A bridge linking the management team

_____ 3. The Hoover Commission on the Organization of the Executive Branch recommended that the President's span of management be
  a. reduced to the ideal of three at the top
  b. somewhat increased by giving the President more power over international matters
  c. increased very little in the future
  d. reduced to about one-third the present number

_____ 4. Which of the following describes "cross relationships" in Graicunas' analysis? (Assume a superior, S, and two subordinates, X and Y.)
  a. S talks to X when Y is present; S talks to Y when X is present.
  b. X consults with Y about the work; Y consults with X about the work.
  c. S talks to X alone; S talks to Y alone.
  d. X and Y bypass S and consult someone at the same level.

_____ 5. The need to develop initiative and self-reliance among subordinates is used as an argument in favor of
  a. centralization
  b. departmentation
  c. flat structures
  d. a narrow span of management

_____ 6. Which of the following least describes managerial activity today?
  a. Hierarchical organizations
  b. Some degree of decentralization of managerial responsibilities
  c. Cooperation among executives in an organization
  d. Entrepreneurial concept of economic theory

_____ 7. What impact did Leavitt and Whisler feel the computer would have on management and organization?
  a. A recentralization of management decisional responsibilities
  b. A relative decrease in the number of people at the top
  c. A decreased flow of information to the top
  d. A relative decrease in staff personnel

_____ 8. What is the best statement concerning the consensus of empirical investigation and research on the impact the computer has had on organizational structure?
  a. Decisional responsibilities have become markedly decentralized.
  b. Decisional responsibilities have become markedly centralized.
  c. There are some changes, but at this time it is difficult to say to what extent the changes are discretionary.
  d. There appears to be no affect at the present time.

_____ 9. Which of the following statements about "the span of management" idea is *not* true?
  a. It was expressed in the Book of Exodus (in the Bible).
  b. Smaller spans mean more levels in the hierarchy and conversely.
  c. There seems to be an ideal number that represents the best possible span for any company.
  d. A great diversity of spans is actually found in industry.

_____ 10. All the following have been used as arguments for a "flat" hierarchical structure EXCEPT:

a. Less "administrative distance" than tall structure
b. Close supervision impossible because the span is long
c. Helps develop capable and self-confident subordinates
d. Involves the use of relatively more authority than does tall structure

Essay-Discussion

1. Why are management positions structured in the form of a hierarchy?

2. Compare and contrast flat versus tall managerial structures.

3. What impact do you think the computer (information technology) will have on the organizational structure of the future?

Section III   ILLUSTRATIVE CASES

NOT SQUARES[1]

An insurance company has recently revamped its organization chart. The traditional hierarchy with squares for each position on the organization chart have been replaced by a large circle. The president of the company is at the center and is ringed by the 15 men who head each of the major areas of the business. Surrounding this large ring are the individual circles of the eight regional vice-presidents. Each of the regional circles has its own branch office satellites.

The organizational rules state that each employee has a triple responsibility: first, to his own function, second, to the function related to his own and, third, to the big circle—the company itself. A vice-president comments on this organization as follows: "In effect, we are sharing our authority, but we're not abdicating responsibility. It's a kind of democratic action, but without taking a vote."[2] However, another vice-president says, "If a man can't get along under the system, there's a tendency for him to go back into the box he had in the old charts."[3]

Analysis

1. In your opinion, is this company's circular chart just a gimmick or a good organizational structure?

2. Why would you speculate that this form of organization is not widely used?

3. Is this circular concept in direct opposition to flat structures? Tall structures? Why?

ORGANIZATIONAL BREAKDOWN[1]

A manufacturing company recently suffered a 40 per cent drop in quarterly profits. The president explained that the setback was due to the breakdown of the materials management system. It seems that the system, which projected customer needs six to eight months ahead, was not capable of handling a sudden rush of new business. The result was the company's inability to supply certain items and a huge backlog of orders.

The company reacted by letting go the executive vice-president who was in charge of the materials system. The president also reorganized the company. Previously, the vice-president who resigned and another executive vice-president were each in charge of three product divisions. Under the new organization plan, the six product divisions would be split among three vice-presidents.

The president was quoted as saying, "Restructuring of the corporation will provide a better coordinated and responsive leadership."[2]

[1] This case was developed from "The Whole Staff Has a Voice in Running Sentry," *Business Week*, July 30, 1966, pp. 112–114.
[2] *Ibid.*, p. 113.
[3] *Ibid.*, p. 114.

[1] Based on "Joy Calls in a New Team" *Business Week*, March 11, 1967, p. 136.
[2] *Ibid.*

Analysis

1. If you were president, would you have asked for the resignation of the vice-president in charge of the materials system?

2. What do you think of the president's reorganization? What organizational concept did he apply?

3. Do you foresee any future problems for this company?

ALL WORK AND NO PLAY[1]

Many companies today are having trouble getting their executives to take a vacation. Many executives feel they are so indispensable and so burdened with responsibilities that they cannot afford to take even a week off.

Are they really that indispensable? Most corporate medical directors do not think so. In fact, the medical profession feels that habitual nonvacationers are hurting, rather than helping, the company. A medical director states: "It's the guys who chain themselves to their desks without any good reason that we worry about. They don't do the company any good, and they can do a great deal of harm to themselves."[2] A classic example is the case of a sales executive in his early fifties. He had always taken his regular vacation until a group of hard-charging young executives joined his department. The sales executive became convinced that the young men were trying to get his job. He started skipping his vacation and working longer hours. The company doctor recalls, "The harder he worked, the less productive he became—and that just made things worse."[3]

Analysis

1. How would you diagnose this sales executive's case? Why?

2. Do you think that executives experience fatigue? Of what kind?

3. What implications does this case have for span of control?

---

[1] Based on news report of "Indispensable Men," *The Wall Street Journal*, July 22, 1968, pp. 1, 15.

[2] *Ibid.*, p. 1.
[3] *Ibid.*

Chapter Six

Departmentation

D EPARTMENTATION OCCURS AT every level of the management hierarchy below the apex; it results in a differentiation of executive responsibility and a grouping of operating activities. The basic types of departmentation and managerial specialization such as functional, product, service, territorial, time, equipment, and alpha-numerical are described and analyzed.

Section I MAJOR CONCEPTS

Departmentation
Functionalization

Product specialization
Territorial specialization

Section II SELF-TEST

True-False

____ 1. Departmentation is best thought of as vertical organization.

____ 2. Work performed at different times can become a basis for departmentation.

____ 3. The study of cultural anthropology might be very helpful to someone who specializes on the basis of territory.

____ 4. In the near future, computerized planning and informational systems will make all of the decisions that were traditionally made by the functional departments.

____ 5. United States–based international business operations seem to be on the decline.

Multiple Choice

____ 1. Which of the following is *not* a consequence of departmentation?
   a. Elimination of coordination problems

b. A higher degree of work division

c. Delineation of managerial responsibility

d. Grouping of operating activities

_____ 2. The major operating divisions of General Motors Corporation are divided on the basis of _____ and the factory level utilizes the _____ _____ approach of organization.

a. Function – territory

b. Product – functional

c. Territory – product

d. Function – product

_____ 3. Functional departments in different kinds of business tend to be most similar

a. at upper levels

b. at lower levels

c. at the apex

d. are the same at all levels

_____ 4. In a comparison of functional centralization and decentralization, which of the following statements is *least* acceptable?

a. Size is not an important variable in determining the extent to which functional centralization is feasible.

b. Company growth often leads to a higher degree of functional specialization.

c. Greater efficiency can result from a reduction in the diversity of functions in a department.

d. Functional centralization is sometimes used to promote control and coordination.

_____ 5. Taylor's functional foremanship idea conflicts with the concept of

a. decentralization

b. specialization

c. departmentation

d. unity of command

_____ 6. Which of the following ideas best expresses the logic of "job enlargement"?

a. Functional specialization no longer has any merit.

b. A larger amount of work should be assigned to managers and other personnel.

c. Taylor's system of functional foremanship.

d. Motivation may be improved by "job enlargement."

_____ 7. Which of the following statements about product departmentation at the primary level of the management hierarchy is *not* valid?

a. It is frequently found in large organizations.

b. It gives some executives decisional experiences that relate to more than one functional area.

c. It has been used to reap the advantages of both small and large size.

d. It results in a higher degree of functional specialization among executives.

_____ 8. A study of different industries, such as steel and automobiles, would be most pertinent for which of the following types of specialization?

a. Functional

b. Product

c. Territorial

d. Time

_____ 9. What would probably be good advice for an executive who is operating in a foreign country?

a. Do not attempt to speak the native language unless you can speak it perfectly.

b. Treat everyone alike. Do not attempt to make "class" distinctions.

c. Play the role of critic because this is what foreign people expect.

d. Attempt to understand the foreign society before you go there.

_____ 10. What is the best statement concerning departmentation:

a. There does not seem to be one best pattern of departmentation.

b. There is one best pattern of departmentation for similar situations.

c. The primary purpose of departmentation is the grouping of factory operations.

d. Departmental units should be called departments (not divisions, etc.)

Essay-Discussion

1. What would be some factors to consider in choosing between product or functional departmentation?

2. What should be done about interest and personal conflicts between various departmental executives?

3. What can and should the business schools do to help to educate and train executives for international operations?

Section III   ILLUSTRATIVE CASES

GEOGRAPHIC VERSUS PRODUCT[1]

A rapidly expanding (in thirteen months, five companies were added through mergers) manufacturing firm started having difficulties. The basic problem was that the parent company was departmentalizaed by three geographic profit centers, while its new acquisitions were organized on product lines. The president remarked, "The more I thought about our organization, the more concerned I became that, looking ahead, we had a real problem facing us."[2]

To decide whether to reorganize, the president headed a committee consisting of the three geographic vice-presidents and two corporate staff members. Over the next several months the committee analyzed all aspects of the company, including present operations and measuring other possible forms of departmentation against the present form. The final decision was made to reorganize into **product** departmentation.

Analysis

1. What would be some possible reasons why this company chose to reorganize into product departments?

2. Do you think the president was wise in including his current geographical department vice-presidents in the decision? Why?

INTERNATIONAL PRODUCT DEPARTMENTATION[1]

A huge fiber and chemical company has created a unique type of departmentation. In the early 1960's the company was organized by all line operations being product-departmentalized. The two broad product departments were headed by an executive vice-president who had worldwide responsibility. The management decided on this type of organization because most of the company's operations were then in the Western hemisphere, and production technology was so complex and diverse that it was felt they would overburden a geographic structure.

As the company became more international in scope, the domestic product departments became the nuclei for product groups now operating around the world. Each domestic department is headed by its own president. These presidents are responsible to a corporate executive vice-president who reports to corporate top management.

Analysis

1. Why do you suppose this company has maintained its product departmentation on an international basis?

---

[1] Developed from "Management's Teams of Trouble" *Dun's Review*, August 1968, pp. 25–27, 70–71.
[2] *Ibid.*, p. 70

---

[1] Based on "The Global Company in a Changing World" *Dun's Review*, August 1967, pp. 27–30, 64–66.

2. What advantage is there of giving the title of president to a head of a product department?

3. In this situation, what advantage does product departmentation have over functional or geographical?

MICROWAVE PLUS JETS[1]

A Rhode Island manufacturer recently installed an ordering system which combines tape-controlled microwave communications with jet freight delivery as follows:

1. A distributor phones, wires or mails an order to a customer service specialist at the manufacturer's nearest district customer service center.

2. The specialist edits the order, which is then processed on Flexowriter, producing tape output. The order is then transmitted to the company's Rhode Island plants via microwave at 1050 words per minute (ten times faster than most people talk).

3. In seconds, the tape is reproduced at the receiving end and fed to automatic writing machines. The machines produce order documents three times faster than a good stenographer and without errors.

4. The stockroom fills the orders. Shipments are picked up daily by airline truck and delivered by jet to the customer service center.

5. Goods are reshipped from the center to the distributor by surface transportation, or picked up directly by the distributor at his option.[2]

Order-delivery time formerly averaged 26 days to Los Angeles and 20 days to Chicago. With the new system, the time between order and delivery in those two cities comes to less than 24 hours.

Analysis

1. What impact will this system have on customer satisfaction? On the goals of the company?

2. What effect will this information technology and high speed transportation have on territorial departmentation? Other types of departmentation?

---

[1] Reported in "B & S Wireless Communication Cuts Distribution Order Time to Three Days" *Industrial Distribution*, February 1968, pp. 72–73.

[2] *Ibid.*

Chapter Seven

Line-Staff-Functional Relationships

THIS CHAPTER IS concerned with the manner in which line, staff, and functional relationships relate to the managerial process. Military and business staff organizations are described and analyzed in some detail. Emphasis is given to the use of staff to take advantage of functional specialization without destroying unity of command. The final portion is concerned with the impact of information technology on line-staff relationships.

Section I MAJOR CONCEPTS

Line
Staff
Military staff

Staff functionalism
Unity of command

Section II SELF-TEST

True-False

_____ 1. A major reform of Scharnhorst, the Prussian general, was to give important command prerogatives to staff officers.

_____ 2. The general staff of the United States Army is the primary planning and coordinating group at division and higher levels.

_____ 3. The military has been more inclined toward the idea of unity of command than business organizations.

_____ 4. The General Motors Corporation has a rule against functional decision making for executives who head staff sections.

_____ 5. The trend seems to be in the direction of clear distinctions being made between line and staff.

Multiple Choice

_____ 1. Which of the following has often been used to solve the problem of functionalization versus unity of command?

a. Functional foremanship
b. Line-staff organization
c. Time and motion analysis
d. Democratic leadership techniques

_____ 2. Which of the following statements is *not* in accord with pure staff-line doctrine?

    a. A staff executive may have more influence than a subordinate line executive under certain circumstances.

    b. Staff executives issue orders directly to subordinate line executives.

    c. Staff suggestions and recommendations should be taken into consideration by line executives.

    d. Staff recommendations to subordinate line executives can be made effective through the command prerogatives of superior line executives.

_____ 3. Which of the following was the last to develop a modern military staff system?

    a. United States
    b. Germany
    c. France
    d. England

_____ 4. Which of the following statements about the general staff system in the United States army is contrary to fact?

    a. The general staff sections encompass all of the activities necessary for command.

    b. The United States has varied the number of sections in the general staff.

    c. The general staff system violates the idea of unity of command.

    d. The United States has given equal status to the various general staff sections?

_____ 5. The primary planning and coordinating group at the division level (in the United States Army) is officially called

a. the general staff
b. coordination staff
c. the commander's staff
d. the general's special staff

_____ 6. Which of the following best defines the manner in which functional executives may be classified?

    a. Line
    b. Staff
    c. A combination of line and staff
    d. All of the above

_____ 7. The General Motors Corporation top-management organization includes three types of staff executives:

    a. Personnel staff, legal staff, and product staff

    b. Personnel staff, financial staff, and operations staff

    c. Legal staff, financial staff, and production staff

    d. Financial staff, legal staff, and operations staff

_____ 8. Differences that may arise between a subordinate line executive and a staff executive are generally resolved by

    a. dismissal of one or the other executive

    b. "discussion to agreement"

    c. appeal to the superior line executive

    d. formally established dueling procedures

_____ 9. What is probably the best reason for the blurring of line-staff distinctions and the coming "death of bureaucracy" which relied on the traditional structure of relationships?

    a. The simplification of industrial products and processes

    b. The need to adapt to rapid and frequent changes

    c. The increasing need for strict discipline in industry

    d. The decreasing importance of "the human element"

_____ 10. What is the best answer to the question of whether information technology is line or staff?

a. Definitely a line function
b. A good example of the pure staff function
c. Line concerning policy decisions and staff on operating matters
d. Staff with some responsibilities that can be called line

Essay-Discussion

1. What functions are generally performed by staff officers or executives?
2. Why do line-staff conflicts develop? How would you eliminate these conflicts?
3. What impact will information technology (computers) have on line-staff relationships and functions? Why?

Section III ILLUSTRATIVE CASES

STAFF POWER[1]

With the help of improved decisional and information systems, many large companies are increasing the size and importance of their specialized staffs at corporate headquarters. There is often a shift in authority and power from the decentralized divisions to the centralized staff. This shift has already occurred in many companies. For example, a large firm in the rubber industry has certain staff specialists now holding the power of line authority over their counterparts in the divisions. Another company has taken the product planning and market forecasting functions away from the fieldmen and turned them over to the corporate staff.

Because of the expanding corporate staff, many entirely new staff functions are beginning to surface. Most of the new positions deal with information flows. An example of the new breed of staff personnel is the technical information officer. His primary function is to keep top line management informed in understandable language of the details and progress of technical engineering projects.

Analysis

1. What are the advantages and disadvantages of shifting from a decentralized staff to a centralized corporate staff?
2. How much influence and power do you think staff positions, such as the technical information officer, have in the modern organization? Why?

"ME"[1]

Bell Laboratories are currently developing the see-while-you-talk telephone called the Picturephone. The research staff team consists of engineers, physicists, chemists, physiologists, and psychologists. They were completely baffled by what to label the button that lets a user see himself on his own screen. They were not satisfied with names they could think of, such as View-self, One-Way, and View and Monitor. As a last resort, one of the researchers brought in his secretary and had her fiddle with an experimental Picturephone. He then asked her what she would call the unnamed button. The secretary thought for a moment and answered brightly, "me." The staff man says her idea has "real possibilities."

Analysis

1. How do you explain the research staff's failure to come up with a suitable name?
2. Can staff personnel only give advice, or can they also seek advice? Can line personnel contribute to the staff's function, as well as vice versa?

---

[1] Developed from "The Crisis in Corporate Controls," *Dun's Review*, July 1963, pp. 38–39, 61–62.

[1] Based on "Stymied Scientists at Bell Get Aid from a Secretary", *The Wall Street Journal*, June 4, 1968, p. 23.

GLOBAL STAFF[1]

The typical corporation of today is becoming much more global-minded. As a bank president recently stated, "The potential for U. S. industry abroad is just enormous. The overseas market is growing twice as fast as the domestic, and it should double or triple in the years ahead. . . it is most important that every corporation structure itself to get on that escalator."[2]

Most companies are still experimenting with what type of structure they should utilize. One large company, when faced with an increasingly large foreign operation, decided to organize a separate international division. According to the chairman, this gave the company a "split personality." The international division was

labeled inefficient and duplicative. The fact that the products could be manufactured in the same way both here and abroad became the key to a new structure. A general staff was created with responsibility all over the globe. The staff operated out of company headquarters in Illinois. Departments, such as engineering and research, manufacturing, marketing, parts and services, and finance, were given the task of supporting line operations anywhere in the world.

Analysis

1. What was the company's rationale for reorganizing?

2. What problems could you foresee in the new organization?

3. What impact would the international variable have on line-staff conflicts?

---

[1] Based on the article "The Global Company in a Changing World", *Dun's Review*, August 1967, pp. 27–30, 64–66.

[2] *Ibid.*, p. 28.

Chapter Eight

Centralization and Decentralization

THE FACTORS THAT influence the degree of decentralization in a management hierarchy are considered in this chapter. Decentralization has many advantages, such as reducing communication difficulties, improving coordination and control, and facilitating executive development. The extreme importance of centralization is also brought out.

Contributing factors of the centralization and decentralization of functional areas are analyzed. The General Motors Corporation is used to illustrate many ideas related to centralization and decentralization. The final section gives an historical perspective and prospects for the future.

Section I MAJOR CONCEPTS

Centralization
Decentralization
Delegation
Functional centralization-decentralization

Geographical centralization-decentralization
Centralized control
The General Motors model of decentralization
Strategy and structure

Section II SELF-TEST

True-False

_____ 1. The management hierarchy involves both centralization and decentralization of decision making.

_____ 2. There is a great deal of empirical evidence to show that large corporations have reached the point of decreasing returns to scale.

_____ 3. A majority of chief executives surveyed by Baker and France thought that industrial relations generally requires more centralization than operating functions.

_____ 4. Major financial decisions tend to be made on a decentralized basis.

_____ 5. The four companies studied by Alfred D. Chandler, Jr., all had the same problems and reached the solution in the same way.

Multiple Choice

_____ 1. Centralization and decentralization of decision making refers to
   a. the geographical dispersion of company operations
   b. the combination of similar kinds of functional activities
   c. the amount of decision making at different hierarchical levels
   d. municipal planning practices

_____ 2. Decentralization _____ involves some degree of centralized planning and control
   a. always
   b. seldom
   c. never
   d. usually

_____ 3. Which of the following is *not* true of delegation?
   a. Delegation reduces work-load but also adds to work-load because of the increase in the span of management.
   b. It is often needed to develop initiative and self-reliance among subordinates.
   c. Lack of competent executives may explain the reluctance to delegate.
   d. Control is eliminated with the act of delegation.

_____ 4. Which of the following statements is least acceptable?
   a. A survey of the American Management Association indicates that decentralization is widespread.
   b. Delegation without control is irresponsible.
   c. Decentralization is an absolute concept.
   d. Decentralization involves the risk of delegation.

_____ 5. Which of the following is *not* a criterion suggested by Ernest Dale

to determine the degree of centralization and decentralization?
   a. The amount of checking required on a decision
   b. The amount of geographical dispersion of operations
   c. The importance of decisions made at lower levels
   d. The number of decisions made at lower levels

_____ 6. Which of the following statements about the GMC structure is contrary to facts?
   a. Some GMC executives have estimated that 95 per cent of all decisions are made at the division level.
   b. The group executives perform an important liaison function between the operating divisions and central management.
   c. Staff executives do not have decision-making prerogatives over matters pertaining to their own department.
   d. GMC has three staffs: operations, financial, and legal.

_____ 7. Which of the following would probably *not* contribute to greater decentralization in the production area?
   a. More than one plant
   b. Radically different production processes
   c. Different products
   d. Extensive amounts of research and development necessary

_____ 8. Harlow Curtice of General Motors has said: "Prior to 1921 there existed no real concept of sound management in General Motors." Which of the following *best* describes the organizational changes made by General Motors?
   a. Greater decentralization
   b. Greater centralization
   c. Both a and b
   d. More functional differentiation at the top level

_____ 9. What is the reason why changes in

structure do not immediately come about after a change in strategy?

    a. The vested interest of executives in an existing structure

    b. A failure to see beyond operating problems

    c. A lack of sufficient knowledge to make necessary structural changes

    d. All of the above

____ 10. What did Chandler find in the four companies he studied?

    a. General Motors had too little decentralization over a diversity of functions and products.

    b. Dupont moved from a decentralized to a centralized structure because of product diversification.

    c. Standard Oil (New Jersey) based its structure on an all-encompassing "plan of organization."

    d. Sears Roebuck moved from an unsuccessful decentralized structure to centralization and then back to a highly successful decentralized structure.

Essay-Discussion

1. What difficulties arise in attempts to measure the degree of decentralization in an organization?

2. How may decentralization improve communication within the management hierarchy?

3. What impact will information technology (computers) have on centralization-decentralization?

Section III   ILLUSTRATIVE CASES

CONGLOMERATE[1]

A new form of corporate organization characterized by a highly diversified product line appealing to multiple markets has recently made a large impact on the business scene. A good example of these conglomerates is Textron Inc., which has 31 divisions operating more than 70 major product lines ranging from helicopters and watchbands to aftershave cologne and chickens.

The key to success for such a conglomerate becomes one of organization and control. Textron has been successful with a blend of decentralized operations and corporate financial controls. Each division headed by its own president does its own planning, manufacturing, research and development, and sales and marketing. Corporate headquarters plays the triple role of banker-consultant-supervisor. Any financial transaction by the divisions that is over $5000 must be handled by corporate headquarters. This was explained by the head of the company as follows: "It provides us with the right kind of control over corporate funds and it relieves the division heads of financial concerns. They can concentrate full time on operations."[2]

Analysis

1. Compare this plan of organization with Alfred P. Sloan's "Plan of Organization" for General Motors.

2. Would you call this company highly decentralized? What is centralized?

3. Considering their type of operation, could you suggest any alternative plans of organization?

CENTRAL CONTROL OF FACULTY PROMOTIONS[1]

Central administrative controls over faculty promotions in large state universities was the

---

[1] Based on "Textron: A Time of Testing?," *Dun's Review,* May 1968, pp. 21-24, 115-121.

[2] *Ibid.,* p. 23.

[1] Based on Fred Luthans, "Faculty Promotions: An Analysis of Central Administrative Control," *Academy of Management Journal,* Vol. 10, No. 4, December 1967, pp. 385-394.

subject of a recent study. This study found that almost half the presidents and academic vice-presidents seldom, if ever, reject recommendations from college deans and/or department heads. Supplementary comments implied that this situation was not necessarily the result of informal control or of a complete accord between university standards and decentral administrator's recommendations. On the contrary, the central administrators were generally depicted as a "rubberstamp" with "automatic approval." This interpretation was substantiated when control of research standards was analyzed. The investigation found that research was an important purpose in these universities and the most widely recognized standard for promotion. Yet, over half the central administrators reported that they promote faculty members who have few, if any, publications. Moreover, the publication record of the sample implied many more full professors with no significant publication record prior to being promoted than central administration realized or cared to admit.

Analysis

1. Does this imply that decentralization should not be applied to faculty administration? Why?

2. How does the concept of control relate to centralization?

DECENTRALIZATION: PHILOSOPHY OF GE CHAIRMAN OF THE BOARD

In a recent interview Gerald L. Phillippe, Chairman of the Board of General Electric, was asked to explain what decentralization has meant to GE. His reply was the following:

> I think maybe two things. In 1950, when Ralph Cordiner first did it, there was great resistance. But G. E. would never have grown as it has—lacking decentralization. It is just physically impossible, in my judgement, for any man or small group of men . . . smart enough to know intimately all the things you should to make intelligent decisions in the marketplace, in your procurement, in your labor relations, in all the varied industries in which we participate.
>
> The second thing is the decision making opportunity such a system provides for people. It provides us with a mechanism by which authority can be given and measured. The individual will know whether he has succeeded or has failed.[1]

Analysis

1. Evaluate these two reasons for decentralization.

2. Can you think of other reasons why a large company should decentralize?

---

[1] Reprinted with permission of the publisher. "Inspiring Teamwork," *Nation's Business,* March 1968, p. 42.

Chapter Nine

Committee Organization

THE PART THAT can be played by committees in the managerial process is considered
in this chapter. Some of the advantages and disadvantages of committees are analyzed, and the
relative effectiveness of committee and individual action is evaluated. The final section
stresses planning and procedures for more
efficient committee action.

Section I MAJOR CONCEPTS

Committee
Plural executives
Advantages of committees

Disadvantages of committees
Committee procedures

Section II SELF-TEST

True-False

_____ 1. Effective committee action can only
be achieved through a strict "Robert's
rules of order" approach.

_____ 2. Committees seem to be particularly
effective in coordinating interdepart-
mental activities.

_____ 3. A committee becomes a plural executive when it performs the decision-
making function.

_____ 4. A committee with 50 or more members can never be justified.

_____ 5. Committees are generally restricted to
top management levels.

Multiple Choice

_____ 1. Which of the following provides the
most logical basis for distinguishing
between committees and informal
meetings?
   a. Social interaction
   b. Participants
   c. Place of meeting
   d. Purpose of meeting

_____ 2. Which of the following statements
about participation by subordinates
in the decisional process is most acceptable?

53

a. The greater the participation by subordinates, the higher is the degree of cooperation.

b. Participation should be viewed as a possible corollary of leadership.

c. Participation is always expected by subordinates.

d. Participation is a substitute for executive leadership.

____ 3. The composition of the board of directors of the Federal Reserve banks provides a good example of

a. an ownership-dominated board

b. lack of interest-group representation

c. diversified interest-group representation

d. an inside board

____ 4. According to the Laboratory of Social Relations at Harvard, which of the following is the first step in a good group decision-making procedure?

a. Attempts to solve the problem

b. Agreement on what and how it shall be done

c. Determination of the facts

d. Determination of possible solutions

____ 5. The American Management Association study of the effectiveness of committees versus individual action indicated that committees were superior in handling _____ and ineffective in handling _____.

a. Leadership–jurisdictional questions

b. Control–executive

c. Jurisdictional questions–leadership

d. None of the above

____ 6. Which of the following is *least* likely to be an advantage of committees?

a. Integrated group judgment

b. Individual responsibility clearly defined

c. Facilitates coordination

d. Instrumental in disseminating and acquiring information

____ 7. Which of the following terms is often used to denote a committee playing the part of an executive?

a. Plural executive

b. Cooperative management

c. Adjunct

d. Coordinating committee

____ 8. When would committees *tend* to become *negative* rather than positive instruments of organizational cooperation?

a. When viewed as achieving integrated group judgement

b. When viewed as a means for achieving personal ends

c. When viewed as achieving coordination between departments

d. When viewed as promoting the development of teamwork among the members

____ 9. What is the most accurate statement about a committee decision?

a. Majority rule always results in the best decision.

b. The minority group will sometimes sabotage the goals of the majority.

c. Majority rule serves no useful purpose.

d. A group with very similar opinions usually *requires* a majority rule to reach a decision.

____ 10. In selecting committee membership, what would be the *most* important consideration when the purpose of the committee is to promote cooperation?

a. Functional proficiency

b. Executives from different departments

c. Required knowledge and technical skills

d. Sociological structure of the organization

Essay-Discussion

1. To what extent should committees be used as a substitute for individual action?

2. What is the appropriate size for a committee?

3. Discuss the cost aspects of committees.

Section III ILLUSTRATIVE CASES

"QUADRUMVIRATE"[1]

Today's major corporations are becoming increasingly complex and are experiencing dynamic change. To meet this challenge many companies are abandoning the traditional single chief executive approach for the plural executive concept at top management levels. As one steel company president recently stated: "There is a tendency to include more than a single man in the role of chief executive in order to provide greater breadth. I suspect that this will become more and more popular in larger and more complex companies."[2]

Union Carbide is an example of a company that has moved in this direction. The company has the president and three executive vice-presidents make up what is called the Office of the President. These four executives symbolically occupy the four corners of the fiftieth floor of the glass-enclosed Park Avenue home office. Every Monday morning the four meet to discuss company strategy and thrash out broad corporate policy. In the President's view, the Office of the President (he and his three executive vice-presidents) is a "central point of management authority."[3]

Analysis

1. Is this a good example of the concept of the plural executive? Why? Why not?

2. What status implications do you think may occur in a typical Monday meeting?

3. What are some advantages and disadvantages in this type of management by committees?

---

[1] Based on "More Room at the Top?," *Dun's Review*, March 1967, pp. 29-31.
[2] *Ibid.*, p. 29.
[3] *Ibid.*, p. 30.

ORGANIZATION FOR STANDARDS[1]

A technical journal concerned with electronic data processing (EDP) discussed an organiza-

---

[1] Reported in "The World of Standards," *Journal of Data Management*, January 1968, p. 11.

tion problem of the two associations responsible for standardization of EDP. The associations set up two sectional committees for standards known as X3 and X4. The organization chart for X3 is similar to most company organization charts. The X3 stands as the top box with eight functional subcommittees reporting to it, and each subcommittee is divided into working groups, which are divided into task groups.

The journal comments that this organization "appears a little time worn and obsolete now as one major sub-committee is completely inactive while others are bursting at the seams, still others are seeking tasks to justify their existence, and some spawning standards are desperately seeking a home in this outmoded structure."[2]

Recently a Systems Advisory Committee was added at the X3 level. This committee is currently reviewing the activities of all the subcommittees.

Analysis

1. Sketch the organization chart for X3.

2. As a member of the Systems Advisory Committee, what recommendations would you make?

3. Do committees always justify their existence? If they do not, what should be done about it?

---

[2] *Ibid.*

MATHEMATICAL FORMULATION OF COMMITTEES[1]

An experienced practicing manager recently wrote a cutting article about executive committee meetings. He states that committees are based on the "not unreasonable theory that two or more heads are infinitely better than

---

[1] Based on Herbert R. Spencer, Jr., "The Open-Window Theory of Executive Conferences," *Dun's Review*, October 1966, pp. 34-35, 106.

one, and that the meshing of many minds on a given subject can produce a creative consensus."[2] He quickly adds the opposing argument that committees are "merely convocations of people who singly can do nothing and collectively decide that nothing can be done."[3]

In conjunction with another executive, he then expressed his feelings about executive committees in terms of a clever mathematical formula:

$$D = \frac{10M}{K^2 + (N-2)^2 + (T-1)^3}$$

Where $D =$ the scope of the decision reached, in "Parkinson units"

---

[2] *Ibid.*, p. 34.
[3] *Ibid.*

$M =$ money involved, in thousands of dollars

$K =$ the difference between the temperature of the meeting room and 72 degrees Fahrenheit

$N =$ number of executives present

$T =$ time elapsed, in whole hours.

In facetious simplicity the formula means that executive meetings vary in direct proportion to the heat of the argument and the temperature in the room.

Analysis

1. Do you think that this mathematical formula is a good representation of committee meetings?

2. Expand on the advantages and disadvantages that the executive presented.

Chapter Ten

Boards of Directors and Other Committees

A GREATER PART of this chapter deals with the nature and functions of boards of directors. Particular attention is given to the legal status of boards, methods of board action, informal activities, the question of size and board composition, and the basis for more effective boards. Committees of the board and top management committees are described and evaluated. Another section considers committees at the operating level, including an analysis of the much discussed Scanlon plan. A final section analyzes committee management in the future.

Section I MAJOR CONCEPTS

Board of directors
Corporations
Board action
Board committees

Top management committees
Committee management
Junior board of directors
Scanlon plan

Section II SELF-TEST

True-False

_____ 1. The laws of most states provide that the corporate powers shall be exercised by directors who come from outside the company.

_____ 2. The Du Pont executive committee may be viewed as tacticians who put board policy into practice at the operating level.

_____ 3. The executive committee of the Standard Oil Company (New Jersey) is composed of executives who have spent most of their careers with the company.

_____ 4. The Scanlon plan accepts the basic assumptions of traditional economic theory.

_____ 5. The evidence seems to indicate that the board of directors' role in the management of large corporations is decreasing rather than increasing in importance.

Multiple Choice

_____ 1. The laws of most states provide that the corporate powers shall be exercised by
   a. the stockholders
   b. the bondholders
   c. the directors
   d. the employees

_____ 2. Under the "balanced board" concept, which of the following would generally not be represented on the board of directors of a large corporation?
   a. Corporation executives
   b. Employee representatives
   c. Representatives of large ownership interests
   d. Experts in management

_____ 3. Which of the following board committees were found to be most prevalent in a survey by the National Industrial Conference Board?
   a. Auditing
   b. Wage
   c. Finance
   d. Executive

_____ 4. The largest number of outside directors in a study by the National Industrial Conference Board were
   a. retired businessmen
   b. corporation presidents
   c. managers
   d. bankers

_____ 5. Which of the following has not generally been given "interest group" representation on corporate boards of directors in the United States?

   a. Creditors
   b. Stockholders
   c. Businessmen
   d. Union leaders

_____ 6. Which of the following would not be true when analyzing the Scanlon plan in the light of the results obtained from the Hawthorne study?
   a. The plan attempts to take advantage of, rather than work at cross purposes with, the behavioral patterns actually found in industrial relations.
   b. The Scanlon plan utilizes effective individual behavior plans to counteract the group pressures found in the Hawthorne studies.
   c. The Scanlon plan provides a setting within which informal interactions can expedite formal goals.
   d. Under the Scanlon plan the individual is not pitted against the group but is directed to behave formally as he generally must behave informally.

_____ 7. McCormick and Company, a Baltimore concern engaged in the spice and extract business,
   a. installed a Junior Board of Directors
   b. initiated the Scanlon plan
   c. eliminated the position of president
   d. developed an authoritarian approach to management

_____ 8. Which of the following was not one of the basic functions performed by boards of directors as determined by a Harvard study?
   a. Negotiating labor contracts
   b. Selection of executives
   c. Policy formulation
   d. Appraising company and executive performance

_____ 9. In the Harvard study, which of the following was not mentioned as a major method of board action?
   a. Decide

b. Arbitrate

c. Confirm

d. Review

_____ 10. What is the best statement about the impact of information technology on committee management in the future?

    a. Leavitt and Whisler, in their pioneering article on management in the 1980s, ignored committee management.

    b. Information technology preceded the birth of top management committees.

    c. It does not appear likely that information technology will rad-

ically reconstruct the group processes that already exist in major corporations.

    d. Information technology will have no impact on top management committee decision making.

Essay-Discussion

1. What managerial functions are performed by boards of directors?

2. What factors influence the sizes of boards of directors?

3. Do you think that committee management will replace man-to-man or "individualistic" management? Why?

Section III ILLUSTRATIVE CASES

PRESIDENT'S VIEWS OF THE BOARD[1]

A panel of top corporation presidents were recently asked to comment on the function of the board of directors. One important area of concern was the relationship between the chief operating executives and the board of directors. Most of the chief executives felt that they should lead the board and not necessarily be impartial. As one president explained, "The chief executive officer (and his staff) is employed by the board to direct the affairs of the company within the broad policy limitations established by the board. . . . An impartial chief executive officer or management staff will defeat this objective."[2]

Another area of interest was the board's obligations to the company. Beside the usual legal responsibilities such as setting policy, electing operating officers, and overseeing the overall conduct of the business, the board was viewed quite differently by many of the company presidents. For example, one large corporation president stated that the board's prime duty is to "manage the company through direction, selection and analysis of hired man-

agement."[3] However, another chief executive replied in a different manner that was more than just semantics: "A board should not manage, but should review and provide overall judgment."[4]

Analysis

1. Do you agree with the executives that they should lead rather than be impartial in their relations with the board? What about conflicts of interest?

2. Explain the positions of the last two executives quoted concerning the primary function of the board of directors? What is the difference between the two viewpoints?

3. What role should the board of directors play in the management of today's corporation?

TASK FORCE[1]

One of the newer types of committee management is the specialized task force or trouble-

---

[1] Based on "The Dilemma with Directors," *Dun's Review*, October 1966, pp. 48–49, 133–134.

[2] *Ibid.*, p. 48.

[3] *Ibid.*, p. 134.

[4] *Ibid.*

[1] Based on "Management's Teams of Trouble," *Dun's Review*, August 1968, pp. 25–27, 70–71.

shooting teams. The task force approach is to utilize various management personnel in a temporary, *ad hoc*, manner, dissolving the group once the given task is accomplished.

Recently, a paper producer suffered a substantial drop in profits. Management placed the blame on an inadequate information system. The corporate planner for the organization formed nine special teams to tackle the information problem in each of the major corporate functions, such as marketing, manufacturing, personnel, and finance. The teams consisted of eight to fifteen men with widely divergent backgrounds. The corporate planner stated, "To really be effective, a team should be multiskilled and diversified."[2] By working from the bottom up, each task force designed a reporting and control system for its assigned function. No superiors and subordinates were on the same team. All teams got together every two weeks to discuss their functional investigations. By the end of three months the task force presented the first stage of their recommendations to top management.

Analysis

1. Do you agree with the corporate planner that task forces should be "multiskilled and diversified"? Why?

2. What problems could you foresee if a superior and his subordinate were on the same team?

3. What kind of organizational problems would this type of committee management be especially suited for? Why?

---

[2] *Ibid.*, p. 27.

"A" COMMITTEE[1]

A large international company holds monthly meetings of its appropriations committee, which it calls the "A" committee. Group executives submit their annual budgets, forecasts, and supplemental requests for capital appropriation (RCA's). The group head also turns in to the committee each month a "green book." This lengthy report details the group's activities for the month. Should the "green book" indicate that performance is more than 10 per cent below budget, the group receives an invitation to go in and talk things over with the "A" committee. The vice-president in charge of corporate administration states, "We try to establish a dialogue with our group heads. I think it's fair to say that we acquire as much knowledge and information of our divisions as their managements have in terms of plant costs, sales forecasts, market development and capital expenditures programs."[2]

Analysis

1. What would you say the major function of the "A" committee seems to be?

2. What would be the purpose of calling in a group executive who is 10 per cent below budget?

3. Cite some advantages and disadvantages of this type of committee management?

---

[1] Developed from "The Changing Face of W. R. Grace," *Dun's Review*, July 1967, pp. 23–24, 54–59.
[2] *Ibid.*, p. 56.

READING: ORGANIZATION THEORY: AN OVERVIEW AND AN APPRAISAL

WILLIAM G. SCOTT

Man is intent on drawing himself into a web of collectivized patterns. "Modern man has learned to accommodate himself to a world increasingly organized. The trend toward ever more explicit and consciously drawn relationships is profound and sweeping; it is marked by depth no less than by extension."[1] This comment by Seidenberg nicely summarizes the pervasive influence of organization in many forms of human activity.

Some of the reasons for intense organizational activity are found in the fundamental transitions which revolutionized our society, changing it from a rural culture, to a culture based on technology, industry, and the city. From these changes, a way of life emerged characterized by the *proximity* and *dependency* of people on each other. Proximity and dependency, as conditions of social life, harbor the threats of human conflict, capricious antisocial behavior, instability of human relationships, and uncertainty about the nature of the social structure with its concomitant roles.

Of course, these threats to social integrity are present to some degree in all societies, ranging from the primitive to the modern. But, these threats become dangerous when the harmonious functioning of a society rests on the maintenance of a highly intricate, delicately balanced form of human collaboration. The civilization we have created depends on the preservation of a precarious balance. Hence, disrupting forces impinging on this shaky form of collaboration must be eliminated or minimized.

Traditionally, organization is viewed as a vehicle for accomplishing goals and objectives. While this approach is useful, it tends to obscure the inner workings and internal purposes of organization itself. Another fruitful way of treating organization is as a mechanism having the ultimate purpose of offsetting those forces which undermine human collaboration. In this sense, organization tends to minimize conflict, and to lessen the significance of individual behavior which deviates from values that the organization has established as worthwhile. Further, organization increases stability in human relationships by reducing uncertainty regarding the nature of the system's structure and the human roles which are inherent to it. Corollary to this point, organization enhances the predictability of human action, because it limits the number of behavioral alternatives available to an individual. As Presthus points out:

> Organization is defined as a system of structural interpersonal relations . . . individuals are differentiated in terms of authority, status, and role with the result that personal interaction is prescribed. . . . Anticipated reactions tend to occur, while ambiguity and spontaneity are decreased.[2]

In addition to all of this, organization has built-in safeguards. Besides prescribing acceptable forms of behavior for those who elect to submit to it, organization is also able to counterbalance the influence of human action which transcends its established patterns.[3]

Reprinted from *Academy of Management Journal*, Vol. 4, No. 1, April 1961, pp. 7–26, with permission of the publisher. William G. Scott was an Associate Professor of Management at De Paul University when he wrote this article.

[1] Roderick Seidenburg, *Post Historic Man* (Boston: Beacon Press, 1951), p. 1.

[2] Robert V. Presthus, "Toward a Theory of Organizational Behavior," *Administrative Science Quarterly*, June, 1958, p. 50.

[3] Regulation and predictability of human behavior

Few segments of society have engaged in organizing more intensively than business.[4] The reason is clear. Business depends on what organization offers. Business needs a system of relationships among functions; it needs stability, continuity, and predictability in its internal activities and external contacts. Business also appears to need harmonious relationships among the people and processes which make it up. Put another way, a business organization has to be free, relatively, from destructive tendencies which may be caused by divergent interests.

As a foundation for meeting these needs rests administrative science. A major element of this science is organization theory, which provides the grounds for management activities in a number of significant areas of business endeavor. Organization theory, however, is not a homogeneous science based on generally accepted principles. Various theories of organization have been, and are being evolved. For example, something called "modern organization theory" has recently emerged, raising the wrath of some traditionalists, but also capturing the imagination of a rather elite *avant-garde*.

The thesis of this paper is that modern organization theory, when stripped of its irrelevancies, redundancies, and "speech defects," is a logical and vital evolution in management thought. In order for this thesis to be supported, the reader must endure a review and appraisal of more traditional forms of organization theory which may seem elementary to him.

In any event, three theories of organization are having considerable influence on management thought and practice. They are arbitrarily labeled in this paper as the classical, the neo-classical, and the modern. Each of these is fairly distinct; but they are not unrelated. Also, these theories are on-going, being actively supported by several schools of management thought.

THE CLASSICAL DOCTRINE

For lack of a better method of identification, it will be said that the classical doctrine deals almost exclusively with the *anatomy of formal organization*. This doctrine can be traced back to Frederick W. Taylor's interest in functional foremanship and planning staffs. But most students of management thought would agree that in the United States, the first systematic approach to organization, and the first comprehensive attempt to find organizational universals, is dated 1931 when Mooney and Reiley published *Onward Industry*.[5] Subsequently, numerous books, following the classical vein, have appeared. Two of the more recent are Brech's, *Organization*[6] and Allen's, *Management and Organization*.[7]

Classical organization theory is built around four key pillars. They are the division of labor, the scalar and functional processes, structure, and span of control. Given these major elements just about all of classical organization theory can be derived.

(1) *The division of labor* is without doubt the cornerstone among the four elements.[8] From it the other elements flow as corollaries. For example, *scalar* and *functional* growth requires specialization and departmentalization of functions. Organization *structure* is naturally dependent upon the direction which specializa-

---

are matters of degree varying with different organizations on something of a continuum. At one extreme are bureaucratic type organizations with tight bonds of regulation. At the other extreme are voluntary associations, and informal organizations with relatively loose bonds of regulation.

This point has an interesting sidelight. A bureaucracy with tight controls and a high degree of predictability of human action appears to be unable to distinguish between destructive and creative deviations from established values. Thus the only thing which is safeguarded is the *status quo*.

[4] The monolithic institutions of the military and government are other cases of organizational preoccupation.

[5] James D. Mooney and Alan C. Reiley, *Onward Industry* (New York: Harper and Brothers, 1931). Later published by James D. Mooney under the title *Principles of Organization*.

[6] E. F. L. Brech, *Organization* (London: Longmans, Green and Company, 1957).

[7] Louis A. Allen, *Management and Organization* (New York: McGraw-Hill Book Company, 1958).

[8] Usually the division of labor is treated under a topical heading of departmentation, see for example: Harold Koontz and Cyril O'Donnell, *Principles of Management* (New York: McGraw-Hill Book Company, 1959), Chapter 7.

tion of activities travels in company development. Finally, *span of control* problems result from the number of specialized functions under the jurisdiction of a manager.

(2) *The scalar and functional processes* deal with the vertical and horizontal growth of the organization, respectively.[9] The scalar process refers to the growth of the chain of command, the delegation of authority and responsibility, unity of command, and the obligation to report.

The division of the organization into specialized parts and the regrouping of the parts into compatible units are matters pertaining to the functional process. This process focuses on the horizontal evolution of the line and staff in a formal organization.

(3) *Structure* is the logical relationship of functions in an organization, arranged to accomplish the objectives of the company efficiently. Structure implies system and pattern. Classical organization theory usually works with two basic structures, the line and the staff. However, such activities as committee and liaison functions fall quite readily into the purview of structural considerations. Again, structure is the vehicle for introducing logical and consistent relationships among the diverse functions which comprise the organization.[10]

(4) *The span of control* concept relates to the number of subordinates a manager can effectively supervise. Graicunas has been credited with first elaborating the point that there are numerical limitations to the subordinates one man can control.[11] In a recent statement on the subject, Brech points out, "span" refers to ". . . the number of persons, themselves carrying managerial and supervisory responsibilities, for whom the senior manager retains his over-embracing responsibility of direction and planning, co-ordination, motivation, and control."[12] Regardless of interpreta-

tion, span of control has significance, in part, for the shape of the organization which evolves through growth. Wide span yields a flat structure; short span results in a tall structure. Further, the span concept directs attention to the complexity of human and functional interrelationships in an organization.

It would not be fair to say that the classical school is unaware of the day-to-day administrative problems of the organization. Paramount among these problems are those stemming from human interactions. But the interplay of individual personality, informal groups, intraorganizational conflict, and the decision-making processes in the formal structure appears largely to be neglected by classical organization theory. Additionally, the classical theory overlooks the contributions of the behavioral sciences by failing to incorporate them in its doctrine in any systematic way. In summary, classical organization theory has relevant insights into the nature of organization, but the value of this theory is limited by its narrow concentration on the formal anatomy of organization.

NEOCLASSICAL THEORY OF ORGANIZATION

The neoclassical theory of organization embarked on the task of compensating for some of the deficiencies in classical doctrine. The neoclassical school is commonly identified with the human relations movement. Generally, the neoclassical approach takes the postulates of the classical school, regarding the pillars of organization as givens. But these postulates are regarded as modified by people, acting independently or within the context of the informal organization.

One of the main contributions of the neoclassical school is the introduction of behavioral sciences in an integrated fashion into the theory of organization. Through the use of these sciences, the human relationists demonstrate how the pillars of the classical doctrine are affected by the impact of human actions. Further, the neoclassical approach includes a systematic treatment of the informal organiza-

[9] These processes are discussed at length in Ralph Currier Davis, *The Fundamentals of Top Management* (New York: Harper and Brothers, 1951), Chapter 7.

[10] For a discussion of structure see: William H. Newman, *Administrative Action* (Englewood Cliffs: Prentice-Hall, Incorporated, 1951), Chapter 16.

[11] V. A. Graicunas, "Relationships in Organization," *Papers on the Science of Administration* (New York: Columbia University, 1937).

[12] Brech, *op. cit.*, p. 78.

tion, showing its influence on the formal structure.

Thus, the neoclassical approach to organization theory gives evidence of accepting classical doctrine, but superimposing on it modifications resulting from individual behavior, and the influence of the informal group. The inspiration of the neoclassical school were the Hawthorne studies.[13] Current examples of the neoclassical approach are found in human relations books like Gardner and Moore, *Human Relations in Industry*,[14] and Davis, *Human Relations in Business*.[15] To a more limited extent, work in industrial sociology also reflects a neoclassical point of view.[16]

It would be useful to look briefly at some of the contributions made to organization theory by the neoclassicists. First to be considered are modifications of the pillars of classical doctrine; second is the informal organization.

Examples of the Neoclassical Approach to the Pillars of Formal Organization Theory

(1) The *division of labor* has been a long standing subject of comment in the field of human relations. Very early in the history of industrial psychology study was made of industrial fatigue and monotony caused by the specialization of the work.[17] Later, attention shifted to the isolation of the worker, and his feeling of anonymity resulting from insignificant jobs which contributed negligibly to the final product.[18]

Also, specialization influences the work of management. As an organization expands, the need concomitantly arises for managerial motivation and coordination of the activities of others. Both motivation and coordination in turn relate to executive leadership. Thus, in part, stemming from the growth of industrial specialization, the neoclassical school has developed a large body of theory relating to motivation, coordination, and leadership. Much of this theory is derived from the social sciences.

(2) Two aspects of the *scalar and functional* processes which have been treated with some degree of intensity by the neoclassical school are the delegation of authority and responsibility, and gaps in or overlapping of functional jurisdictions. The classical theory assumes something of perfection in the delegation and functionalization processes. The neoclassical school points out that human problems are caused by imperfections in the way these processes are handled.

For example, too much or insufficient delegation may render an executive incapable of action. The failure to delegate authority and responsibility equally may result in frustration for the delegatee. Overlapping of authorities often causes clashes in personality. Gaps in authority cause failures in getting jobs done, with one party blaming the other for shortcomings in performance.[19]

The neoclassical school says that the scalar and functional processes are theoretically valid, but tend to deteriorate in practice. The ways in which they break down are described, and some of the human causes are pointed out. In addition the neoclassicists make recommendations, suggesting various "human tools" which will facilitate the operation of these processes.

(3) *Structure* provides endless avenues of analysis for the neoclassical theory of organization. The theme is that human behavior disrupts the best laid organizational plans, and thwarts the cleanness of the logical relationships founded in the structure. The neoclassical critique of structure centers on frictions which

[13] See: F. J. Roethlisberger and William J. Dickson, *Management and the Worker* (Cambridge: Harvard University Press, 1939).

[14] Burleigh B. Gardner and David G. Moore, *Human Relations in Industry* (Homewood: Richard D. Irwin, 1955).

[15] Keith Davis, *Human Relations in Business* (New York: McGraw-Hill Book Company, 1957).

[16] For example see: Delbert C. Miller and William H. Form, *Industrial Sociology* (New York: Harper and Brothers, 1951).

[17] See: Hugo Munsterberg, *Psychology and Industrial Efficiency* (Boston: Houghton Mifflin Company, 1913).

[18] Probably the classic work is: Elton Mayo, *The Human Problems of an Industrial Civilization* (Cambridge: Harvard University, 1946, first printed 1933).

[19] For further discussion of the human relations implications of the scalar and functional processes see: Keith Davis, *op. cit.*, pp. 60–66.

appear internally among people performing different functions.

Line and staff relations is a problem area, much discussed, in this respect. Many companies seem to have difficulty keeping the line and staff working together harmoniously. Both Dalton[20] and Juran[21] have engaged in research to discover the causes of friction, and to suggest remedies.

Of course, line-staff relations represent only one of the many problems of structural frictions described by the neoclassicists. As often as not, the neoclassicists will offer prescriptions for the elimination of conflict in structure. Among the more important harmony-rendering formulae are participation, junior boards, bottom-up management, joint committees, recognition of human dignity, and "better" communication.

(4) An executive's *span of control* is a function of human determinants, and the reduction of span to a precise, universally applicable ratio is silly, according to the neoclassicists. Some of the determinants of span are individual differences in managerial abilities, the type of people and functions supervised, and the extent of communication effectiveness.

Coupled with the span of control question are the human implications of the type of structure which emerges. That is, is a tall structure with a short span or a flat structure with a wide span more conducive to good human relations and high morale? The answer is situational. Short span results in tight supervision; wide span requires a good deal of delegation with looser controls. Because of individual and organizational differences, sometimes one is better than the other. There is a tendency to favor the looser form of organization, however, for the reason that tall structures breed autocratic leadership, which is often pointed out as a cause of low morale.[22]

The Neoclassical View of the Informal Organization

Nothing more than the barest mention of the informal organization is given even in the most recent classical treatises on organization theory.[23] Systematic discussion of this form of organization has been left to the neoclassicists. The informal organization refers to people in group associations at work, but these associations are not specified in the "blueprint" of the formal organization. The informal organization means natural groupings of people in the work situation.

In a general way, the informal organization appears in response to the social need—the need of people to associate with others. However, for analytical purposes, this explanation is not particularly satisfying. Research has produced the following, more specific determinants underlying the appearance of informal organizations.

(1) The *location* determinant simply states that in order to form into groups of any lasting nature, people have to have frequent face-to-face contact. Thus, the geography of physical location in a plant or office is an important factor in predicting who will be in what group.[24]

(2) *Occupation* is key factor determining the rise and composition of informal groups. There is a tendency for people performing similar jobs to group together.[25]

(3) *Interests* are another determinant for informal group formation. Even though people might be in the same location, performing similar jobs, differences of interest among them explain why several small, instead of one large, informal organizations emerge.

(4) *Special issues* often result in the formation of informal groups, but this determinant is set apart from the three previously mentioned. In this case, people who do not neces-

[20] Melville Dalton, "Conflicts between Staff and Line Managerial Officers," *American Sociological Review*, June, 1950, pp. 342–351.

[21] J. M. Juran, "Improving the Relationship between Staff and Line," *Personnel*, May, 1956, pp. 515–524.

[22] Gardner and Moore, *op cit.*, pp. 237–243.

[23] For example: Brech, *op. cit.*, pp. 27–29; and Allen, *op. cit.*, pp. 61–62.

[24] See: Leon Festinger, Stanley Schachter, and Kurt Back, *Social Pressures in Informal Groups* (New York: Harper and Brothers, 1950), pp. 153–163.

[25] For example see: W. Fred Cottrell, *The Railroader* (Palo Alto: The Stanford University Press, 1940), Chapter 3.

sarily have similar interests, occupations, or locations may join together for a common cause. Once the issue is resolved, then the tendency is to revert to the more "natural" group forms.[26] Thus, special issues give rise to a rather impermanent informal association; groups based on the other three determinants tend to be more lasting.

When informal organizations come into being they assume certain characteristics. Since understanding these characteristics is important for management practice, they are noted below:

(1) Informal organizations act as agencies of *social control*. They generate a culture based on certain norms of conduct which, in turn, demands conformity from group members. These standards may be at odds with the values set by the formal organization. So an individual may very well find himself in a situation of conflicting demands.

(2) The form of human interrelationships in the informal organization requires *techniques of analysis* different from those used to plot the relationships of people in a formal organization. The method used for determining the structure of the informal group is called sociometric analysis. Sociometry reveals the complex structure of interpersonal relations which is based on premises fundamentally unlike the logic of the formal organization.

(3) Informal organizations have *status and communication* systems peculiar to themselves, not necessarily derived from the formal systems. For example, the grapevine is the subject of much neoclassical study.

(4) Survival of the informal organization requires stable continuing relationships among the people in them. Thus, it has been observed that the informal organization *resists change*.[27]

Considerable attention is given by the neoclassicists to overcoming informal resistance to change.

(5) The last aspect of analysis which appears to be central to the neoclassical view of the informal organization is the study of the *informal leader*. Discussion revolves around who the informal leader is, how he assumes this role, what characteristics are peculiar to him, and how he can help the manager accomplish his objectives in the formal organization.[28]

This brief sketch of some of the major facets of informal organization theory has neglected, so far, one important topic treated by the neoclassical school. It is the way in which the formal and informal organizations interact.

A conventional way of looking at the interaction of the two is the "live and let live" point of view. Management should recognize that the informal organization exists, nothing can destroy it, and so the executive might just as well work with it. Working with the informal organization involves not threatening its existence unnecessarily, listening to opinions expressed for the group by the leader, allowing group participation in decision-making situations, and controlling the grapevine by prompt release of accurate information.[29]

While this approach is management centered, it is not unreasonable to expect that informal group standards and norms could make themselves felt on formal organizational policy. An honestly conceived effort by managers to establish a working relationship with the informal organization could result in an association where both formal and informal views would be reciprocally modified. The danger which at all costs should be avoided is that "working with the informal organization" does not degenerate into a shallow disguise for human manipulation.

Some neoclassical writing in organization

---

[26] Except in cases where the existence of an organization is necessary for the continued maintenance of employee interest. Under these conditions the previously informal association may emerge as a formal group, such as a union.

[27] Probably the classic study of resistance to change is: Lester Coch and John R. P. French, Jr., "Overcoming Resistance to Change," in Schuyler Dean Hoslett (editor), *Human Factors in Management* (New York: Harper and Brothers, 1951) pp. 242–268.

[28] For example see: Robert Saltonstall, *Human Relations in Administration* (New York: McGraw-Hill Book Company, 1959), pp. 330–331; and Keith Davis, *op. cit.*, pp. 99–101.

[29] For an example of this approach see: John T. Doutt, "Management Must Manage the Informal Group, Too," *Advanced Management*, May, 1959, pp. 26–28.

theory, especially that coming from the management-oriented segment of this school, gives the impression that the formal and informal organizations are distinct, and at times, quite irreconcilable factors in a company. The interaction which takes place between the two is something akin to the interaction between the company and a labor union, or a government agency, or another company.

The concept of the social system is another approach to the interactional climate. While this concept can be properly classified as neoclassical, it borders on the modern theories of organization. The phrase "social system" means that an organization is a complex of mutually interdependent, but variable, factors.

These factors include individuals and their attitudes and motives, jobs, the physical work setting, the formal organization, and the informal organizations. These factors, and many others, are woven into an overall pattern of interdependency. From this point of view, the formal and informal organizations lose their distinctiveness, but find real meaning, in terms of human behavior, in the operation of the system as a whole. Thus, the study of organization turns away from descriptions of its component parts, and is refocused on the system of interrelationships among the parts.

One of the major contributions of the Hawthorne studies was the integration of Pareto's idea of the social system into a meaningful method of analysis for the study of behavior in human organizations.[30] This concept is still vitally important. But unfortunately some work in the field of human relations undertaken by the neoclassicists has overlooked, or perhaps discounted, the significance of this consideration.[31]

The fundamental insight regarding the social system, developed and applied to the industrial scene by the Hawthorne researchers, did not find much extension in subsequent work in the neoclassical vein. Indeed, the neoclassical

school after the Hawthorne studies generally seemed content to engage in descriptive generalizations, or particularized empirical research studies which did not have much meaning outside their own context.

The neoclassical school of organization theory has been called bankrupt. Criticisms range from, "human relations is a tool for cynical puppeteering of people," to "human relations is nothing more than a trifling body of empirical and descriptive information." There is a good deal of truth in both criticisms, but another appraisal of the neoclassical school of organization theory is offered here. The neoclassical approach has provided valuable contributions to lore of organization. But, like the classical theory, the neoclassical doctrine suffers from incompleteness, a shortsighted perspective, and lack of integration among the many facets of human behavior studied by it. Modern organization theory has made a move to cover the shortcomings of the current body of theoretical knowledge.

MODERN ORGANIZATION THEORY

The distinctive qualities of modern organization theory are its conceptual-analytical base, its reliance on empirical research data and, above all, its integrating nature. These qualities are framed in a philosophy which accepts the premise that the only meaningful way to study organization is to study it as a system. As Henderson put it, the study of a system must rely on a method of analysis, ". . . involving the simultaneous variations of mutually dependent variables."[32] Human systems, of course, contain a huge number of dependent variables which defy the most complex simultaneous equations to solve.

Nevertheless, system analysis has its own peculiar point of view which aims to study organization in the way Henderson suggests. It treats organization as a system of mutually dependent variables. As a result, modern organization theory, which accepts system analysis, shifts the conceptual level of organization study

[30] See: Roethlisberger and Dickson, *op. cit.*, Chapter 24.

[31] A check of management human relations texts, the organization and human relations chapters of principles of management texts, and texts on conventional organization theory for management courses reveals little or no treatment of the concept of the social system.

[32] Lawrence J. Henderson, *Pareto's General Sociology* (Cambridge: Harvard University Press, 1935), p. 13.

above the classical and neoclassical theories. Modern organization theory asks a range of interrelated questions which are not seriously considered by the two other theories.

Key among these questions are: (1) What are the strategic parts of the system? (2) What is the nature of their mutual dependency? (3) What are the main processes in the system which link the parts together, and facilitate their adjustment to each other? (4) What are the goals sought by systems?[33]

Modern organization theory is in no way a unified body of thought. Each writer and researcher has his special emphasis when he considers the system. Perhaps the most evident unifying thread in the study of systems is the effort to look at the organization in its totality. Representative books in this field are March and Simon, *Organizations*,[34] and Haire's anthology, *Modern Organization Theory*.[35]

Instead of attempting a review of different writers' contributions to modern organization theory, it will be more useful to discuss the various ingredients involved in system analysis. They are the parts, the interactions, the processes, and the goals of systems.

The Parts of the System and Their Interdependency

The first basic part of the system is the *individual*, and the personality structure he brings to the organization. Elementary to an individual's personality are motives and attitudes which condition the range of expectancies he hopes to satisfy by participating in the system.

The second part of the system is the formal arrangement of functions, usually called the *formal organization*. The formal organization is the interrelated pattern of jobs which make up the structure of a system. Certain writers, like Argyris, see a fundamental conflict resulting from the demands made by the system, and the structure of the mature, normal personality. In any event, the individual has expectancies regarding the job he is to perform; and, conversely, the job makes demands on, or has expectancies relating to, the performance of the individual. Considerable attention has been given by writers in modern organization theory to incongruencies resulting from the interaction of organizational and individual demands.[36]

The third part in the organization system is the *informal organization*. Enough has been said already about the nature of this organization. But it must be noted that an interactional pattern exists between the individual and the informal group. This interactional arrangement can be conveniently discussed as the mutual modification of expectancies. The informal organization has demands which it makes on members in terms of anticipated forms of behavior, and the individual has expectancies of satisfaction he hopes to derive from association with people on the job. Both these sets of expectancies interact, resulting in the individual modifying his behavior to accord with the demands of the group, and the group, perhaps, modifying what it expects from an individual because of the impact of his personality on group norms.[37]

Much of what has been said about the various expectancy systems in an organization can also be treated using status and role concepts. Part of modern organization theory rests on research findings in social-psychology relative to reciprocal patterns of behavior stemming from role demands generated by both the formal and informal organizations, and role perceptions peculiar to the individual. Bakke's *fusion process* is largely concerned with the modification of role expectancies. The fusion process is a force, according to Bakke, which acts to weld divergent elements together for the preservation of organizational integrity.[38]

---

[33] There is another question which cannot be treated in the scope of this paper. It asks, what research tools should be used for the study of the system?

[34] James G. March and Herbert A. Simon, *Organizations* (New York: John Wiley and Sons, 1958).

[35] Mason Haire (editor), *Modern Organization Theory* (New York: John Wiley and Sons, 1959).

[36] See Chris Argyris, *Personality and Organization* (New York: Harper and Brothers, 1957), esp. Chapters 2, 3, 7.

[37] For a larger treatment of this subject see: George C. Homans, *The Human Group* (New York: Harcourt, Brace and Company, 1950), Chapter 5.

[38] E. Wight Bakke, "Concept of the Social Or-

The fifth part of system analysis is the *physical setting* in which the job is performed. Although this element of the system may be implicit in what has been said already about the formal organization and its functions, it is well to separate it. In the physical surroundings of work, interactions are present in complex man-machine systems. The human "engineer" cannot approach the problems posed by such interrelationships in a purely technical, engineering fashion. As Haire says, these problems lie in the domain of the social theorist.[39] Attention must be centered on responses demanded from a logically ordered production function, often with the view of minimizing the error in the system. From this standpoint, work cannot be effectively organized unless the psychological, social, and physiological characteristics of people participating in the work environment are considered. Machines and processes should be designed to fit certain generally observed psychological and physiological properties of men, rather than hiring men to fit machines.

In summary, the parts of the system which appear to be of strategic importance are the individual, the formal structure, the informal organization, status and role patterns, and the physical environment of work. Again, these parts are woven into a configuration called the organizational system. The processes which link the parts are taken up next.

The Linking Processes

One can say, with a good deal of glibness, that all the parts mentioned above are interrelated. Although this observation is quite correct, it does not mean too much in terms of system theory unless some attempt is made to analyze the processes by which the interaction is achieved. Role theory is devoted to certain types of interactional processes. In addition,

modern organization theorists point to three other linking activities which appear to be universal to human systems of organized behavior. These processes are communication, balance, and decision making.

(1) Communication is mentioned often in neoclassical theory, but the emphasis is on description of forms of communication activity, i.e., formal-informal, vertical-horizontal, line-staff. Communication, as a mechanism which links the segments of the system together, is overlooked by way of much considered analysis.

One aspect of modern organization theory is study of the communication network in the system. Communication is viewed as the method by which action is evoked from the parts of the system. Communication acts not only as stimuli resulting in action, but also as a control and coordination mechanism linking the decision centers in the system into a synchronized pattern. Deutsch points out that organizations are composed of parts which communicate with each other, receive messages from the outside world, and store information. Taken together, these communication functions of the parts comprise a configuration representing the total system.[40] More is to be said about communication later in the discussion of the cybernetic model.

(2) The concept of *balance* as a linking process involves a series of some rather complex ideas. Balance refers to an equilibrating mechanism whereby the various parts of the system are maintained in a harmoniously structured relationship to each other.

The necessity for the balance concept logically flows from the nature of systems themselves. It is impossible to conceive of an ordered relationship among the parts of a system without also introducing the idea of a stabilizing or an adapting mechanism.

Balance appears in two varieties—quasi-automatic and innovative. Both forms of balance act to insure system integrity in face of changing conditions, either internal or external to the system. The first form of balance,

ganization," in *Modern Organization Theory*, Mason Haire (editor) (New York: John Wiley and Sons, 1959) pp. 60–61.

[39] Mason Haire, "Psychology and the Study of Business: Joint Behavioral Sciences," in *Social Science Research on Business: Product and Potential* (New York: Columbia University Press, 1959), pp. 53–59.

[40] Karl W. Deutsch "On Communication Models in the Social Sciences." *Public Opinion Quarterly,* 16 (1952), pp. 356–380.

quasi-automatic, refers to what some think are "homoeostatic" properties of systems. That is, systems seem to exhibit built-in propensities to maintain steady states.

If human organizations are open, self-maintaining systems, then control and regulatory processes are necessary. The issue hinges on the degree to which stabilizing processes in systems, when adapting to change, are automatic. March and Simon have an interesting answer to this problem, which in part is based on the type of change and the adjustment necessary to adapt to the change. Systems have programs of action which are put into effect when a change is perceived. If the change is relatively minor, and if the change comes within the purview of established programs of action, then it might be fairly confidently predicted that the adaptation made by the system will be quasi-automatic.[41]

The role of innovative, creative balancing efforts now needs to be examined. The need for innovation arises when adaptation to a change is outside the scope of existing programs designed for the purpose of keeping the system in balance. New programs have to be evolved in order for the system to maintain internal harmony.

New programs are created by trial and error search for feasible action alternatives to cope with a given change. But innovation is subject to the limitations and possibilities inherent in the quantity and variety of information present in a system at a particular time. New combinations of alternatives for innovative purposes depend on:

(a) the possible range of output of the system, or the capacity of the system to supply information.

(b) the range of available information in the memory of the system.

(c) the operating rules (program) governing the analysis and flow of information within the system.

(d) the ability of the system to "forget" previously learned solutions to change problems.[42] A system with too good a memory

might narrow its behavioral choices to such an extent as to stifle innovation. In simpler language, old learned programs might be used to adapt to change, when newly innovated programs are necessary.[43]

Much of what has been said about communication and balance brings to mind a cybernetic model in which both these processes have vital roles. Cybernetics has to do with feedback and control in all kinds of systems. Its purpose is to maintain system stability in the face of change. Cybernetics cannot be studied without considering communication networks, information flow, and some kind of balancing process aimed at preserving the integrity of the system.

Cybernetics directs attention to key questions regarding the system. These questions are: How are communication centers connected, and how are they maintained? Corollary to this question: what is the structure of the feedback system? Next, what information is stored in the organization, and at what points? And as a corollary: how accessible is this information to decision-making centers? Third, how conscious is the organization of the operation of its own parts? That is, to what extent do the policy centers receive control information with sufficient frequency and relevancy to create a real awareness of the operation of the segments of the system? Finally, what are the learning (innovating) capabilities of the system?[44]

Answers to the questions posed by cybernetics are crucial to understanding both the balancing and communication processes in systems.[45] Although cybernetics has been applied largely to technical-engineering problems of automation, the model of feedback, control, and regulation in all systems has a good deal of generality. Cybernetics is a fruit-

---

[41] March and Simon, op. cit., pp. 139–140.

[42] Mervyn L. Cadwallader "The Cybernetic Analysis of Change in Complex Social Organization,"

The American Journal of Sociology, September, 1959, p. 156.

[43] It is conceivable for innovative behavior to be programmed into the system.

[44] These are questions adapted from Deutsch, *op. cit.*, 368–370

[45] Answers to these questions would require a comprehensive volume. One of the best approaches currently available is Stafford Beer, *Cybernetics and Management* (New York: John Wiley and Sons, 1959).

ful area which can be used to synthesize the processes of communication and balance.

(3) A wide spectrum of topics dealing with types of decisions in human systems makes up the core of analysis of another important process in organizations. Decision analysis is one of the major contributions of March and Simon in their book *Organizations*. The two major classes of decisions they discuss are decisions to produce and decisions to participate in the system.[46]

Decisions to produce are largely a result of an interaction between individual attitudes and the demands of organization. Motivation analysis becomes central to studying the nature and results of the interaction. Individual decisions to participate in the organization reflect on such issues as the relationship between organizational rewards versus the demands made by the organization. Participation decisions also focus attention on the reasons why individuals remain in or leave organizations.

March and Simon treat decisions as internal variables in an organization which depend on jobs, individual expectations and motivations, and organizational structure. Marschak[47] looks on the decision process as an independent variable upon which the survival of the organization is based. In this case, the organization is viewed as having, inherent to its structure, the ability to maximize survival requisites through its established decision processes.

The Goals of Organization

Organization has three goals which may be either intermeshed or independent ends in themselves. They are growth, stability, and interaction. The last goal refers to organizations which exist primarily to provide a medium for association of its members with others. Interestingly enough these goals seem to apply to different forms of organization at varying levels of complexity, ranging from simple clockwork mechanisms to social systems.

These similarities in organizational purposes

have been observed by a number of people, and a field of thought and research called general system theory has developed, dedicated to the task of discovering organizationed universals. The dream of general system theory is to create a science of organizational universals, or if you will, a universal science using common organizational elements found in all systems as a starting point.

Modern organization theory is on the periphery of general system theory. Both general system theory and modern organization theory studies:

(1) the parts (individuals) in aggregates, and the movement of individuals into and out of the system.

(2) the interaction of individuals with the environment found in the system.

(3) the interactions among individuals in the system.

(4) general growth and stability problems of systems.[48]

Modern organization theory and general system theory are similar in that they look at organization as an integrated whole. They differ, however, in terms of their generality. General system theory is concerned with every level of system, whereas modern organizational theory focuses primarily on human organization.

The question might be asked, what can the science of administration gain by the study of system levels other than human? Before attempting an answer, note should be made of what these other levels are. Boulding presents a convenient method of classification:

(1) The static structure—a level of framework, the anatomy of a system; for example, the structure of the universe.

(2) The simple dynamic system—the level of clockworks, predetermined necessary motions.

(3) The cybernetic system—the level of the thermostat, the system moves to maintain a given equilibrium through a process of self-regulation.

[46] March and Simon, *op. cit.*, Chapters 3 and 4.
[47] Jacob Marschak, "Efficient and Viable Organizational Forms," in *Modern Organization Theory,* Mason Haire (editor) (New York: John Wiley and Sons, 1959), pp. 307–320.

[48] Kenneth E. Boulding, "General System Theory— The Skeleton of a Science," *Management Science,* April, 1956, pp. 200–202.

(4) The open system—level of self-maintaining systems, moves toward and includes living organisms.

(5) The genetic-societal system—level of cell society, characterized by a division of labor among cells.

(6) Animal systems—level of mobility, evidence of goal-directed behavior.

(7) Human systems—level of symbol interpretation and idea communication.

(8) Social system—level of human organization.

(9) Transcendental systems—level of ultimates and absolutes which exhibit systematic structure but are unknowable in essence.[49]

This approach to the study of systems by finding universals common at all levels of organization offers intriguing possibilities for administrative organization theory. A good deal of light could be thrown on social systems if structurally analogous elements could be found in the simpler types of systems. For example, cybernetic systems have characteristics which seem to be similar to feedback, regulation, and control phenomena in human organizations. Thus, certain facets of cybernetic models could be generalized to human organization. Considerable danger, however, lies in poorly founded analogies. Superficial similarities between simpler system forms and social systems are apparent everywhere. Instinctually based ant societies, for example, do not yield particularly instructive lessons for understanding rationally conceived human organizations. Thus, care should be taken that analogies used to bridge system levels are not mere devices for literary enrichment. For analogies to have usefulness and validity, they must exhibit inherent structural similarities or implicitly identical operational principles.[50]

Modern organization theory leads, as it has been shown, almost inevitably into a discussion of general system theory. A science of organization universals has some strong advocates, particularly among biologists.[51] Organization theorists in administrative science cannot afford to overlook the contributions of general system theory. Indeed, modern organization concepts could offer a great deal to those working with general system theory. But the ideas dealt with in the general theory are exceedingly elusive.

Speaking of the concept of equilibrium as a unifying element in all systems, Easton says, "It (equilibrium) leaves the impression that we have a useful general theory when in fact, lacking measurability, it is a mere pretence for knowledge."[52] The inability to quantify and measure universal organization elements undermines the success of pragmatic tests to which general system theory might be put.

Organization Theory: Quo Vadis?

Most sciences have a vision of the universe to which they are applied, and administrative science is not an exception. This universe is composed of parts. One purpose of science is to synthesize the parts into an organized conception of its field of study. As a science matures, its theorems about the configuration of its universe change. The direction of change in three sciences, physics, economics, and sociology, are noted briefly for comparison with the development of an administrative view of human organization.

The first comprehensive and empirically verifiable outlook of the physical universe was presented by Newton in his *Principia*. Classical physics, founded on Newton's work, constitutes a grand scheme in which a wide range of

---

[49] *Ibid.*, pp. 202–205.
[50] Seidenberg, *op. cit.*, p. 136. The fruitful use of the type of analogies spoken of by Seidenberg is evident in the application of thermodynamic principles, particularly the entropy concept, to communication theory. See: Claude E. Shannon and Warren Weaver, *The Mathematical Theory of Communication* (Urbana: The University of Illinois Press, 1949). Further, the existence of a complete analogy between the operational behavior of thermodynamic systems, electrical communication systems, and biological systems has been

noted by: Y. S. Touloukian, *The Concept of Entropy in Communication, Living Organisms, and Thermodynamics*, Research Bulletin 130, Purdue Engineering Experiment Station.
[51] For example see: Ludwig von Bertalanffy, *Problem of Life* (London: Watts and Company, 1952).
[52] David Easton, "Limits of the Equilibrium Model in Social Research," in *Profits and Problems of Homeostatic Models in the Behavioral Sciences*, Publication 1, Chicago Behavioral Sciences, 1953, p. 39.

physical phenomena could be organized and predicted. Newtonian physics may rightfully be regarded as "macro" in nature, because its system of organization was concerned largely with gross events of which the movement of celestial bodies, waves, energy forms, and strain are examples. For years classical physics was supreme, being applied continuously to smaller and smaller classes of phenomena in the physical universe. Physicists at one time adopted the view that everything in their realm could be discovered by simply subdividing problems. Physics thus moved into the "micro" order.

But in the nineteenth century a revolution took place motivated largely because events were being noted which could not be explained adequately by the conceptual framework supplied by the classical school. The consequences of this revolution are brilliantly described by Eddington:

> From the point of view of philosophy of science the conception associated with entropy must I think be ranked as the great contribution of the nineteenth century to scientific thought. It marked a reaction from the view that everything to which science need pay attention is discovered by microscopic dissection of objects. It provided an alternative standpoint in which the centre of interest is shifted from the entities reached by the customary analysis (atoms, electric potentials, etc.) to qualities possessed by the system as a whole, which cannot be split up and located—a little bit here, and a little bit there. . . .
>
> We often think that when we have completed our study of *one* we know all about *two*, because "two" is "one and one." We forget that we have still to make a study of "and." Secondary physics is the study of "and"—that is to say, of organization.[53]

Although modern physics often deals in minute quantities and oscillations, the conception of the physicist is on the "macro" scale. He is concerned with the "and," or the organization of the world in which the events occur. These developments did not invalidate classical physics as to its usefulness for explaining a certain range of phenomena. But

classical physics is no longer the undisputed law of the universe. It is a special case.

Early economic theory, and Adam Smith's *Wealth of Nations* comes to mind, examined economic problems in the macro order. The *Wealth of Nations* is mainly concerned with matters of national income and welfare. Later, the economics of the firm, micro-economics, dominated the theoretical scene in this science. And, finally, with Keynes' *The General Theory of Employment Interest and Money,* a systematic approach to the economic universe was reintroduced on the macro level.

The first era of the developing science of sociology was occupied by the great social "system builders." Comte, the so-called father of sociology, had a macro view of society in that his chief works are devoted to social reorganization. Comte was concerned with the interrelationships among social, political, religious, and educational institutions. As sociology progressed, the science of society compressed. Emphasis shifted from the macro approach of the pioneers to detailed, empirical study of small social units. The compression of sociological analysis was accompanied by study of social pathology or disorganization.

In general, physics, economics, and sociology appear to have two things in common. First, they offered a macro point of view as their initial systematic comprehension of their area of study. Second, as the science developed, attention fragmented into analysis of the parts of the organization, rather than attending to the system as a whole. This is the micro phase.

In physics and economics, discontent was evidenced by some scientists at the continual atomization of the universe. The reaction to the micro approach was a new theory or theories dealing with the total system, on the macro level again. This third phase of scientific development seems to be more evident in physics and economics than in sociology.

The reason for the "macro-micro-macro" order of scientific progress lies, perhaps, in the hypothesis that usually the things which strike man first are of great magnitude. The scientist attempts to discover order in the vastness. But after macro laws or models of systems are postulated, variations appear which demand

---

[53] Sir Arthur Eddington, *The Nature of the Physical World* (Ann Arbor: The University of Michigan Press, 1958), pp. 103–104.

analysis, not so much in terms of the entire system, but more in terms of the specific parts which make it up. Then, intense study of microcosm may result in new general laws, replacing the old models of organization. Or, the old and the new models may stand together, each explaining a different class of phenomenon. Or, the old and the new concepts of organization may be welded to produce a single creative synthesis.

Now, what does all this have to do with the problem of organization in administrative science? Organization concepts seem to have gone through the same order of development in this field as in the three just mentioned. It is evident that the classical theory of organization, particularly as in the work of Mooney and Reiley, is concerned with principles common to all organizations. It is a macro-organizational view. The classical approach to organization, however, dealt with the gross anatomical parts and processes of the formal organization. Like classical physics, the classical theory of organization is a special case. Neither are especially well equipped to account for variation from their established framework.

Many variations in the classical administrative model result from human behavior. The only way these variations could be understood was by a microscopic examination of particularized, situational aspects of human behavior. The mission of the neoclassical school thus is "micro-analysis."

It was observed earlier, that somewhere along the line the concept of the social system, which is the key to understanding the Hawthorne studies, faded into the background. Maybe the idea is so obvious that it was lost to the view of researchers and writers in human relations. In any event, the press of research in the microcosmic universes of the informal organization, morale and productivity, leadership, participation, and the like forced the notion of the social system into limbo. Now, with the advent of modern organization theory, the social system has been resurrected.

Modern organization theory appears to be concerned with Eddington's "and." This school claims that its operational hypothesis is based on a macro point of view; that is, the

study of organization as a whole. This nobility of purpose should not obscure, however, certain difficulties faced by this field as it is presently constituted. Modern organization theory raises two questions which should be explored further. First, would it not be more accurate to speak of modern organization theor*ies*? Second, just how much of modern organization theory is modern?

The first question can be answered with a quick affirmative. Aside from the notion of the system, there are few, if any, other ideas of a unifying nature. Except for several important exceptions,[54] modern organization theorists tend to pursue their pet points of view,[55] suggesting they are part of system theory, but not troubling to show by what mystical means they arrive at this conclusion.

The irony of it all is that a field dealing with systems has, indeed, little system. Modern organization theory needs a framework, and it needs an integration of issues into a common conception of organization. Admittedly, this is a large order. But it is curious not to find serious analytical treatment of subjects like cybernetics or general system theory in Haire's, *Modern Organizational Theory* which claims to be a representative example of work in this field. Beer has ample evidence in his book *Cybernetics and Management* that cybernetics, if imaginatively approached, provides a valuable conceptual base for the study of systems.

The second question suggests an ambiguous answer. Modern organization theory is in part a product of the past; system analysis is not a new idea. Further, modern organization theory relies for supporting data on microcosmic research studies, generally drawn from the journals of the last ten years. The newness of modern organization theory, perhaps, is its effort to synthesize recent research contributions of many fields into a system theory characterized by a reoriented conception of organization.

One might ask, but what is the modern

---

[54] For example: E. Wight Bakke, *op. cit.*, pp. 18–75.

[55] There is a large selection including decision theory, individual-organization interaction, motivation, vitality, stability, growth, and graph theory, to mention a few.

theorist reorienting? A clue is found in the almost snobbish disdain assumed by some authors of the neo-classical human relations school, and particularly, the classical school. Re-evaluation of the classical school of organization is overdue. However, this does not mean that its contributions to organization theory are irrelevant and should be overlooked in the rush to get on the "behavioral science bandwagon."

Haire announces that the papers appearing in *Modern Organization Theory* constitute, "the ragged leading edge of a wave of theoretical development."[56] Ragged, yes; but leading no! The papers appearing in this book do not represent a theoretical breakthrough in the concept of organization. Haire's collection is an interesting potpourri with several contributions of considerable significance. But readers should beware that they will not find vastly new insights into organizational behavior in this book, if they have kept up with the literature of the social sciences, and have dabbled to some extent in the esoteria of biological theories of growth, information theory, and mathematical model building. For those who have not maintained the pace, *Modern Organization Theory* serves the admirable purpose of bringing them up-to-date on a rather diversified number of subjects.

Some work in modern organization theory is pioneering, making its appraisal difficult and future uncertain. While the direction of this endeavor is unclear, one thing is patently true. Human behavior in organizations, and indeed, organization itself, cannot be adequately understood within the ground rules of classical and neo-classical doctrines. Appreciation of human organization requires a *creative* synthesis of massive amounts of empirical data, a high order of deductive reasoning, imaginative research studies, and a taste for individual and social values. Accomplishment of all these objectives, and the inclusion of them into a framework of the concept of the system, appears to be the goal of modern organization theory. The vitality of administrative science

rests on the advances modern theorists make along this line.

Modern organization theory, 1960 style, is an amorphous aggregation of synthesizers and restaters, with a few extending leadership on the frontier. For the sake of these few, it is well to admonish that pouring old wine into new bottles may make the spirits cloudy. Unfortunately, modern organization theory has almost succeeded in achieving the status of a fad. Popularization and exploitation contributed to the disrepute into which human relations has fallen. It would be a great waste if modern organization theory yields to the same fate, particularly since both modern organization theory and human relations draw from the same promising source of inspiration—system analysis.

Modern organization theory needs tools of analysis and a conceptual framework uniquely its own, but it must also allow for the incorporation of relevant contributions of many fields. It may be that the framework will come from general system theory. New areas of research such as decision theory, information theory, and cybernetics also offer reasonable expectations of analytical and conceptual tools. Modern organization theory represents a frontier of research which has great significance for management. The potential is great, because it offers the opportunity for uniting what is valuable in classical theory with the social and natural sciences into a systematic and integrated conception of human organization.

Outside Reading: Essay-Discussion Questions

1. Compare and contrast the classical with the neoclassical theory of organization.

2. What are the specific determinants underlying the appearance of informal organizations?

3. What does Scott mean by "Organization Theory: Quo Vadis?"

4. Do the concepts of span of control, departmentation, line-staff, centralization-decentralization, and committee play any significant role in modern organization theory? Explain.

---

56 Mason Haire, "General Issues," in Mason Haire (editor), *Modern Organization Theory* (New York: John Wiley and Sons, 1959), p. 2.

PART III

MANAGERIAL ORGANIZATION: BEHAVIORAL ASPECTS

Chapter Eleven

Authority, Status, and Power

POWER AND AUTHORITY are defined in the first part of the chapter. Attention is then directed to the social foundations of authority. The importance of social conditioning and sanctions, the law of private property, the impact of markets, unionism and collective bargaining, and the influence of professional associations are considered. The discussion then turns to the status system in organizations and the manner in which it affects authority. Such formal status instruments as scalar and functional titles, ceremonies, insignia, academic degrees, and special facilities are scrutinized.

Section I MAJOR CONCEPTS

Authority
Power
Sanctions

Status
Foundations of authority
Collective bargaining

Section II SELF-TEST

True-False

____ 1. Authority is power, but not all power is authority.
____ 2. Some executives have more power than the power (or authority) that evolves from their position.
____ 3. Authority can always be reestablished by sanctions.
____ 4. Status is a product of group behavior; an isolated individual has no status.
____ 5. Business organizations, unlike reli-gious and military organizations, do not have a formal status system.

Multiple Choice

____ 1. Which of the following terms defines the power that evolves from a man-agerial position?
a. Status
b. Authority

c. Responsibility

d. Function

____ 2. Professors John Dollard and Neal E. Miller make the following conclusions on the matter of child training:

a. Teenagers are more irresponsible today than a few years ago.

b. A child should be seen but not heard.

c. Children are generally able to correct the mistakes of their parents when they themselves become parents.

d. Current child-training procedures represent a long history of conflict and confusion.

____ 3. Which of the following things did *not* happen on the *Prince Potemkin?*

a. The firing squad refused to fire upon the rebellious crew.

b. The crew saw maggoty meat in the galley.

c. The *Potemkin* was being shelled by the Japanese fleet.

d. Some of the officers were killed during the mutiny.

____ 4. Which of the following best describes the nature and purpose of sanctions?

a. They can be expressed in terms of negative rewards.

b. They are instrumental in creating authority.

c. They result from authority.

d. All of the above.

____ 5. Which of the following best expresses the relationship between property and authority?

a. Property directly confers authority upon its owner.

b. Property has nothing to do with authority.

c. Property provides sanctions that can be used to maintain authority.

d. The quest for property is the only basis of authority.

____ 6. Which of the following would probably *not* contribute to the support of authority in a business organization?

a. Surplus of jobs

b. Law of property

c. Positive sanctions

d. Negative sanctions

____ 7. Which of the following techniques is *not* generally used by professional associations?

a. Strike

b. "Blacklists"

c. Politicking

d. Boycott

____ 8. All of the following describe the formal status system in organization EXCEPT:

a. A social or group phenomenon

b. Attribute of managerial positions

c. Relate and rank persons

d. Promotes equality among executives

____ 9. What is the best statement concerning authority in a given society?

a. Breakdowns of authority happened quite frequently in historical events.

b. A society should probably encourage breakdown of authority for the general welfare.

c. Extreme use of negative sanctions indicates a breakdown of existing authority.

d. Authority should be maintained at any cost.

____ 10. What is true of the concept of status?

a. A garbage man has no status.

b. Status has nothing to do with authority.

c. All ceremonies are useful.

d. A status system makes possible some degree of stability.

Essay-Discussion

1. What is the relationship between authority and power?

2. What role do sanctions play in relation to authority?

3. Discuss some methods of determining status.

Section III ILLUSTRATIVE CASES

STARTING THEM YOUNG

The Presidents' Professional Association, an American Management Association subsidiary, is a sponsor of Camp Enterprise, a two-week camp for high school boys. The purpose is to teach the boys something about the business world of today and tomorrow, to tell them what management really is, and to show them how managers operate a business at a profit. *Business Week* reports that "Behind this stated objective lies the hope that the camp will help rectify the neglect that businessmen feel their field suffers in high school and college."[1]

Analysis

1. Relate this illustrative case to the authority concept.
2. How does the Soviet Union cope with the acceptance of authority?

[1] *Business Week,* June 27, 1964, pp. 152-154.

DOWN WITH EXECUTIVE WASHROOM KEYS

A very successful electronics firm makes a deliberate effort to minimize status *symbols*.[1] For instance, all employees share the same dining and coffee-bar facilities, parking and office space is assigned by need rather than responsibility, and there is no standardized attire, which often consists of informal sportswear at all levels. The head of management research explains: "The net effect of such a system is to orient employees on a competence basis rather than to sensitize them to, and sandwich them into, an authority hierarchy."[2]

Analysis

1. Discuss and critically analyze the statement by the head of management research.

[1] M. Scott Myers, "Conditions for Manager Motivation," *Harvard Business Review*, Vol. 44, No. 1, January-February 1966, p. 66.
[2] *Ibid.*

2. What is the difference between status and status symbols? Relate to the illustrative case above.
3. What role do status symbols play in reinforcing authority?

"CORPORATE SYMBOLOGY"[1]

Many of today's corporations are developing symbols that identify the image they are trying to project. Consulting firms made up of market research analysts, photographers, psychologists, and commercial artists specialize in what they call corporate identification programs. The price for a new symbol runs high—some companies have paid up to $2 million in consultation fees and expenses.

Are these symbols worth the money and effort? Since Chrysler adopted its pentastar symbol, its share of the automobile market has increased from 10 to 18 per cent. On the other hand, an industrial psychologist observed that "My guess is that the consultant makes a lot of money and that's about all."[2] New York's Consolidated Edison is an example of corporate symbology that may backfire. Their slogan of "Dig We Must" was so effective that the public soon began to blame Consolidated Edison for every excavation in the city. Consolidated Edison later changed its slogan to "Clean Energy."

Analysis

1. Are these corporate symbols status symbols? Why?
2. What are some advantages of a well known corporate symbol?
3. Why do you suppose Consolidated Edison came up with "Clean Energy" as its slogan?

[1] Reported in "Many Firms Adopt New Corporate Symbols in Bid to Improve Recognition, Lift Sales" *The Wall Street Journal*, August 1, 1968, p. 18.
[2] *Ibid.*

Chapter Twelve

Organizational Dynamics

THE FIRST PART of this chapter considers the manner in which sociopsychological forces affect managerial organization. The next section shows the relationship between the planned structure of authority and the actual structure of power. Particular attention is given to an empirical study on this subject and to informal status and power instruments. Planned changes in the organization structure and the means by which they are achieved are then discussed. The last section presents some common organizational problems and indicates policies that can help overcome them.

Section I MAJOR CONCEPTS

Functional organizational structure
Informal organization
Organizational behavior
Authority structure

Power structure
Organizational planning
Reorganization
Organizational change

Section II SELF-TEST

True-False

_____ 1. The functional theorist assumes that personality will have no impact on the structure he has planned.

_____ 2. The informal organization often compensates for deficiencies in the formal plan.

_____ 3. The authority and power structures in the Milo plant were the same.

_____ 4. Most companies use a pyramid-type organization chart, with rectangular boxes to denote positions.

_____ 5. Companies often assign organizing activities to the personnel or industrial engineering departments.

Multiple Choice

_____ 1. Which of the following best describes the differences between the leadership structure of the Norton gang and the managerial organization of the business firm?

a. One is hierarchical; the other is not hierarchical.

b. One involves inequality; the other does not.

c. One is a by-product of social process; the other is systematically planned.

d. One involves informal behavior; the other does not.

2. The argument of the "functional theorists" is that

a. the right functional arrangements will assure cooperation

b. personality will have no impact on the planned structure

c. organizations should begin with a good functional structure

d. personality is more important than function in the long run

3. Which of the following statements about the Milo plant power structure is *not* in accord with the facts?

a. Stevens has a higher formal position than Hardy.

b. Hardy tended to dominate the scene even when Stevens was present.

c. Rees wielded a great deal of power in the industrial relations area.

d. Revere had more power because he no longer aspired to dominate.

4. In a shipyard during World War II, Indians were employed with bad results. The situation was remedied by which of the following actions?

a. The draft was threatened.

b. The chief was made foreman.

c. The Indians were given training.

d. Wages were increased by a small percentage.

5. Which of the following best describes "an earthquake approach" to reorganization?

a. Radical organizational changes arbitrarily put into effect

b. Changes involving only those at the ground level

c. Reorganization after a shocking incident

d. Putting the lid on an otherwise explosive situation

6. Vincent Peele, the new manager of a gypsum plant studied by Alvin W. Gouldner, imposed bureaucratic restrictions not present under the old manager. Which of the following statements best defines the response?

a. All accepted the situation without complaint.

b. Everyone refused to go along with the restrictions.

c. One group was less willing than the other to accept the restraints.

d. The union opposed the new manager and finally called a strike

7. Which of the following best describes the results achieved in the Westinghouse Electric Company reorganization in the late 1930's?

a. There was a great deal of evidence that the organization was premature.

b. During the first year the gains from reorganization were far below the additional costs.

c. The second stage, the second and third years, resulted in temporary gains beyond the extra expenses of reorganization.

d. The final stage, which began after three or four years, gave rise to many benefits that had only begun to bear fruit during earlier periods.

8. What is the major purpose of a functional organizational design?

a. To achieve the organizational objective

b. To temper the impact of individual personality

c. To temper the impact of the participant's social behavior

d. To design the most efficient system possible

9. What is the best statement about

informal organization?

a. It is the behavior that is planned by superiors.

b. It is almost always disruptive and dysfunctional.

c. It is the behavior that subordinates have planned to contend with organizational and personal problems.

d. It exists only in organizations that are having problems.

_____ 10. What is true of organizational change?

a. The organizer should recognize the importance of the informally organized social system.

b. In some situations an organizer may deliberately attempt to break up the informal social pattern.

c. In some situations the organizer may change the leadership and membership of informal groups by forced resignations.

d. All of the above.

Essay-Discussion

1. What is the basic argument of the functional theorist on the matter of organizational planning?

2. What factors affect the power that subordinates may have in the organizational structure?

3. What are some of the limitations of organization charts?

Section III   ILLUSTRATIVE CASES

TAILOR-MADE ORGANIZATION[1]

The president of a small but growing textile company recently outlined his company's form of "functional management." The company felt that organization in the past had become an end in itself rather than a means to an end. The result is a tailor-made system that fits the job to the executive instead of the executive to the job. This form of organization, the president claims, allows each man to make the most effective use of his own talents.

Many executives in this textile firm are responsible for more than one functional area. For example, one executive handles product styling and development, financial management, and is operating head of one division. Each manager, therefore, becomes a generalist rather than a specialist. The president summed up this managerial philosophy as flexibility within control.

Analysis

1. Would this organization be considered a functional organizational design? Why?

2. Can this form of organization be applied to any type of operation? What would be some necessary prerequisites?

3. What are some advantages and disadvantages of this type of organization?

"A BEHAVIORAL SCIENCE LABORATORY"[1]

A $6 million, privately held electronics firm, Non-Linear Systems, Inc. of San Diego, has become a famous proving ground for the behavioral approach to organization and management. The president of the company, aided by the writings and advice of noted scholars, such as A. H. Maslow, Rensis Likert, Douglas McGregor, and Frederick Herzberg, set up a revolutionary program for his company. The ensuing changes took place at all levels of the company but were most pronounced on the factory floor. The program called for throwing out all time cards and putting production workers on a relatively high salary. The as-

[1] Developed from "Rx for Boxed in Executives," *Dun's Review*, October 1967, pp. 55–56, 77.

[1] Based on "When Workers Manage Themselves," *Business Week*, March 20, 1965, pp. 93-94.

sembly line procedure was also eliminated and replaced with 16 independent production units of six or seven workers each. The independent teams are free to organize and work as they wish. Job inspectors were also eliminated.

Initially the program resulted in "sky high" morale but disrupted production. After three months, the output attained the old assembly line level, and the president estimates that now it is at least 30 per cent higher. Other tangible side effects were greater flexibility, uncovering unsuspected talents, a 70 per cent decrease in customer complaints, and rejects becoming almost nonexistent.

The same type of organization was also tried in engineering, sales, and upper management with *mixed* results. In most instances, the company reverted to the conventional structure in these areas.

No other corporation has yet gone this far. However, most companies agree with an executive who said: "They're courageous in trying it."[2]

Analysis

1. Why does it take courage to try this type of organization?

2. Why do you suppose the program worked very well at lower levels of the organization but not so well in the upper levels of the organization?

3. What do you think the future holds for this type of organization?

_____
[2] *Ibid.*, p. 94.

"CLEAN HOUSE"[1]

The *Wall Street Journal* recently ran a story on a "tough tycoon" who lives by the for-

_____
[1] Reported in Dennis Farney, "Tough Tycoon," *The Wall Street Journal,* May 28, 1968, p. 1.

mula—"I buy run-down, poor-management companies, analyze them, then come in and clean house."[2] An example of this philosophy was the tycoon's acquisition of a long-complacent company whose headquarters was a tidy red-brick building with a flag in front. The acquired company was started in the basement of the founder and had a long history of following the leading company in their specialized industry. When a salesman from the acquired company was asked why customers bought his product, he replied: "They don't want [the leading company] to have all the business."[3]

The tycoon is confident that he can change this situation. He states that "In a period of five years, I expect to have $1 billion in sales behind me, and profits in line with sales. By that time, I think we should have a hell of a good organization and a springboard to go places."[4]

Within nine months, the tycoon fired the acquired company's president and assumed the job himself. With pleasure, the tycoon recalled telling the former president over lunch one day that he was getting ready to fire him. He also canned, or retired, almost 150 other company personnel. The tycoon explained that "You can't get entrenched people to change. All you can do is let them go fishing and bring in new people."[5]

Analysis

1. What type of reorganization would this be called?

2. What would you do if you acquired this company?

3. Can you foresee any difficulties that the tycoon may encounter?

_____
[2] *Ibid.*
[3] *Ibid.*
[4] *Ibid.*
[5] *Ibid.*

Chapter Thirteen

From Organization to Process

THE FUNCTIONS THAT make up the management process are viewed as organized phenomena in this chapter. The first part of the chapter is concerned with formal and informal communication channels and their relationship to the communication function. The second part deals with the nature of decision-making responsibilities in a hierarchical system.

Section I MAJOR CONCEPTS

Informational communication channels
Hierarchical communication channels
Decision-making centers

Decisional obligations
Delegation

Section II SELF-TEST

True-False

_____ 1. A communication channel has been defined as the line of persons through which oral or written messages pass.

_____ 2. Informal communication is generally unnecessary in formal organizations.

_____ 3. There are generally strong taboos against the dissemination of information that might "embarrass" one's superior.

_____ 4. A superior should always be willing to help a subordinate executive make a decision.

_____ 5. A decentralized decision-making system involves delegation to subordinates.

Multiple Choice

_____ 1. Members of the RCA organization may make contacts between units in the most direct way. In making such contacts the member of the organization should keep his superior informed on certain matters.

Which answer does not fit the basic categories spelled out by RCA?

a. Any matters on which his senior may be held accountable by those senior to him

b. Any matters of disagreement or those likely to cause controversy within or between any units of the corporation

c. Any matters concerning the political activities of executives

d. any matters involving recommendation for change in, or variance from, established policies

2. Which of the following is the most acceptable statement on informal communication?

a. The elimination of informal communication is a must for successful organization.

b. Keith Davis pointed out through his "cluster chain" that informal communication tends to be non-selective.

c. The psychological restraints of a hierarchical system give impetus to a "cluster chain."

d. The results of the Hawthorne study would seem to negate the "cluster chain" as a prominent type of informal communication for the worker level.

3. Which of the following is *not* the name of one of the categories used by Davis to classify informal communication channels in his study of a leather goods company?

a. Gossip

b. Probability

c. Single strand

d. Isolate

4. Which statement concerning informal communication channels is *incorrect?*

a. Much of the communication system is informal in the sense that it is not planned by superior executives.

b. Some channels evolve from the

efforts of people to satisfy purely personal motives.

c. Most of the informal communication among management personnel follows the pattern of the gossip chain.

d. Informal communications channels frequently seem to have an infinite capacity for carrying information.

5. The local representative of the insurance company carrying the employee group contract planned a picnic for Jason Company executives. The president invited 36 executives from higher levels—31 were not invited. The grapevine carried the news

a. to all the uninvited executives

b. to none of the uninvited executives

c. to a majority of those who were not invited

d. to only two of the 31 not invited

6. Which of the following decisional obligations does Barnard call the "important test of executive capacity"?

a. Decisions evolving from appellate cases

b. Problems transmitted to an executive from higher levels

c. Decisions that involve the responsibilities of the executive's own position

d. Decisions on technological matters

7. When Sir Ian Hamilton took over the duties of his former chief in addition to his existing responsibilities, he found that

a. his chief had performed the work in much less time

b. his chief had simply said yes or no in making a decision

c. the work departed with his chief

d. he should have appreciated the outstanding achievements of his former chief

_____ 8. In a functionally differentiated decision-making system
   a. a subordinate has only one superior from whom he receives orders and to whom he reports
   b. subordinates are subject to a number of functional executives
   c. the unity of command principle is strictly followed
   d. personnel in the sales department are not subject to any decisions made by the head of the production department

_____ 9. What did Professor E. Wight Bakke find in a study of a large telephone company?
   a. Respondents were reacting to the planned system of communication.
   b. Respondents were *not* reacting to unplanned procedures, which they themselves had made.
   c. Respondents were reacting to planned procedures, which they had remade.
   d. All of the above.

_____ 10. What is *not* true of executive decisional obligations?
   a. Executives may sometimes have to practice insubordination in the best interests of the organization.
   b. The executive should make the decision whenever subordinates appeal for help.
   c. Every executive has some decisional responsibilities that are not imposed by superior decisions or referred by subordinates.
   d. The fear of wrong decision is frequently more compelling than the possible adverse consequences of no decision.

Essay-Discussion

1. What is a communication channel?
2. How should executives view informal communication channels?
3. What is the nature of the organized decision-making process?

Section III   ILLUSTRATIVE CASES

SUPPLEMENTARY CHANNELS[1]

The president of a highly diversified company prides himself in keeping in contact with his widely scattered division managers. He states: "The airplane and today's communications networks keep you in touch with your people no matter where you are."[2] He also developed three supplementary communication techniques: (1) an annual meeting of all major operating personnel; (2) an "Honors Night," which is a formal banquet where outstanding employees are given special recognition; and (3) division head meetings with the board of directors. The president comments on this third communicating device as follows:

These meetings are a two-way street. The operating people report to the board and they also get to absorb some of the board's general attitude.[3]

Analysis

1. Can these three types of meetings be considered as communication channels? Why?
2. What are some communication advantages that probably result from these meetings?

"SMOKE IN THE FILAMENT"[1]

A classic case of the way to approach a decisional problem was recently discussed by a

---

[1] Based on "A Conglomerate Called Martin-Marietta," *Dun's Review*, August 1968, pp. 28–31, 69.
[2] *Ibid.*, p. 30.
[3] *Ibid.*
[1] Based on a case discussed in "Charting Pitfalls of Decision," *Business Week*, June 5, 1965, p. 66.

management consulting firm. The situation took place in a plastics plant. A normally translucent filament turned up black in one of six machines producing the filament. The filament stayed black for a few minutes but eventually returned to its translucent color. The foreman immediately reacted by checking equipment for impurities. Finding nothing wrong, the foreman summoned the general manager. The general manager deduced that the whole machine was affected and incorrectly suspected that either the raw material or the acid bath was to blame. Next on the scene was an inquisitive technical man. The technical man determined that the blackening agent was carbon, which he traced to an air vent. What had happened was a coal-burning switch engine had stopped under the vent, which in turn sucked in the carbon smoke to blacken the filament.

Analysis

1. If you were a consultant on this case how would you analyze the foreman's decisional behavior? The general manager's?

2. What was there in the technical man's decisional obligations that led to the solution where the others had failed?

3. Would you consider this to be a typical decisional problem in industrial organizations? Discuss in terms of decision making centers.

DELEGATION, FACTS, AND COMMON SENSE

M. J. Warnock, the Chairman of Armstrong Cork, was recently asked how he makes his decisions. His reply was as follows: "Well first, you must ask yourself 'Is this a decision I ought to make or is it one that should be delegated?' If it's one I ought to make, then I try to get all the facts and get all the opinions of the people who have the most knowledge on the subject. Based on this and on experience and, I guess, common sense, I decide."[1]

Analysis

1. What implications does the question he asks himself have for the concept of delegation?

2. Do most of the "facts" come from formal or informal communication channels? Give examples of both.

3. Where do most of the "opinions" come from?

---

[1] Reprinted with permission of the publisher from "Knowing Your Peoples' Abilities," *Nation's Business*, February 1968, p. 72.

READING: CHANGING ORGANIZATIONS

WARREN G. BENNIS

A foreign visitor in Boston once walked up to an American sailor and asked why the ships of the latter's country were built to last for only a short time. According to the foreign tourist, "The sailor answered without hesitation that the art of navigation is making such rapid progress that the finest ship would become obsolete if it lasted beyond a few years. In these words, which fell accidentally from an uneducated man, I began to recognize the general and systematic idea upon which your great people direct all their concerns."

The visitor was that shrewd observer of American morals and manners, Alexis de Tocqueville. The year was 1835, but he caught the central theme of our country, its preoccupation, its *obsession* with change. One thing that *is* new since de Tocqueville's time is the prevalence of newness, the changing scale and scope of change itself, so that, as Oppenheimer has said, ". . . the world alters as we walk in it, so that the years of man's life measure not some small growth or rearrangement or moderation of what was learned in childhood, but a great upheaval."

We are all aware of the momentum of the Scientific Revolution, moving like a juggernaut, transforming or ossifying everything in its way. Its magnitude, its scale, its accelerating rate, to say nothing of its consequences, are truly staggering. By 1980 it will cut even a wider path and require an even wider berth, for in that year the government alone will spend close to 35 billion dollars for research and development: 10 billion for arms and arms control, 7 billion for basic research, and 18 billion on vast civilian welfare programs and new technology.

"Everything nailed down is coming loose," an historian said recently, and it does seem that no exaggeration, no hyperbole, no outrage can appraise realistically the extent and pace which modernization involves. It takes only a year or two for the exaggerations to come true. Nothing will remain in the next 10 years. Or there will be twice as much of it.

How will these changes taking place in our society influence human organizations? First of all, we should consider the dominant form of human organization employed throughout the industrial world. We spend all of our working day in it and a great deal of our nonworking day. It is a unique and extremely durable arrangement called "bureaucracy."

As I use the term here, bureaucracy is a social invention, perfected during the industrial revolution to organize and direct the activities of the business firm. Today it is also the prevailing and supreme type of organization wherever people direct concerted effort toward the achievement of some goal. This holds for university systems, for hospitals, for large voluntary organizations, and for governmental organizations.

Corsica, according to Gibbon, is much easier to deplore than to describe. The same holds true for bureaucracy. Basically, it is a system that relies exclusively on the power to influence through rules, reason, and the law. Max Weber, a German sociologist who developed the theory of bureaucracy around the turn of the century, once described it thus:

> Bureaucracy is like a modern judge who is a vending machine into which the pleadings are inserted together with the fee and which then disgorges the judgment together with its reasons mechanically derived from the code.

Reprinted by permission of the publisher from *The Technology Review*, April 1966, pp. 37–41; 64. Copyright 1966, Alumni Association of the Massachusetts Institute of Technology. Dr. Bennis was Professor of Management at the Massachusetts Institute of Technology when he wrote this paper.

The bureaucratic "machine model" that Weber outlined was developed as a reaction against the personal subjugation, nepotism, cruelty, and the capricious and subjective judgments that passed for managerial practices in the early days of the industrial revolution. The true hope for man, it was thought, lay in his ability to rationalize, to calculate, to use his head as well as his hands and heart. Bureaucracy emerged out of the need for more predictability, order, and precision. It was an organization ideally suited to the values of the Victorian Empire.

It is my premise that the bureaucratic form of organization is out of joint with contemporary realities; that emerging shapes, patterns, and models promise drastic changes in the conduct of the corporation and of managerial practices in general. In the next 25 to 50 years we should witness and participate in the end of bureaucracy as we know it and the rise of new social systems better suited to Twentieth Century demands of industrialization.

I see two main reasons for the changes in organizational life. One involves the population and knowledge explosions. The other is more subtle and muted, perhaps less significant; but for me, it is profoundly exciting. It is not easy to designate. It has to do with man's individual historical quest for self-awareness, for using reason to achieve and stretch his potentialities, his possibilities. I think that this deliberate self-analysis has spread to large and complex social systems, to organizations.

Over the last two decades there has been a dramatic upsurge of this spirit of inquiry. At new depths and over a wider range of affairs, organizations are opening their operations to self-inquiry and to analysis. This really involves two parallel shifts in values and outlooks, between the men who make history and the men who make knowledge. One change is the scientist's realization of his affinity with men of affairs, and the other is the latter's receptivity and new-found respect for men of knowledge. I call this new development *"organizational revitalization,"* a complex social process that involves a deliberate and self-conscious examination of organizational behavior and a collaborative relationship between managers and scientists to improve performance.

This development is unprecedented. Never before in history or in any society has man in his organizational context so willingly searched, scrutinized, examined, inspected, or contemplated—for meaning, for purpose, for improvement.

This shift in outlook has taken a good deal of courage. The manager has had to shake off old prejudices about "eggheads" and "longhair" intellectuals. More important, he has had to make himself and his organization vulnerable and receptive to external sources, and to new, unexpected, even unwanted information. The academician has had to shed some of his natural hesitancies. Scholarly conservatism is admirable, except to hide behind, and for a long time caution was a defense against reality.

The field of management education is a case in point; until recently, not only was it disregarded by large portions of the American public, but also it was unknown to or snubbed by the academic establishment. There, management education and research was regarded at best with dark suspicion, as if contact with the world of reality—particularly monetary realities—was equivalent to a dreadful form of pollution. In fact, historically academic man has taken one of two stances toward The Establishment, *any* Establishment: that of a rebellious critic or of a withdrawn snob. The rebel can be "bought," but only at paperback book stores under such titles as *The Power Elite, The Lonely Crowd, The Organization Man, Hidden Persuaders, Tyranny of Testing,* and many others.

The withdrawn stance can be observed in some of our American universities, but less so these days. It is still the prevailing attitude, though, in many European universities. There, the university seems intent to preserve the monastic ethos of its medieval origins, offering a false but lulling security to its inmates and sapping the curriculum of virility and relevance. Max Beerbohm's whimsical and idyllic fantasy of Oxford, *Zuleika Dobson,* dramatizes this:

> It is this mild, miasmal air, not less than the grey beauty and the gravity of the buildings that has helped Oxford to produce, and foster, eternally, her peculiar race of artist-scholars,

scholar-artists . . . . The buildings and their traditions keep astir in his mind whatsoever is gracious; the climate enfolding and enfeebling him, lulling him, keeps him careless of the sharp, harsh exigent realities of the outer world. These realities may be seen by him. . . . But they cannot fire him. Oxford is too damp for that.

"Adorable Dreamer," said Matthew Arnold, in his valedictory to Oxford: "Adorable Dreamer, whose heart has been so romantic! who has given thyself so prodigally, given thyself to sides and to heroes not mine, only never to the Philistine! . . . what teacher could ever so save us from that bondage to which we are all prone . . . the bondage of what binds us all, the narrow, the mundane, the merely practical."

It is probably true that in the United States we have had a more pragmatic attitude toward knowledge than anyone else. Even in Russia, where one would least expect it, there is little interest in the "merely useful" and Harrison Salisbury in his recent travels there saw only one great agricultural experimental station on the American model. In that case, professors were working in the fields. They told Salisbury: "People call us Americans."

There may not be many American professors working in the fields, but they can be found, when not waiting in airports, almost everywhere else: In factories, in government, in less advanced countries—and more recently, in backward areas of our own country, in mental hospitals, in the State Department, in educational systems, and in practically all the institutional crevices Ph.D candidates can worm their way into. This is not to say that the deep ambivalence which some Americans hold toward the intellectual has disappeared, but it does indicate that academic man has become more committed to action, in greater numbers, with more diligence, and with higher aspirations than at any other time in history.

As to managerial philosophy, over the past decade we have seen a fundamental change in the basic attitudes which underlie managerial behavior, reflected most of all in the following three areas:

1. A new concept of *man*, based on in-creased knowledge of his complex and shifting needs, which replaces the oversimplified, innocent push-button idea of man.

2. A new concept of *power*, based on collaboration and reason, which replaces a model of power based on coercion and fear.

3. A new concept of *organizational values,* based on humanistic-democratic ideals, that replaces the depersonalized mechanistic value system of bureaucracy.

These changes may be light-years away from actual adoption but they have gained wide intellectual acceptance in enlightened management quarters and they have been used as a basis of policy formulation by many large-scale organizations.

All the foregoing changes affect organizations but the real *coup de grâce* to bureaucracy has come as much from our turbulent environment as from incorrect assumptions about human behavior. The pyramidal structure of bureaucracy, where power was concentrated at the top, seemed perfect to "run a railroad." And undoubtedly, for tasks like building railroads, for the routinized tasks of the Nineteenth and early Twentieth Centuries, bureaucracy was and is an eminently suitable social arrangement.

Nowadays, due primarily to the growth of science, technology, and research and development activities, the organizational environment of the firm is rapidly changing. Rather than a placid and predictable environment, today it is turbulent and there is a deepening interdependence among the economic and other facets of society. This means that economic organizations are increasingly enmeshed in legislation and public policy. Put more simply, it means that the government will be in about everything, more of the time. It might also mean (and this is radical) that maximizing co-operation rather than competition between firms—particularly if their fates are correlated—may become a strong possibility.

Also, we face the problem of revitalization: Alfred North Whitehead sets the problem neatly before us:

The art of free society consists first in the maintenance of the symbolic code, and secondly, in the fearlessness of revision . . . Those societies which cannot combine reverence to their symbols with freedom of revision must ultimately decay.

Organizations, as well as societies, must be concerned with those social conditions that engender a buoyancy, resilience, and a fearlessness of revision.

What can we expect in organizations of the future? A forecast falls somewhere between a prediction and a prophecy. It lacks the divine guidance of the latter and the empirical foundation of the former. On thin empirical ice, I want to set forth some of the conditions that will dictate organization life in the next 25-50 years.

THE ENVIRONMENT. Rapid technological change and diversification will lead to interpenetration of the government—its legal and economic policies—with business. Partnerships between business and government will be typical. And because of the immensity and expense of the projects, there will be fewer identical units competing for the same buyers and sellers. The three main features of the environment will be interdependence rather than competition, turbulence rather than steadiness, and large-scale rather than small-scale enterprises.

POPULATION CHARACTERISTICS. The most distinctive characteristic of our society is, and will become even more so, its education. Peter Drucker calls us the "educated society," and for good reason: Within 15 years, two-thirds of our population living in metropolitan areas will have attended college. Adult education is growing even faster. It is now almost routine for the experienced physician, engineer, and executive to go back to school for advanced training every two or three years. Some 50 universities, in addition to a dozen large corporations, offer advanced management courses to successful men in the middle and upper ranks of business. Before World War II, only two such programs existed, both new, and struggling to get students.

All of this education is not just "nice," but necessary. For as Secretary of Labor Wirtz recently pointed out, computers can do the work of most high school graduates—cheaper and more effectively. Fifty years ago education used to be regarded as "nonwork" and intellectuals on the payroll (and many staff workers) were considered "overhead." Today, the survival of the firm depends more than ever before on the proper exploitation of brain power.

WORK VALUES. The lowered expense and ease of transportation, coupled with the real needs of a dynamic environment, will change drastically the idea of "owning" a job—or of "having roots," for that matter. Participants will be shifted from job to job and even from employer to employer with little concern for roots and homestead. People will be more intellectually committed to their jobs and will probably require more involvement, participation, and autonomy in their work.

Also, they will tend to be more "other-directed," taking cues for their norms and values from their immediate environment more than from tradition. We will tend to rely more heavily on temporary social arrangements, on our immediate and constantly changing colleagues. We will tend to be more concerned and involved with relationships rather than with relatives.

TASKS AND GOALS. The tasks of the firm will be more technical, complicated, and unprogrammed. They will rely more on the intellect than on muscle. And they will be too complicated for one person to comprehend, to say nothing of, control. Essentially, they will call for the collaboration of specialists in a project or team-form of organization.

There will be a complication of goals. Business will increasingly concern itself with its adaptive or innovative-creative capacity. In addition, meta-goals will have to be articulated and developed—that is, supra-goals which shape and provide the foundation for the goal structure. One meta-goal might be a system for detecting new and changing goals; another could be a system for deciding priorities among goals.

Finally, there will be more conflict and contradiction among diverse standards of organizational effectiveness, just as in hospitals and universities today there is conflict between teaching and research. The reason for this is the increased number of professionals involved, who tend to identify more with the goals of their profession than with those of their immediate employer. University professors can be used as a case in point. More and more of their income comes from outside sources, such as foundations and consultant work. They tend not to be good "company men" because they divide their loyalty between professional values and organizational goals.

ORGANIZATION. The key word will be "temporary"; there will be adaptive, rapidly changing *temporary systems*. These will be "task forces," organized around problems to be solved, of groups of relative strangers who represent a diverse set of professional skills. The groups will be arranged on an organic rather than mechanical model. The "executive" thus becomes a co-ordinator or "linking pin" between various task forces. He must be a man who can speak the diverse languages of research, with skills to relay information and to mediate between groups. People will be differentiated not vertically according to rank and status, but flexibly and functionally according to skill and professional training. This is the organizational form that will gradually replace bureaucracy as we know it. As no catchy phrase comes to mind, I call it an organic-adaptive structure.

MOTIVATION. Such an organization should increase motivation, and thereby effectiveness, because it enhances satisfactions intrinsic to the task. There is a harmony between the educated individual's need for meaningful, satisfactory, and creative tasks and a flexible organizational structure. However, there will also be reduced commitment to work groups, for these groups will be transient and changing. While skills in human interaction will become more important, due to the growing needs for collaboration in complex tasks, there will be a concomitant reduction in group cohesiveness. I would predict that in the organic-adaptive system people will have to learn to develop quick and intense relationships on the job, and learn to bear the loss of more enduring work relationships. Because of the added ambiguity of roles, more time will have to be spent on the continual rediscovery of the appropriate organizational mix.

In general, I do not agree with those who emphasize a New Utopianism, in which leisure, not work, becomes the emotional-creative sphere of life. Jobs should become more rather than less involving; man is a problem-solving animal and the tasks of the future guarantee a full agenda of problems. In addition, the adaptive process itself may become captivating to many.

At the same time, I think that the future I describe is not necessarily a "happy" one. Coping with rapid change, living in temporary work systems (set up in quickstep time), developing meaningful relations—and then breaking them—all augur social strains and psychological tensions. Learning how to live with ambiguity, to identify with the adaptive process, to make a virtue out of contingency, and to be self-directing will be the task of education, the goal of maturity, and the achievement of the successful manager. To be a wife in this era will become a profession of providing stability and continuity.

In these new organizations, participants will be called on to use their minds more than at any other time in history. Fantasy, imagination, and creativity will be legitimate in ways that today seem strange. Social structures will no longer be instruments of psychic repression but will increasingly promote play and freedom on behalf of curiosity and thought.

Bureaucracy was a monumental discovery for harnessing the muscle power of the industrial revolution. In today's world, it is a lifeless crutch that is no longer useful. For we now require structures of freedom to permit the expression of play and imagination and to exploit the new pleasure of work.

Outside Reading: Essay-Discussion Questions

1. According to Professor Bennis, what are the two major reasons for the changes in organizational life?

2. Professor Bennis observes a fundamental

change in the basic attitudes that underlie managerial behavior. In what three areas is this reflected?

3. What does Professor Bennis predict the organization condition for organizational life will be in the next 25 to 50 years? What is the key word in describing this organization condition?

4. What role will the behavioral sciences play in the future of managerial organization?

PART IV

DECISION MAKING: PLANNING STRATEGIES

Chapter Fourteen

Surveying the Environment

THIS CHAPTER GIVES emphasis to environmental factors that relate to planning. After a discussion of sales forecasting, attention is given to financial, labor, raw material, and other resource markets. Government intervention, innovation, cultural factors, and weather conditions are also considered.

Section I MAJOR CONCEPTS

Market forecasting
Sales forecasting
Economic forecasting

Financial markets
Labor markets
Innovation

Section II SELF-TEST

True-False

_____ 1. Vertical integration means control of various steps in the production and marketing process.

_____ 2. Most of the purchases made by business firms are hedged in the future markets.

_____ 3. The public utilities are generally subject to more direct government regulation then ordinary business firms.

_____ 4. The high excess-profit tax rates of the postwar years caused companies to reduce expenditures for such things as advertising and expense accounts.

_____ 5. Innovation affects productive efficiency but not consumer demand.

Multiple Choice

_____ 1. Which of the following statements about economic forecasting is most acceptable?
   a. The large majority of companies make their own economic forecasts.
   b. Most professional economic forecasters refuse to use government data.

c. Economic forecasts are almost completely reliable *if* the forecaster uses all available scientific techniques.

d. Many companies rely on outside economic forecasts in making their sales projections.

_____ 2. A "sales forecast" is most like which of the following?

a. The organizational objective

b. Economic forecast

c. Total demand in a competitive industry

d. Gross national product

_____ 3. The existence of "a lag" between sales and some economic phenomenon may be important in the use of which of the following forecasting techniques?

a. Survey and interview techniques

b. Crystal gazing

c. Trend-cycle analysis

d. Correlation analysis

_____ 4. The demand for furniture is a function of disposable personal income per household, the value of private residential construction per household, and the ratio of the furniture price index to the Consumer Price Index. This statement represents which of the following forecasting techniques?

a. Multiple correlation

b. Simple correlation

c. Interview techniques

d. Survey techniques

_____ 5. Which of the following statements about "survey and interviewing techniques" is most acceptable?

a. It is almost completely reliable for forecasting the demand for such products as automobiles and furniture.

b. It is the newest and therefore the best forecasting tool.

c. It gives the best results during a period of major economic change.

d. Persons being interviewed generally make implicit or explicit assumptions about the future.

_____ 6. The following tend to reduce imperfections in the labor market EXCEPT:

a. Employment offices

b. Labor mobility

c. Competition

d. Lack of knowledge

_____ 7. The extent to which investment is financed from internal sources

a. is the same for different industries

b. is constant over a period of time

c. is influenced by past profits

d. is not a factor in money market demand

_____ 8. Which of the following best expresses the percentages of large corporate capital needs acquired from internal sources during the past decade?

a. Less than 50 per cent

b. More than 50 per cent

c. Less than 10 per cent

d. More than 90 per cent

_____ 9. Business planning may be influenced directly or indirectly by government action. For example, as a result of the antitrust suit against Du Pont and General Motors, a firm might *not*

a. diversify products

b. integrate vertically

c. use magnetic tape for data processing

d. resist union demands

_____ 10. What is the most accurate statement about the concept of innovation?

a. It is always easy to measure a cause-and-effect relationship between innovation and productivity.

b. Innovation should be only concerned with increasing productivity efficiency.

c. Innovations may cause declines in the demand for existing products or services.

d. Advertising innovations are playing a decreasing role in business competition.

Essay-Discussion

1. How does a sales forecast differ from economic and market forecasts?

2. To what extent do interest rates influence planning?

3. What affect do you think the government will have on business environment in the near future? Include specific areas, such as planning, pricing, and collective bargaining.

Section III ILLUSTRATIVE CASES

EVERYBODY TALKS ABOUT IT

The following passage taken from a large fruit company shareholder's report points to the problems a firm could have with the weather and the strategies that could be used to overcome them.

> Weather problems are always present in any agricultural business. But losses from wind this year hurt much more than usual because they came abnormally early and were concentrated in two of the lower cost divisions where boxing facilities were completed.

The company's difficulties were further complicated by trying to maintain good customer service.

> Replacement supplies were obtained in the open market in an effort to keep our customers supplied but the quality was not satisfactory; much of it had to be sold in stem form at a discount, and our expenses were doubled by the fact that we already paid out the money necessary to produce a crop in the first place and then had to pay a second time to obtain fruit in the open market.

The company attempted to counteract these environmental contingencies by (1) planting wind-resistant and disease-resistant bananas in places where they can be produced at the lowest cost and (2) developing new production in geographically dispersed areas to provide more protection against weather abnormalities in a particular local area.

Analysis

1. Evaluate this company's approach to its environment.

2. In order to carry out some of the strate-gies, the company was forced to expand its international operations. What cultural factors will affect them and what strategies would you develop to overcome any forecasted cultural problems?

"QE2"[1]

The abbreviation QE2 stands for *Queen Elizabeth the Second*—Britain's brand-new $72 million transatlantic superliner.

Market forecasting is largely based on past performance. The past performance of transatlantic passenger ships is very bleak. The ship company lost $7.2 million in 1965, and the jetliners finally "drydocked" the QE2's older sisters. The *Queen Mary* is now a waterfront museum in San Diego, and the first *Elizabeth* is a floating hotel in Philadelphia.

This past performance has not seemed to affect the enthusiasm the company has for the new market potential of QE2. The president indicated four factors that will make QE2 overcome the fate of her older sisters:

1. A fly-cruise arrangement with Pan American;

2. A tie-in with a competing shipping line to guarantee regularity of transatlantic schedules;

3. A new concept of ocean-going service designed to attract the wealthy "go-go" American, not the dowager and her lap robe; and

---

[1] Reported in "Long Live the Queen (No. 2 That Is)," *Lincoln Journal and Star,* August 11, 1968, p. 6C.

4. Construction techniques which provide more economical and comfortable passenger service.[2]

Analysis

1. How much technical market forecasting do you think this company utilized? What specific techniques *could* be used?

2. Based on the company's four-point argument, do you think that the company is justified in the QE2 venture or are they "beating a dead horse"? Explain.

---

[2] *Ibid.*

"SWISS-CHEESE BATS AND PEEKERS"[1]

The U. S. Patent Office has a deluge of inventions—some excellent but many border on the ridiculous. The absurd inventions, however, often pay off. One patent official recalled a simple contraption of wood and wire that did nothing more than make some black powder jump onto a sheet of paper and stick there. This device was the breakthrough for xerography, a process by which many office copying machines now work.

Another innovation led to the redesign of the conventional ash baseball bat. The ash bat is only good for about a year's use. A manufacturer of bowling pins and toilet seats de-

cided to try to remedy the complaints of coaches that they were spending too much on bats. The owner and his staff developed a plastic laminated hickory bat that costs 25 per cent more but lasts twice as long. The problem was that hickory added more weight. The innovation was to bore several holes to reduce the weight but not affect the hitting prowess. The company has sold 30,000 to 40,000 of the new bats since they were initiated on the market about two years ago.

A hosiery manufacturer came up with an eye-opening innovation. The head of the company took "technical" interest in the miniskirt and the problems it raises for the wearer when she sits down. He developed Peekers, which are a pair of garterlike circlets, heavily trimmed with lacy material, that are worn thigh-high. The patent discreetly describes them as "an attractive, vision-blocking screen or veil . . . to prevent the exposure of the upper portion of the leg and the undergarments . . . ."[2] The manufacturer comments: "They're selling pretty good. Advertised in *Playboy,* you know."[3]

Analysis

1. How do you suppose these innovations came about? In dreams or what?

2. Can you think of any similar innovations that have improved a company's sales and profit picture?

---

[1] Based on "The Innovators," *The Wall Street Journal,* July 30, 1968, p. 1, 11.

[2] *Ibid.*, p. 11.
[3] *Ibid.*

Chapter Fifteen

The Development of Planning Strategies

T HIS CHAPTER DEFINES the planning prob-lem and then considers some of the strate-gies that may be used to solve the problem.

Emphasis is given to marketing and resource procurement strategies and to techniques for increasing productivity.

Section I MAJOR CONCEPTS

Planning
Product line strategies
Price policies
Advertising

Product research and development
Resource procurement strategies
Productive efficiency strategies

Section II SELF-TEST

True-False

_____ 1. The Ford Motor Company pursued a policy of high profit per unit during much of its early history.

_____ 2. The extent to which sales can be changed by advertising varies little from product to product.

_____ 3. A steel-producing company that ex-tends ownership over iron and coal mining facilities is engaged in hori-zontal integration.

_____ 4. A process chart shows graphically what happens to a person, part, mate-rial, or printed form as it proceeds from one selected point in a process to another.

_____ 5. The problem of excess plant capacity is made more difficult if the plant is highly specialized.

Multiple Choice

_____ 1. A higher price means lower revenues under which of the following conditions?
   a. Elastic demand curve
   b. Inelastic demand curve
   c. Favorable consumer preferences
   d. Upward shift in the demand schedule

_____ 2. A failure to raise price, even though it is economically possible, may be justified for the following reasons EXCEPT:
   a. Keeping out potential competitors
   b. Fear of adverse public reaction
   c. Maximizing profits
   d. Why tempt fate in the face of the unknown?"

_____ 3. The basic steel producers did not increase price as much as they might have during the "gray market" period for which of the following reasons?
   a. They sought to maximize profits in the short run.
   b. They could supply a sufficient amount of steel for the demand.
   c. They feared increased regulation by government.
   d. The "gray market" price was lower than the price they were charging.

_____ 4. The Ford move to reduce the price of the Model T Ford is most closely related to which of the following concepts?
   a. High profits per unit
   b. Lower plant utilization
   c. Mass markets
   d. Reduced consumer welfare

_____ 5. Which of the following is _not_ one of the "house rules" developed by the Du Pont Company to guide its research and development activities?
   a. A small commercial or revenue base
   b. Select problems with great care

   c. Recognize that a program may run as long as five or six years
   d. Know when to quit

_____ 6. Which of the following does _not_ express the philosophy of "Boulwareism"?
   a. Strike a wedge between the union and the employees
   b. Attempt to enhance management prerogatives in the labor relations area
   c. Use advertising and other communication devices
   d. Use a passive program to avoid conflict with the union

_____ 7. Which of the following is _not_ an argument for the use of more than one supplier?
   a. Possibility of a strike in the supplier's establishment
   b. Forcing competition
   c. Protection against interruptions in production
   d. Economic gains from quantity production

_____ 8. All of the following favor lower inventories EXCEPT:
   a. Expected price increases
   b. Expected decline in demand
   c. Expected price reductions
   d. Interest and storage costs

_____ 9. The Ford Motor Company, during its early history, practiced
   a. little vertical integration
   b. much vertical integration
   c. horizontal, but not vertical, integration
   d. a policy of "purchase from the outside whenever possible"

_____ 10. Which of the following does _not_ describe a standard?
   a. It is a unit of measurement or a system of classification.
   b. It is commonly accepted.
   c. It precludes product diversification.
   d. It promotes simplification.

Essay-Discussion

1. What is the nature of the planning problem?

2. How does product diversification give companies a greater growth potential?

3. What can a company do to solve the problem of excess plant capacity?

Section III   ILLUSTRATIVE CASES

"PROGRESS: THE MOST IMPORTANT PRODUCT"

General Electric, which employs 350,000 people and operates 252 manufacturing plants in 24 different countries or territories, is living proof of its well-known slogan. A few of GE's accomplishments are the following:

1. It is the largest manufacturer of man-made industrial diamonds.

2. It is a leader in jet engines.

3. It holds more patents than any other company in the United States.

4. It is the largest manufacturer of electronic medical equipment.

5. It has developed a three-dimensional x-ray machine called the "Stereo Fluoricon."

6. It produces a machine gun that sprays 6000 bullets a minute.

7. It developed "Lucalox," a lamp bulb that is as bright as 25 of the conventional 100 watt household bulbs but uses only as much electricity as four 100-watt bulbs.[1]

Analysis

1. What are the implications of the GE slogan?

2. Would the accomplishments listed above suggest that GE is highly diversified?

3. What would you speculate are the reasons why GE has become one of the elite corporations in America?

[1] "Computer a Bad Word at General Electric," *The Magazine of Wall Street*, April 27, 1968, p. 17.

THE HOUSE CRAPS OUT[1]

The idea of "game theory" is that planning should take into consideration the strategies

[1] See John MacDonald, *Strategy in Poker, Business and War* (New York: W. W. Norton and Company, Inc., 1950).

developed by others. To illustrate this concept, an analogy is often made between the strategies involved in playing poker and those that relate to competitive business practices. The poker parlors of a California city provided an ironic situation in this respect. They became involved in a price war in which they reduced the price of dinners served to poker players. The price of a full-course meal dropped to 10 cents. In addition to losing money on meals, the poker parlors almost lost their licenses as the result of pressure put on city hall by restaurants in the area.

Analysis

1. Discuss the planning of these poker parlors according to the concept of "game theory."

2. What are some considerations that affect pricing policies?

HASN'T MADE A NICKEL[1]

A *Wall Street Journal* article recently told of a corporate researcher who has a beautiful laboratory, a very high salary, and the high esteem of his colleagues and his empoyer. He also is credited with not making a nickle for the company in his nine years of employment. The research manager says: "Over the years [he] has come up with some very nice theoretical accomplishments—none of which has a commercial application."[2]

[1] Based on "The Innovators," *The Wall Street Journal*, June 4, 1968, p. 1.
[2] *Ibid.*

This is contrasted to the Du Pont case, a recognized leader in research and development. A chemist puttered fruitlessly in the Du Pont laboratories for more than six years before he finally invented nylon, the base for the entire synthetic fabrics industry.

Analysis

1. How should research and development (R&D) fit into a company's planning strategies?

2. What guidelines would you suggest for the management of research?

MODERN CHAMPAGNE

Champagne may no longer bring visions of native Frenchmen crushing grapes with their bare feet and then aging the rich juices in oaken casks in a musty cave. Instead, the bubbly beverage, one of the last holdouts for craftsmanship of a mass-produced item, has finally succumbed to modern productive techniques. This changeover was expressed by one French producer as follows: "To survive, we certainly must bring more and more of our operations up to date, and are doing so. But not at the expense of quality in champagne."[1] Some of the new techniques utilized are (1) improved fertilizers and frost-fighting processes for the vineyards, (2) stainless steel and glass-lined fermentation tanks instead of oak casks, and (3) assembly-line bottling and new packaging.[2]

Analysis

1. Do you think that modern industry is sacrificing quality for productive efficiency?

2. Can you foresee any problems the champagne manufacturers may have as a result of their new methods of production?

---

[1] "Bubbling with Ideas," *Business Week*, November 16, 1963, p. 30.
[2] *Ibid.*

Chapter Sixteen

Dynamic Planning I

THIS CHAPTER IS CONCERNED with the nature of the planning process and the manner In which companies plan their programs. Particular attention is given to such subjects as lead time, the transformation period, and planning criteria. The discussion then turns to operations research and other model-solving planning techniques. In the final section, comprehensive consideration is given to the importance of subjective processes and techniques in solving planning problems.

Section I MAJOR CONCEPTS

Lead time
Transformation period
Planning criteria
Operations research

Subjective problem-solving
Creative thinking
"Brainstorming"

Section II SELF-TEST

True-False

_____ 1. Iconic models portray various properties of something by a different set of properties.

_____ 2. Operations research is primarily concerned with the construction of analogue models.

_____ 3. Operations research was developed by Henry L. Gantt at the Bethlehem Steel Company.

_____ 4. Successful executives always know how they make decisions.

_____ 5. There is evidence that the subconscious mind has the capacity to create new ideas.

Multiple Choice

_____ 1. Which of the following best expresses "from the drawing board to

the completed new model"?
a. Lead time
b. Mechanical drawing
c. Budgeting
d. Transformation period

_____ 2. Which of the following was used to reduce the lead time involved in producing the atomic bomb?
a. Turning back the clock
b. Break-even chart
c. Harmonious overlap
d. Transformation period

_____ 3. The time necessary to depreciate a fixed capital asset is defined by which of the following terms?
a. Consumption period
b. Transformation period
c. Sequence of operations
d. Lead time

_____ 4. Which of the following words best describes the solutions to most planning problems?
a. A definite solution
b. Alternatives
c. Scientific solution
d. Objective

_____ 5. Which of the following best dates the beginning of operations research as an important managerial tool?
a. 1900
b. 1945
c. 1832
d. 1903

_____ 6. All of the following are valid statements about operations research EXCEPT:
a. It was extensively used to solve tactical and strategic military problems during World War II.
b. It involves the use of "high-powered" mathematics.
c. It is primarily concerned with the construction of "analogue models."
d. A team of people from various disciplines is often used.

_____ 7. The models of operations research can be classified into three categories. Which category is correctly described?

a. Iconic—used to predict consequences to the extent that the logic of mathematics corresponds in some degree to the dynamics of the reality it represents.
b. Analogue—employs one set of properties to represent another set of properties.
c. Symbolic—a scaled-down reproduction of that which it represents.
d. Systems—nonconnecting and noninterrelated entities.

_____ 8. Which of the following best defines the problems that can be solved by operations research techniques?
a. Inventory problems
b. Competitive problems
c. Replacement problems
d. All of the above

_____ 9. The "brainstorming" technique developed by Alex Osborn, an advertising executive, involves the following EXCEPT:
a. No criticism during session
b. Pouring out large volume of ideas
c. Combining and improving ideas
d. Restraints when ideas become too wild

_____ 10. Shackle's theory dealing with the problem of uncertainty involves the selection of an alternative that seems to offer the least
a. monopoly profit
b. risk and uncertainty
c. potential surprise
d. accounting cost

Essay-Discussion

1. How does the transformation period relate to the forecasting problem?

2. What factors limit the applicability of the profit norm as a measure of management efficiency?

3. Compare and contrast operations research with scientific management.

Section III ILLUSTRATIVE CASES

DYNAMIC HARDWARE[1]

A hardware company founded in 1904 originally existed by selling wagonloads of supplies to coal mines and company-owned stores. Whether it was furniture, tools, or equipment, if the mines would buy it, the hardware company "stocked" it. During the great depression, the mining operation started to change with more and more mechanization, until, shortly after World War II, the mine stores virtually disappeared. The miners no longer purchased their own tools. For instance, the two to three carloads of shovels that miners purchased per month soon disappeared. Guided by the president of the hardware company's policy that "A distributor must stay abreast—preferably ahead—of changes in his market area,"[2] the company steadily and rapidly moved from being a general hardware operation to becoming a full-line industrial supply firm with specialists in individual lines, such as power transmission. The president states: "Any type of expansion move whether it is the addition of a line, the opening of a branch, or the acquisition of another company should be the result of careful analysis and planning."[3]

Analysis

1. What are the implications of the title of this illustrative case?

2. Do you think that the president of this company recognizes that we live in an ever-changing world?

3. Can you think of other types of companies or operations beside hardware that have faced a dramatically changing market for their product or service?

[1] Based on "Expansion: Major Problem or Mini-Headache?" *Industrial Distribution*, May 1968, p. 52.
[2] *Ibid.*
[3] *Ibid.*

"THE FLYING EDSEL"?

The TFX or F-111 jet bomber-fighter has created much controversy. The cost was origi-nally estimated to be $2.8 million per plane. However, after approximately $1 billion had been spent in research and development, the cost actually turned out to be about $6 million per plane.

Admirers of the plane proclaim that the "bird can fly in any weather, hang in the sky or surge to supersonic speed, soar across any ocean, climb into thin air or skim the ground with unerring calm, stop on a dime and carry on its back a crew of humans in shirtsleeve comfort."[1] At this writing, three of the six "superplanes" flown to Vietnam for battle-testing have crashed or been shot down and have been grounded for further testing.

Analysis

1. If you were responsible for the F-111, whom would you "call on the carpet"?

2. What does this say about the planning that went into this plane?

3. Should the project be abandoned? What is its current status?

[1] "Our Most Fantastic Flying Machine," *Nation's Business*, March 1968, p. 48.

INSTANT CREATIVITY[1]

According to a recent magazine article, corporate jargon or cant is currently the "in" type of communication. The executive who sticks to the old adverbial standbys, such as "actually" and "basically," may leave his creativity and imagination open to question. A vice-president of a computer company recently devised a special tool to help the executive to become more creative in his communication. He developed a handy pocket card called the "Instant Buzzword Generator," which lists 27 numbered words in three columns. The executive need only to select at

[1] Based on "The New Babel of Business," *Dun's Review*, October 1967, pp. 38–39.

random one word from each column and combine them. The result for 9-6-6 is "balanced transitional time-phase," and 4-7-8 yields "functional incremental hardware." The founder of the tool points out that "This has no meaning whatsoever, but you'll find that no one will dare to challenge the use of such a profound term."[2]

---

[2] *Ibid.*, p. 39.

Analysis

1. What impact does such "creative" language have on the subjective decision-making process?

2. Is this case a good example of creativity in business organizations? Explain.

3. Can you think of any other tools, such as the buzzword generator, which can be useful in triggering creativity?

Chapter Seventeen

Dynamic Planning II

THIS CHAPTER DEALS with the planning problem from the viewpoint of a particular organization's program. Strategic or limiting factors and computerized planning systems are given special emphasis. The impact of planning on objectives and policies is also discussed.

Section I MAJOR CONCEPTS

Satisficing
Strategic factors
Organizational objectives
Sales forecast

Planning systems
Standards
Policies

Section II SELF-TEST

True-False

_____ 1. Planning is not concerned with organizational objectives.

_____ 2. A strategic factor is the missing link in whatever system of integrated conditions or actions is necessary to achieve an objective.

_____ 3. A company sales forecast is the same as a forecast of market or economic conditions.

_____ 4. Budgeting tends to systematize the planning process.

_____ 5. Executives at higher levels of the hierarchy are more concerned with means than those at middle or lower levels.

Multiple Choice

_____ 1. In retrospect, Willi Schlicker, chief of German iron and steel production, concluded that strategic Allied bombing was most effective in the area of

a. oil refineries

b. ball-bearing plants
c. railroads
d. mines

____ 2. Which of the following would probably be the most strategic factor during a major depression?
a. Workers
b. Plant capacity
c. Customers
d. Supplies

____ 3. What is the best statement about policies?
a. They are standards or norms.
b. They are never implicit.
c. They are usually enforced absolutely.
d. They are always explicit.

____ 4. What is the most accurate statement about change?
a. A major change in objectives is usually very easy to accomplish.
b. Time plays no factor in change.
c. High degrees of specialization tend to make change easier.
d. People generally do not like change.

____ 5. What is an example of planning?
a. Slight modification in the procedure for making customer refunds
b. A major change in the production program
c. A foreman who orders a worker to do something in a certain way
d. All of the above

____ 6. What approach would Herbert Simon say executives take toward solving planning problems?
a. Satisficing
b. Maximizing
c. Minimizing
d. Criticizing

____ 7. What is the most accurate statement about the profit criterion in relation to planning?
a. It is a highly abstract concept.
b. It generally directly indicates what needs to be done.

c. It has nothing to do with planning.
d. It is the only criterion of planning.

____ 8. In what way is a computerized planning system *most* helpful?
a. Determining organizational objectives
b. Translating organizational objectives into subsidiary objectives
c. Making subjective decisions for executives
d. Making policy decisions

____ 9. There are two phases to the organized planning process. The first phase is concerned with the formulation of objectives, and the second occurs after the objective has been given final approval. What is true concerning these two phases?
a. Planning during the first phase generally follows hierarchical lines more rigidly than during the second phase.
b. The top executive is not held responsible for the final decision as to the nature of objectives in the second phase.
c. In the first phase, executives who head functional staff sections actively participate in the formulation of over-all corporate objectives.
d. In the first phase, principal operating executives do not participate in the formulation of over-all corporate objectives.

____ 10. What is *not* true of a budgetary system?
a. It gives emphasis to the importance of planning.
b. It frequently leads to a more systematic approach to planning.
c. It can be used to evaluate the efficiency of managerial personnel.
d. It can be a substitute for good planning.

Essay-Discussion

1. What is the importance of strategic or limiting factors in planning?

2. What is the relationship between the sales forecast and planning?

3. What is meant by the term "company policies"?

Section III ILLUSTRATIVE CASES

DON'T CALL ME, I'LL CALL ON YOU

A large company decided that it was spending too much for supplies. It approached the problem in a unique manner. Instead of having its purchasing agents wait for the supplier's salesmen to call, the company sent some of its top personnel "on the road" to relate the company's needs directly to suppliers.[1] The company uses a traveling display of its needs. This unique method of purchasing seems to be accomplishing two desired aims: (1) increasing the number of suppliers, thus leading to more competitive bids and lower costs to the company; and (2) stimulating supplier innovation by outlining future needs.

Analysis

1. Evaluate how this organization approached its planning problem for supplies.

2. Will the sales forecast play any role in this company's plan? Why?

[1] "TWA Goes on the Road," *Business Week*, January 26, 1963, pp. 138–140.

"THE GREAT DEBATE"[1]

A debate was recently held between an advertising executive with the thesis that "Industrial distributors have outlived their usefulness" and a president of a distributing company who feels that "We're not only surviving—we're thriving." The advertising man stated that "the selling climate improved far beyond the most optimistic expectations, and the industrial distributor complex, a truly archaic business and one that has not changed its basic thinking for 50 years, remained practically unchanged and reaped a tremendously profitable period of growth from the general economic surge. . . . In today's marketplaces it is not worth the 20 per cent (average) the distributor realizes to stock, warehouse, and deliver industrial products locally—when the time, coast-to-coast, has been reduced to the 3-hour and 45-minute jet time today."

The distributing company president countered with the following: "You said a turndown in business might be detrimental and a great flag of warning to the industrial distributor. You said that the zip-up in transportation might also be a factor which could make the industrial distributor much less necessary, and you mentioned the acceleration in technology. If there were ever three basics for proving the indispensability of industrial distributors, they are your very arguments."

Analysis

1. Explain the distribution company president's position.

2. Have other industries, for example, railroads, faced similar planning problems?

3. If you were a company president, what would you do to ensure that your company did not become obsolete in the dynamic world in which we live? What policies would you develop?

[1] Reprinted with permission of the publisher from "Debate on Distribution," *Industrial Distribution*, October 1967, pp. 56–57.

A PIGGYBACK RIDE

The traditionally conservative railroad industry should be congratulated for its novel approach in meeting competition. Their piggy-back system seems to imply that "If you can't lick them, join them." Their industry has been plagued by excess capacity largely resulting from increased highway transportation. To eliminate some of the excess, the railroads used their biggest competitor to their advantage. When one waits at a railroad crossing today, he no longer counts boxcars; he counts truck trailers and new cars going down the tracks.

Analysis

1. What may be considered to be the strategic factor in this illustrative case? Why?

2. Discuss the concepts of organizational objectives and policies in relation to the railroad's freight and passenger service.

READING: SHAPING THE MASTER STRATEGY OF YOUR FIRM

WILLIAM H. NEWMAN

Every enterprise needs a central purpose expressed in terms of the services it will render to society. And it needs a basic concept of how it will create these services. Since it will be competing with other enterprises for resources, it must have some distinctive advantages—in its services or in its methods of creating them. Moreover, since it will inevitably cooperate with other firms, it must have the means for maintaining viable coalitions with them. In addition, there are the elements of change, growth, and adaptation. Master strategy is a company's basic plan for dealing with these factors.

One familiar way of delving into company strategy is to ask, "What business are we in or do we want to be in? Why should society tolerate our existence?" Answers are often difficult. A company producing only grass seed had very modest growth until it shifted its focus to "lawn care" and provided the suburban homeowner with a full line of fertilizers, pesticides, and related products. Less fortunate was a cooperage firm that defined its business in terms of wooden boxes and barrels and went bankrupt when paperboard containers took over the field.

Product line is only part of the picture, however. An ability to supply services economically is also crucial. For example, most local bakeries have shut down, not for lack of demand for bread, but because they became technologically inefficient. Many a paper mill has exhausted its sources of pulpwood. The independent motel operator is having difficulty meeting competition from franchised chains. Yet in all these industries some firms have prospered—the ones that have had the foresight and adaptability (and probably some luck, too) to take advantage of their changing environment. These firms pursued a master strategy which enabled them to increase the services rendered and attract greater resources.

Most central managers recognize that master strategy is of cardinal importance. But they are less certain about how to formulate a strategy for their particular firm. This article seeks to help in the shaping of master strategies. It outlines key elements and an approach to defining these. Most of our illustrations will be business enterprises; nevertheless, the central concept is just as crucial for hospitals, universities, and other nonprofit ventures.

A practical way to develop a master strategy is to:

- Pick particular roles or niches that are appropriate in view of competition and the company's resources.
- Combine various facets of the company's efforts to obtain synergistic effects.
- Set up sequences and timing of changes that reflect company capabilites and external conditions.
- Provide for frequent reappraisal and adaptation to evolving opportunities.

NEW MARKETS OR SERVICES

Pickling Propitious Niches

Most companies fill more than one niche. Often they sell several lines of products; even

Reprinted by permission from the *California Management Review*, Vol. 9, No. 3, Spring 1967, pp. 77–88. Copyright 1967 by the Regents of the University of California. Dr. Newman is Samuel Bronfman Professor of Democratic Business Enterprise in the Graduate School of Business, Columbia University.

when a single line is produced an enterprise may sell it to several distinct types of customers. Especially as a firm grows, it seeks expansion by tapping new markets or selling different services to its existing customers. In designing a company strategy we can avoid pitfalls by first examining each of these markets separately.

Basically, we are searching for customer needs—preferably growing ones—where adroit use of our unique resources will make our services distinctive and in that sense give us a competitive advantage. In these particular spots, we hope to give the customer an irresistible value and to do so at relatively low expense. A bank, for example, may devise a way of financing the purchase of an automobile that is particularly well-suited to farmers; it must then consider whether it is in a good position to serve such a market.

Identifying such propitious niches is not easy. Here is one approach that works well in various situations: Focus first on the industry —growth prospects, competition, key factors required for success—then on the strengths and weaknesses of the specific company as matched against these key success factors. As we describe this approach more fully, keep in mind that we are interested in segments of markets as well as entire markets.

The sales volume and profits of an industry or one of its segments depend on the demand for its services, the supply of these services, and the competitive conditions. (We use "service" here to include both physical products and intangible values provided by an enterprise.) Predicting future demand, supply, and competition is an exciting endeavor. In the following paragraphs, we suggest a few of the important considerations that may vitally affect the strategy of a company.

ELEMENTS OF DEMAND

Demand for Industry Services

The strength of the desire for a service affects its demand. For instance, we keenly want a small amount of salt, but care little for additional quantities. Our desire for more and better automobiles does not have this same sort of cut-off level, and our desires for pay-tele-vision (no commercials, select programs) or supersonic air travel are highly uncertain, falling in quite a different category from that of salt.

Possible *substitutes* to satisfy a given desire must be weighed—beef for lamb, motorboats for baseball, gas for coal, aureomycin for sulfa, weldments for castings, and so forth. The frequency of such substitutions is affected, of course, by the relative prices.

Desire has to be backed up by *ability to pay*, and here business cycles enter in. Also, in some industries large amounts of capital are necessarily tied up in equipment. The relative efficiency, quality of work, and nature of machinery already in place influence the money that will be available for new equipment. Another consideration: If we hope to sell in foreign markets, foreign-exchange issues arise.

The *structure of markets* also requires analysis. Where, on what terms, and in response to what appeals do people buy jet planes, sulphuric acid, or dental floss? Does a manufacturer deal directly with consumers or are intermediaries such as retailers or brokers a more effective means of distribution?

Although an entire industry is often affected by such factors—desire, substitutes, ability to pay, structure of markets—a local variation in demand sometimes provides a unique opportunity for a particular firm. Thus, most drugstores carry cosmetics, candy, and a wide variety of items besides drugs, but a store located in a medical center might develop a highly profitable business by dealing exclusively with prescriptions and other medical supplies.

All these elements of demand are subject to change—some quite rapidly. Since the kind of strategic plans we are considering here usually extends over several years, we need both an identification of the key factors that will affect industry demand and an estimate of how they will change over a span of time.

SUPPLY SITUATION

Supply Related to Demand

The attractiveness of any industry depends on more than potential growth arising from strong demand. In designing a company strategy we also must consider the probable supply of services and the conditions under which they will be offered.

The *capacity* of an industry to fill demand for its services clearly affects profit margins. The importance of over- or undercapacity, however, depends on the ease of entry and withdrawal from the industry. When capital costs are high, as in the hotel or cement business, adjustments to demand tend to lag. Thus, overcapacity may depress profits for a long period; even bankruptcies do not remove the capacity if plants are bought up—at bargain prices—and operated by new owners. On the other hand, low capital requirements—as in electronic assembly work—permit new firms to enter quickly, and shortages of supply tend to be short-lived. Of course, more than the physical plant is involved; an effective organization of competent people is also necessary. Here again, the case of expansion or contraction should be appraised.

Costs also need to be predicted—labor costs, material costs, and for some industries, transportation costs or excise taxes. If increases in operating costs affect all members of an industry alike and can be passed on to the consumer in the form of higher prices, this factor becomes less significant in company strategy. However, rarely do both conditions prevail. Sharp rises in labor costs in Hawaii, for example, place its sugar industry at a disadvantage on the world market.

A highly dynamic aspect of supply is *technology*. New methods for producing established products—for example, basic oxygen conversion of steel displacing open-hearth furnaces and mechanical cotton pickers displacing century-old hand-picking techniques—are part of the picture. Technology may change the availability and price of raw materials; witness the growth of synthetic rubber and industrial diamonds. Similarly, air cargo planes and other new forms of transportation are expanding the sources of supply that may serve a given market.

For an individual producer, anticipating these shifts in the industry supply situation may be a matter of prosperity or death.

CLIMATE OF INDUSTRY

Competitive Conditions in the Industry

The way the interplay between demand and supply works out depends partly on the nature of competition in the industry. *Size, strength, and attitude of companies* in one industry—the dress industry where entrance is easy and style is critical—may lead to very sharp competition. On the other hand, oligopolistic competition among the giants of the aluminum industry produces a more stable situation, at least in the short run. The resources and managerial talent needed to enter one industry differ greatly from what it takes to get ahead in the other.

A strong *trade association* often helps to create a favorable climate in its industry. The Independent Oil Producers' Association, to cite one case, has been unusually effective in restricting imports of crude oil into the United States. Other associations compile valuable industry statistics, help reduce unnecessary variations in size of products, run training conferences, hold trade shows, and aid members in a variety of other ways.

Government regulation also modifies competition. A few industries like banking and insurance are supervised by national or state bodies that place limits on prices, sales promotion, and the variety of services rendered. Airlines are both regulated as a utility and subsidized as an infant industry. Farm subsidies affect large segments of agriculture, and tariffs have long protected selected manufacturers. Our patent laws also bear directly on the nature of competition, as is evident in the heated discussion of how pharmaceutical patents may be used. Clearly, future government action is a significant factor in the outlook of many industries.

CRUCIAL FACTORS

Key Factors for Success in the Industry

This brief review suggests the dynamic nature of business and uncertainties in the outlook for virtually all industries. A crucial task of every top management is to assess the forces at play in its industry and to identify those factors that will be crucial for future success. These we call "key success factors." Leadership in research and development may be very important in one industry, low costs in another, and adaptability to local need in a third; large financial resources may be a *sine qua non* for mining whereas creative imagination is the touchstone in advertising.

We stressed earlier the desirability of making such analyses for narrow segments as well as broad industry categories. The success factors for each segment are likely to differ in at least one or two respects form those for other segments. For example, General Foods Corporation discovered to its sorrow that the key success factors in gourmet foods differ significantly from those for coffee and Jello.

Moreover, the analysis of industry outlook should provide a forecast of the *growth potentials* and the *profit prospects* for the various industry segments. These conclusions, along with key success factors, are vital guideposts in setting up a company's master strategy.

The range of opportunities for distinctive service is wide. Naturally, in picking its particular niche out of this array a company favors those opportunities which will utilize its strength and bypass its limitations. This calls for a candid appraisal of the company itself.

POSITION IN MARKET

Market Strengths of Company

A direct measure of *market position* is the percentage that company sales are of industry sales and of major competitors' sales. Such figures quickly indicate whether our company is so big that its activities are likely to bring prompt responses from other leading companies. Or our company may be small enough to enjoy independent maneuverability. Of course, to be most meaningful, these percentages should be computed separately for geographical areas, product lines, and types of customer—if suitable industry data are available.

More intangible but no less significant are the relative standing of *company products* and

their *reputation* in major markets. Kodak products, for instance, are widely and favorably known; they enjoy a reputation for both high quality and dependability. Clearly, this reputation will be a factor in Eastman Kodak Company strategy. And any new, unknown firm must overcome this prestige if it seeks even a small share in one segment of the film market. Market reputation is tenacious. Especially when we try to "trade up," our previous low quality, service, and sharp dealing will be an obstacle. Any strategy we adopt must have enough persistence and consistency so that our firm is assigned a "role" in the minds of the customers we wish to reach.

The relationship between a company and the *distribution system* is another vital aspect of market position. The big United States automobile companies, for example, are strong partly because each has a set of dealers throughout the country. In contrast, foreign car manufacturers have difficulty selling here until they can arrange with dealers to provide dependable service. A similar problem confronted Whirlpool Corporation when it wanted to sell its trademarketed appliances publicly. (For years its only customer had been Sears, Roebuck and Company.) Whirlpool made an unusual arrangement with Radio Corporation of America which led to the establishment of RCA-Whirlpool distributors and dealers. Considering the strong competition, Whirlpool could not have entered this new market without using marketing channels such as RCA's.

All these aspects of market position—a relative share of the market, comparative quality of product, reputation with consumers, and ties with a distributive system—help define the strengths and limitations of a company.

SERVICE ABILITIES

Supply Strengths of a Company

To pick propitious niches we also should appraise our company's relative strength in creating goods and services. Such ability to supply services fitted to consumer needs will be built largely on the firm's resources of labor and material, effective productive facilities, and perhaps pioneering research and development.

Labor in the United States is fairly mobile. Men tend to gravitate to good jobs. But the process takes time—a southern shoe plant needed ten years to build up an adequate number of skilled workers—and it may be expensive. Consequently, immediate availability of competent men at normal industry wages is a source of strength. In addition, the relationships between the company and its work force are important. All too often both custom and formal agreements freeze inefficient practices. The classic example is New England textiles; here, union-supported work habits give even mills high labor costs. Only recently have a few companies been able to match their more flourishing competitors in the South.

Access to *low-cost materials* is often a significant factor in a company's supply position. The development of the southern paper industry, for example, is keyed to the use of fast-growing forests which can be cut on a rotational basis to provide a continuing supply of pulpwood. Of course, if raw materials can be easily transported, such as iron ore and crude oil by enormous ships, plants need not be located at the original source.

Availability of materials involves more than physical handling. Ownership, or long-term contracts with those who do own, may assure a continuing source at low cost. Much of the strategy of companies producing basic metals —iron, copper, aluminum, or nickel—includes huge investments in ore properties. But all sorts of companies are concerned with the availability of materials. So whenever supplies are scarce a potential opportunity exists. Even in retailing, Sears, Roebuck and Company discovered in its Latin American expansion that a continuing flow of merchandise of standard quality was difficult to assure, but once established, such sources became a great advantage.

Physical facilities—office buildings, plants, mines—often tie up a large portion of a company's assets. In the short run, at least, these facilities may be an advantage or a disadvantage. The character of many colleges, for instance, has been shaped by their location, whether in a plush suburb or in a degenerating urban area, and the cost of moving facilities is so great that adaptation to the existing neighborhood becomes necessary. A steel company, to cite another case, delayed modernizing its plant so long that it had to abandon its share of the basic steel market and seek volume in specialty products.

Established organizations of highly talented people to perform particular tasks also give a company a distinctive capability. Thus, a good research and development department may enable a company to expand in pharmaceuticals, whereas a processing firm without such a technical staff is barred from this profitable field.

Perhaps the company we are analyzing will enjoy other distinctive abilities to produce services. Our central concern at this point is to identify strengths and see how these compare with strengths of other firms.

FINANCES AND MANAGEMENT

Other Company Resources

The propitious niche for a company also depends on its financial strength and the character of its management.

Some strategies will require large quantities of capital. Any oil company that seeks foreign sources of crude oil, for instance, must be prepared to invest millions of dollars. Few firms maintain case reserves of this size, so *financial capacity* to enter this kind of business depends on: an ability to attract new capital— through borrowing or sale of stock—or a flow of profits (and depreciation allowances) from existing operations that can be allocated to the new venture. On the other hand, perhaps a strategy can be devised that calls for relatively small cash advances, and in these fields a company that has low financial strength will still be able to compete with the affluent firms.

A more subtle factor in company capacity is its *management*. The age and vitality of key executives, their willingness to risk profit and capital, their urge to gain personal prestige through company growth, their desire to insure stable employment for present workers—

all affect the suitability of any proposed strategy. For example, the expansion of Hilton Hotels Corporation into a world-wide chain certainly reflects the personality of Conrad Hilton; with a different management at the helm, a modification in strategy is most appropriate because Conrad Hilton's successors do not have his particular set of drives and values.

Related to the capabilities of key executives is the organization structure of the company. A decentralized structure, for instance, facilitates movement into new fields of business, whereas a functional structure with fine specialization is better suited to expansion in closely related lines.

PICKING A NICHE

Matching Company Strengths with Key Success Factors

Armed with a careful analysis of the strengths and limitations of our company, we are prepared to pick desirable niches for company concentration. Naturally, we will look for fields where company strengths correspond with the key factors for success that have been developed in our industry analyses described in the preceding section. And in the process we will set aside possibilities in which company limitations create serious handicaps.

Potential growth and profits in each niche must, of course, be added to the synthesis. Clearly, a low potential will make a niche unattractive even though the company strengths and success factors fit neatly. And we may become keenly interested in a niche where the fit is only fair if the potential is great.

Typically, several intriguing possibilities emerge. These are all the niches—in terms of market lines, market segments, or combinations of production functions—that the company might pursue. Also typically, a series of positive actions is necessary in order for the company to move into each area. So we need to list not only each niche and its potential, but the limitations that will have to be overcome and other steps necessary for the company to succeed in each area. These are our propitious niches—nestled in anticipated business conditions and tailored to the strengths and limitations of our particular company.

An enterprise always pursues a variety of efforts to serve even a single niche, and, typically, it tries to fill several related niches. Considerable choice is possible, at least in the degree to which these many efforts are pushed. In other words, management decides how many markets to cover, to what degree to automate production, what stress to place on consumer engineering, and a host of other actions. One vital aspect of master strategy is fitting these numerous efforts together. In fact, our choice of niches will depend in part, on how well we can combine the total effort they require.

Synergy is a powerful ally for this purpose. Basically, synergy means that the combined effect of two or more cooperative acts is greater than the sum which would result if the actions were taken independently. A simple example in marketing is that widespread dealer stocks *combined* with advertising will produce much greater sales volume than widespread dealer stocks in, say, Virginia and advertising in Minnesota. Often the possibility of obtaining synergistic effects will shape the master strategy of the company—as the following examples will suggest.

COMBINATION OF SERVICES

Total Service to Customer

A customer rarely buys merely a physical product. Other attributes of the transaction often include delivery, credit terms, return privileges, repair service, operating instructions, conspicuous consumption, psychological experience of purchasing, and the like. Many services involve no physical product at all. The crucial question is what combination of attributes will have high synergistic value for the customers we serve.

International Business Machines, for instance, has found a winning combination. Its products are well designed and of high quality. But so are the products of several of its competitors. In addition, IBM provides salesmen who understand the customer's problems and how IBM equipment can help solve them, and fast, dependable repair service. The synergistic effect of these three services is of high value to many customers.

Each niche calls for its own combination of services. For example, Chock Full o' Nuts expanded its restaurant chain on the basis of three attributes: good quality food, cleanliness, and fast service. This combination appealed to a particular group of customers. A very limited selection, crowded space, and lack of frills did not matter. However, if any one of the three characteristics slips at an outlet, the synergistic effect is lost.

ADDING TO CAPABILITIES

Fuller Use of Existing Resources

Synergistic effects are possible in any phase of company operations. One possibility is that present activities include a "capability" that can be applied to additional uses. Thus, American watch companies have undertaken the manufacture of tiny gyroscopes and electronic components for spacecraft because they already possessed technical skill in the production of miniature precision products. They adopted this strategy on the premise that they could make both watches and components for spacecraft with less effort than could separate firms devoted to only one line of products.

The original concept of General Foods Corporation sought a similar synergistic effect in marketing. Here, the basic capability was marketing prepared foods. By having the same sales organization handle several product lines, a larger and more effective sales effort could be provided and/or the selling cost per product line could be reduced. Clearly, the combined sales activity was more powerful than separate sales efforts for each product line would have been.

VERTICAL INTEGRATION

Expansion to Obtain a Resource

Vertical integration may have synergistic effects. This occurred when the Apollo Print-

ing Machine Company bought a foundry. Apollo was unsatisfied with the quality and tardy delivery of its castings and was looking for a new supplier. In its search, it learned that a nearby foundry could be purchased. The foundry was just breaking even, primarily because the volume of its work fluctuated widely. Following the purchase, Apollo gave the foundry a more steady backlog of work, and through close technical cooperation the quality of castings received by them was improved. The consolidated set-up was better for both enterprises than the previous independent operations.

The results of vertical integration are not always so good, however; problems of balance, flexibility, and managerial capacity must be carefully weighed. Nevertheless, control of a critical resource is often a significant part of company strategy.

UNIQUE SERVICES

Expansion to Enhance Market Position

Efforts to improve market position provide many examples of "the whole being better than the sum of its parts." The leading can companies, for example, moved from exclusive concentration on metal containers into glass, plastic, and paper containers. They expected their new divisions to be profitable by themselves, but an additional reason for the expansion lay in anticipated synergistic effects of being able to supply a customer's total container requirements. With the entire packaging field changing so rapidly, a company that can quickly shift from one type of container to another offers a distinctive service to its customers.

International Harvester, to cite another case, added a very large tractor to its line a few years ago. The prospects for profit on this line alone were far from certain. However, the new tractor was important to give dealers "a full line"; its availability removed the temptation for dealers to carry some products of competing manufacturers. So, when viewed in combination with other International Harvester products, the new tractor looked much more significant than it did as an isolated project.

NEGATIVE SYNERGY

Compatibility of Efforts

In considering additional niches for a company, we may be confronted with negative synergy—that is, the combined effort is worse than the sum of independent efforts. This occurred when a producer of high quality television and hi-fi sets introduced a small color television receiver. When first offered, the small unit was as good as most competing sets and probably had an attractive potential market. However, it was definitely inferior in performance to other products of the company and, consequently, undermined public confidence in the quality of the entire line. Moreover, customers had high expectations for the small set because of the general reputation of the company, and they became very critical when the new product did not live up to their expectations. Both the former products and the new product suffered.

Compatibility of operations within the company should also be considered. A large department store, for instance, ran into serious trouble when it tried to add a high-quality dress shop to its mass merchandising activities. The ordering and physical handling of merchandise, the approach to sales promotion, the sales compensation plan, and many other procedures which worked well for the established type of business were unsuited to the new shop. And friction arose each time the shop received special treatment. Clearly, the new shop created an excessive number of problems because it was incompatible with existing customs and attitudes.

BROAD COMPANY GOALS

Summarizing briefly: We have seen that some combinations of efforts are strongly reinforcing. The combination accelerates the total effect or reduces the cost for the same effect or solidifies our supply or market position. On the other hand, we must watch for incompatible efforts which may have a disruptive effect in the same cumulative manner. So, when we select niches—as a part of our master strategy—one vital aspect is the possibility of such synergistic effects.

Master strategy sets broad company goals. One firm may decide to seek pre-eminence in a narrow specialty while another undertakes to be a leader in several niches or perhaps in all phases of its industry. We have recommended that this definition of "scope" be clear in terms of:

- Services offered to customers.
- Operations performed by the company.
- Relationships with supplies of necessary resources.
- The desirability of defining this mission so as to obtain synergistic effects.

But master strategy involves more than defining our desired role in society. Many activities will be necessary to achieve this desired spot, and senior executives must decide what to do first, how many activities can be done concurrently, how fast to move, what risks to run, and what to postpone. These questions of sequence and timing must be resolved to make the strategy operational.

STRATEGY OF SEQUENCE

Choice of Sequence

Especially in technical areas, sequence of actions may be dictated by technology. Thus, process research must precede equipment designs, product specifications must precede cost estimation, and so forth. Other actions, such as the steps necessary to form a new corporation, likewise give management little choice in sequence. When this occurs, normal programming or possibly PERT analysis may be employed. Little room—or need—exists for strategy.

Preordained sequences, however, are exceptional in the master strategy area. A perennial issue when entering a new niche, for instance, is whether to develop markets before working on production economies, or vice versa. The production executive will probably say, "Let's be sure we can produce the product at a low cost before committing ourselves to customers," whereas the typical marketing man will advise, "Better be sure it will sell before tooling up for a big output."

A striking example of strategy involving sequence confronted the Boeing company when it first conceived of a large four-engine jet plane suitable for handling cargo or large passenger loads. Hindsight makes the issue appear simple, but at the time, Air Force officers saw little need for such a plane. The belief was that propeller-driven planes provided the most desirable means for carrying cargo. In other words, the company got no support for its prediction of future market requirements. Most companies would have stopped at this point. However, Boeing executives decided to invest several million dollars to develop the new plane. A significant portion of the company's liquid assets went into the project. Over two years later, Boeing was able to present evidence that caused the Air Force officials to change their minds—and the KC 135 was born. Only Boeing was prepared to produce the new type of craft which proved to be both faster and more economical than propeller-driven planes. Moreover, the company was able to convert the design into the Boeing 707 passenger plane which, within a few years, dominated the airline passenger business. Competing firms were left far behind, and Convair almost went bankrupt in its attempt to catch up. In this instance, a decision to let engineering and production run far ahead of marketing paid off handsomely.

No simple guide exists for selecting a strategic sequence. Nevertheless, the following comments do sharpen the issue:

- Resist the temptation to do first what is easiest simply because it requires the least initiative. Each of us typically has a bias for what he does well. A good sequence of activities, however, is more likely to emerge from an objective analysis.
- If a head start is especially valuable on one front, start early there. Sometimes, being the first in the market is particularly desirable (there may be room for only one company). In other cases, the strategic place to begin is the acquiring of key resources; at a later date limited raw material may already be bought up or the best sites occupied by competitors. The importance of a head start is usually hard to estimate, but probably more money is lost in trying to be first than in catching up with someone else.
- Move into uncertain areas promptly, preferably before making any major commitments. For instance, companies have been so entranced with a desired expansion that they committed substantial funds to new plants before uncertainties regarding the production processes were removed.
- If a particular uncertainty can be investigated quickly and inexpensively, get it out of the way promptly.
- Start early with processes involving long lead-times. For example, if a new synthetic food product must have government approval, the tedious process of testing and reviewing evidence may take a year or two longer than preparation for manufacturing and marketing.
- Delay revealing plans publicly if other companies can easily copy a novel idea. If substantial social readjustment is necessary, however, an early public announcement is often helpful.

In a particular case, these guides may actually conflict with each other, or other considerations may be dominant. And, as the Boeing 707 example suggests, the possible gains may be large enough to justify following a very risky sequence. Probably the greatest value of the above list is to stimulate careful thought about the sequence that is incorporated into a company's master strategy.

RESOURCE LIMITATIONS

Straining Scarce Resources

A hard-driving executive does not like to admit that an objective cannot be achieved. He prefers to believe, "Where there's a will there's a way." Yet, an essential aspect of master strategy is deciding what can be done and how fast.

Every enterprise has limits—perhaps severe limits—on its resources. The amount of capital, the number and quality of key personnel, the physical production capacity, or the adaptability of its social structure—none of these is boundless. The tricky issue is how to use these limited resources to the best advantage. We must devise a strategy which is feasible within the inherent restraints.

A household-appliance manufacturer went bankrupt because he failed to adapt his rate of growth to his financial resources. This man had a first-rate product and a wise plan for moving with an "economy model" into an expanding market (following rural electrification). But, to achieve low production costs, he built an oversized plant and launched sales effort in ten states. His contention was that the kind of company he conceived could not start out on a small scale. Possibly all of these judgments were correct, but they resulted in cash requirements that drained all of his resources before any momentum was achieved. Cost of the partially used plant and of widely scattered sales efforts was so high that no one was willing to bail out the financially strapped venture. His master strategy simply did not fit his resources.

The scarce resource affecting master strategy may be managerial personnel. A management consulting firm, for instance, reluctantly postponed entry into the international arena because only two of its partners had the combination of interest, capacity, and vitality to spend a large amount of time abroad, and these men were also needed to assure continuity of the United States practice. The firm felt that a later start would be better than weak action immediately—even though this probably meant the loss of several desirable clients.

The weight we should attach to scarce resources in the timing of master strategy often requires delicate judgment. Some strain may be endured. But, how much, how long? For example, in its switch from purchased to company-produced tires, a European rubber company fell behind on deliveries for six months, but, through heroic efforts and pleading with customers, the company weathered the squeeze. Now, company executives believe the timing was wise! If the delay had lasted a full year—and this was a real possibility—the consequence would have approached a catastrophe.

Forming Coalitions

A cooperative agreement with firms in related fields occasionally provides a way to overcome scarce resources. We have already referred to the RCA-Whirlpool arrangement for distributing Whirlpool products. Clearly, in this instance, the timing of Whirlpool's entrance into the market with its own brand depended on forming a coalition with RCA.

EXAMPLES OF COALITIONS

The early development of frozen foods provides us with two other examples of fruitful coalitions. A key element in Birdseye master strategy was to obtain the help of cold-storage warehouses; grocery wholesalers were not equipped to handle frozen foods, and before the demand was clearly established they were slow to move into the new activity. And the Birdseye division of General Foods lacked both managerial and financial resources to venture into national wholesaling.

Similarly, Birdseye had to get freezer cabinets into retail stores, but it lacked the capability to produce them. So, it entered into a coalition with a refrigerator manufacturer to make and sell (or lease) the cabinets to retail stores. This mutual agreement enabled Birdseye to move ahead with its marketing program much faster. With the tremendous growth of frozen foods, neither the cold storage warehouse nor the cabinet manufacturer continued to be necessary, but without them in the early days widespread use of frozen foods would have been delayed three to five years.

Coalitions may be formed for reasons other than "buying time." Nevertheless, when we are trying to round out a workable master strategy, coalitions—or even mergers—may provide the quickest way to overcome a serious deficiency in vital resources.

THE RIGHT TIME TO ACT

Receptive Environment

Conditions in a firm's environment affect the "right time" to make a change. Mr. Ralph Cordiner, for example, testifies that he launched his basic reorganization of General Electric Company only when he felt confident of three years of high business activity because, in his opinion, the company could not have absorbed all the internal readjustments during a period of declining volume and profits.

Judging the right time to act is difficult. Thus, one of the contributing factors to the multimillion-dollar Edsel car fiasco was poor timing. The same automobile launched a year or two earlier might have been favorably received. But buyer tastes changed between the time elaborate market research studies were made and the time when the new car finally appeared in dealer showrooms. By then, preference was swinging away from a big car that "had everything" toward compacts. This mistake in timing and associated errors in strategy cost the Ford Motor Company over a hundred million dollars.

A major move can be too early, as well as too late. We know, for instance, that a forerunner of the modern, self-service supermarket—the Piggly Wiggly—was born too soon. In its day, only a few housewives drove automobiles to shopping centers; and those that could afford cars usually shunned the do-it-yourself mode so prevalent today. In other words, the environment at that time simply was not receptive to what now performs so effectively. Other "pioneers" have also received cool receptions—prefabricated housing and local medical clinics are two.

NO SIMPLE RULES

The preceding discussions of sequence and timing provide no simple rules for these critical aspects of basic strategy. The factors we have mentioned for deciding which front(s) to push first (where is a head start valuable, early attention to major uncertainties, lead-times, significance of secrecy) and for deciding how fast to move (strain on scarce resources, possible coalition to provide resources, and receptivity of the environment) bear directly on many strategy decisions. They also highlight the fundamental nature of sequence and timing in the master strategy for a firm.

Master strategy involves deliberately relating a company's efforts to its particular future environment. We recognize, of course, that both the company's capabilities and its environment continually evolve; consequently, strategy should always be based, not on existing conditions, but on forecasts. Such forecasts, however, are never 100 per cent correct; instead, strategy often seeks to take advantage of uncertainty about future conditions.

This dynamic aspect of strategy should be underscored. The industry outlook will shift for any of numerous reasons. These forces may accelerate growth in some sectors and spell decline in others, may squeeze material supply, may make old sources obsolete, may open new possibilities and snuff out others. Meanwhile, the company itself is also changing—due to the success or failure of its own efforts and to actions of competitors and cooperating firms. And with all of these internal and external changes the combination of thrusts that will provide optimum synergistic effects undoubtedly will be altered. Timing of actions is the most volatile element of all. It should be adjusted to both the new external situation and the degrees of internal progress on various fronts.

Consequently, frequent reappraisal of master strategy is essential. We must build into the planning mechanisms sources of fresh data that will tell us how well we are doing and what new opportunities and obstacles are appearing on the horizon. The feedback features of control will provide some of these data. In addition, senior managers and others who have contact with various parts of the environment must be ever-sensitive to new developments that established screening devices might not detect.

Hopefully, such reappraisal will not call for sharp reversals in strategy. Typically, a master strategy requires several years to execute and some features may endure much longer. The kind of plan I am discussing here sets the direction for a whole host of company actions, and external reputations and relations often persist for many years. Quick reversals break momentum, require repeated relearning, and dissipate favorable cumulative effects. To be sure, occasionally a sharp break may be necessary. But, if my forecasts are reasonably sound, the adaptations to new opportunities will be more evolution than revolution. Once embarked on a course, we make our reappraisal from our new position—and this introduces an advantage in continuing in at least the same general direction. So, normally, the adaptation is more an unfolding than a completely new start.

Even though drastic modification of our master strategy may be unnecessary, frequent incremental changes will certainly be required to keep abreast of the times. Especially desirable are shifts that anticipate change before the pressures build up. And such farsighted adjustments are possible only if we periodically reappraise and adapt present strategy to new opportunities.

Master strategy is the pivotal planning instrument for large and small enterprises alike. The giant corporations provide us with examples on a grand scale, but the same kind of thinking is just as vital for small firms.

AN EXAMPLE

A terse sketch of the central strategy of one small firm will illustrate this point. The partners of an accounting firm in a city with a quarter-million population predicted faster growth in data processing than in their normal auditing and tax work, yet they knew that most of their clients were too small to use an electronic computer individually. So they foresaw the need for a single, cooperative computer center serving several companies. And they believed that their intimate knowledge of the procedures and the needs of several of these companies, plus the specialized ability of one partner in data processing, put them in a unique position to operate such a center. Competition was anticipated from two directions: New models of computers much smaller in size would eventually come on the market— but even if the clients could rent such equipment they would still need programmers and other specialized skills. Also, telephonic hookups with International Business Machines service centers appeared likely—but the accounting firm felt its local and more intimate knowledge of each company would give it an advantage over such competition. So, the cooperative computer center looked like a propitious niche.

The chief obstacle was developing a relatively stable volume of work that would carry the monthly rental on the proposed computer. A local insurance company was by far the best prospect for this purpose; it might use half the computer capacity, and then the work for other, smaller companies could be fitted into the remaining time. Consequently, the first major move was to make a deal—a coalition—with the insurance company. One partner was to devote almost his entire time working on details for such an arrangement; meanwhile, the other two partners supported him through their established accounting practice.

We see in this brief example:

- The picking of a propitious niche for expansion.
- The anticipated synergistic effect of combining auditing services with computing service.
- The sequence and timing of efforts to overcome the major limiting factor.

The project had not advanced far enough for much reappraisal, but the fact that two partners were supporting the third provided a built-in check on the question of "how are we doing."

REFERENCE

This article is adapted from a new chapter in *The Process of Management*, second edition, to be published by Prentice-Hall, Inc., in 1967. Executives who wish to explore the meaning and method of shaping master strategies still further can consult the following materials: E. W. Reilley, "Planning the Strategy of the Business," *Advanced Management,* vol. 20, pp. 8–12, December, 1955; T. Levitt, "Marketing Myopia," *Harvard Business Review,* vol. 38, no. 4, pp. 45–66, July-August, 1960; F. F. Gilmore and R. G. Brandenburg, "Anatomy of Corporate Planning," *Harvard Business Review,* vol. 41, no. 6, pp. 61–69, November-December, 1962; and H. W. Newman and T. L. Berg, "Managing External Relations," *California Management Review,* vol. 5, no. 3, pp. 81–86, Spring 1963.

Outside Reading: Essay-Discussion Questions

1. What are the four major elements of demand for industry services discussed by Dr. Newman? Briefly comment on each.

2. Define synergy and discuss how it may be used in planning strategies.

3. Discuss the advantages and disadvantages of vertical integration.

4. Analyze Dr. Newman's statement that "Master strategy involves deliberately relating a company's efforts to its particular future environment."

COMMUNICATION
AND CONTROL

Chapter Eighteen

Information and Communication

AFTER A DISCUSSION of basic factors that relate to communication, the nature of the semantic problem is given comprehensive consideration. Attention is then given to the nature of and the functions performed by communication centers in the transmission of information. A final section is concerned with deliberate and nondeliberate (semantic) information distortion.

Section I MAJOR CONCEPTS

Information theory
Communication
Control
Perception
Language

Semantics
Communication centers
Communication channels
Information distortion

Section II SELF-TEST

True-False

_____ 1. Cybernetics can be applied to informational problems of computers.

_____ 2. Accounting, statistics, and mechanical drawings are languages.

_____ 3. Barnard has emphasized that persons who occupy organizational positions are the *means* through which communication takes place.

_____ 4. Information is often distorted as it flows up the hierarchy, but information from higher levels is never distorted as it flows down.

_____ 5. The semantic problem often results in nondeliberate information distortion.

Multiple Choice

_____ 1. Which of the following best describes the information theory de-

veloped by Norbert Wiener and Claude E. Shannon?
   a. Operations research
   b. Linear programming
   c. Management science
   d. Cybernetics

____ 2. Message construction, as it is concerned with the area of communication, refers to
   a. various channels of communication
   b. method of transmitting the message
   c. transferring ideas into words
   d. transferring words into ideas

____ 3. Which of the following best defines the reason why people often form different perceptions about the same phenomenon?
   a. Physiological factors
   b. Psychological factors
   c. Sociological factors
   d. All of the above

____ 4. Which of the following is primarily concerned with the impact of language on meaning?
   a. Entropy
   b. Cybernetics
   c. Semantics
   d. Phrenology

____ 5. Which of the following used an analogy between language and the map of a territory?
   a. Alfred Korzybski
   b. Norbert Wiener
   c. Claude Shannon
   d. Chester I. Barnard

____ 6. Which of the following describes a higher order of abstraction?
   a. More details
   b. Fewer details
   c. Neither a nor b
   d. Either a or b

____ 7. The _____ in Aristotelian logic leads to two-valued conclu-

sions as true or false, good or bad, rich or poor.
   a. Law of identity
   b. Law of contradiction
   c. Law of the excluded middle
   d. None of the above

____ 8. Decisional information is generally _____ as it flows from lower to higher levels and _____ as it moves in the opposite direction.
   a. Differentiated—integrated
   b. Segregated—integrated
   c. Integrated—differentiated
   d. Abstract—integrated

____ 9. Which of the following is *not* an argument for listening to subordinates?
   a. Executive workload is increased
   b. Motivate subordinates
   c. Ease emotional tensions
   d. Obtain information about attitudes

____ 10. What is the most accurate statement concerning "semantics and executive action"?
   a. Executives should forbid "semantic" distortions of information.
   b. Advertising slogans should be eliminated.
   c. Distortions created by words can have constructive consequences.
   d. Propaganda cannot lead to profits.

Essay-Discussion

1. How may perception affect the communication process?

2. What is the nature of the semantic problem?

3. How may personal qualities influence the communication process?

Section III   ILLUSTRATIVE CASES

"STALAG 18"

"In the microenvironment of Stalag 18, a hydramatic one-one who esotericizes in a shirtsleeve is a high-wire problem who, for all his psychic income, may have to be de-hired."[1]

Make any sense? If you were on the "in" of executive jargon you would know right away that this means, in "square" translation, that in the in-organization of any company, a shiftless, low-performance executive who decides without facts during conferences is a management misfit who, despite such extras as carpeted floor and reserved parking space, may have to be eased out of his post, or out of the company altogether.[2]

Analysis

1. How important is it to know the jargon of your profession?
2. What aspect of semantics does the case above point out?
3. What status implications are inherent in the illustrative case?

[1] "The New Babel of Business," *Dun's Review*, May 1968, p. 21.
[2] *Ibid.*

"SEMANTIC WALLS"

Many specialists are unable to communicate with other persons outside their area of expertise. They tend to use a highly technical language which only the knowledgeable person understands. This communication difficulty was recently brought out by John Diebold, the man credited with coining the term "automation." Discussing the problems of bringing men and machines together, he says that "there are still computer technicians who build semantic walls around the operation to keep management out."[1] Computer jargon,

[1] "Needed: A Yardstick for Computers," *Dun's Review*, August 1968, p. 40.

such as "firmware" meaning hardware that performs some software functions; "input," "output," and "throughput" used to describe information at various stages of processing in a machine; and whole new languages of acronyms to identify programming such as FORTRAN, COBAL, ALGOL, QUIKTRAN, and COMPASS—all tend to impede communication between technicians and the outside world.[2]

Analysis

1. What about Diebold's word "automation"? Can you define what this term means?
2. Why would the computer technicians want to "keep management out"?
3. What would you suggest to improve the communication between specialists and managers?

[2] *Ibid.*, p. 40–41.

HISTORY IS BUNK

H. L. Mencken proved the wisdom of Henry Ford's caustic comment that "history is bunk" when he concocted an absurd and obviously untrue history of the bathtub. The article, which appeared in a New York newspaper, alleged that the bathtub was invented by a cotton broker from Cincinnati in 1842. The splash of the first bathtub, in Mencken's account, brought with it a storm of protest and attempts to protect the citizentry of this great Republic. Medical societies, state legislatures, the city of Boston, and many others took action to stop the spread of bathing. There was much resentment when a bathtub was installed in the White House by President Fillmore. Mencken notes that bathtubs and bathing were finally incorporated into the American mode of living. This tall tale was accepted as the gospel truth by doctors of medicine, bathtub manufacturers, radio commentators, newspaper editors, and many others. In 1926, Mencken publicly proclaimed that the story was a complete hoax. But his contribution to history refused to die. Again he enunciated the tale's untruth. And again to no avail.

Analysis

1. What analogy can you make with the "facts" of a business organization?

2. How much communication in a business firm do you think is deliberately distorted? Why?

Chapter Nineteen

Communication Media: Message Construction and Reception

T HE FIRST SECTION of this chapter deals with alternative media and methods that may be used to transmit information in an organization. The problem of constructing written and oral messages is then scrutinized in terms of such matters as vocabulary, grammar, semantics, and order giving. The final section emphasizes the importance of effective listening and faster reading in the communication process.

Section I MAJOR CONCEPTS

Oral communication
Written communication
Message construction

Order giving
Listening
Reading

Section II SELF-TEST

True-False

_____ 1. Face-to-face communication is not normally a preferred communication method.

_____ 2. Top executives generally require less vocabulary than the rest of the population.

_____ 3. All orders are messages, but not all messages are orders.

_____ 4. Most fast readers read everything at the same rate of speed.

_____ 5. Faster reading speeds reduce the degree of comprehension by a significant amount.

Multiple Choice

_____ 1. A _Fortune_ poll asked executives to select the method most preferred for gathering information. Which of the following is true?

a. Over half preferred verbal reports.

b. Over half preferred written reports.

c. Over half preferred inspection tours.

d. None of the above.

_____ 2. Which of the following represents a conclusion derived from a survey of presidents of large corporations on how they preferred to transmit "very important policies"?

a. Many preferred written methods exclusively.

b. Most of them preferred to use the telephone or intercom.

c. A majority selected a combination of oral and written methods.

d. A majority preferred to use well-written interoffice memos.

_____ 3. Which of the following is most directly concerned with the act of communicating?

a. English language

b. *Webster's International Dictionary*

d. Mathematics

c. A business letter

_____ 4. Bergen and Cornelia Evans have emphasized that the only way to really understand words is to

a. experience their use in as many contexts as possible

b. add a new word to your vocabulary every day

c. look for all of the possible meanings in a standard dictionary

d. carry around a booklet on "how to improve your vocabulary"

_____ 5. Which of the following best expresses the meaning of "correct grammar"?

a. Majority of people

b. The common man

c. The educated

d. Old English

_____ 6. Which of the following statements

best expresses the present attitude of grammarians?

a. Much more dogmatic about grammar than grammarians in the past

b. Agree that usage should be the final criterion of correctness

c. Willing to abandon the idea that there is "better" and "worse" grammar

d. Generally more inclined than in the past to accept usage as a criterion

_____ 7. The *positive* role that "rumors and gossip" may play in an organization is best expressed by which of the following?

a. Getting the truth

b. Lack of information

c. Motivation of personnel

d. Information is distorted

_____ 8. Which of the following best expresses the difference between an order and an ordinary message?

a. Grammar

b. Semantics

c. Authority

d. Language

_____ 9. According to Professor Nila B. Smith, effective reading is fundamentally

a. a mental process

b. a matter of eye movements

c. a problem of reading down the page

d. related to the size of print

_____ 10. Which of the following is a "directional word"?

a. Lecturing

b. Scent

c. Running

d. However

Essay-Discussion

1. Analyze and discuss oral versus written communication.

2. How can a person become a better listener?

3. How would you give orders to your subordinates? Why?

Section III ILLUSTRATIVE CASES

"AN AVALANCHE"[1]

All large corporations of today are utilizing highly sophisticated information technology. Yet, in spite of all the advances made in communication technology, the plain and simple written report is far from perfected. Many firms have become so concerned with this problem that they have created special corporate offices to raise the quality of written reports. The goals of these offices are three-fold: (1) make reports readable. (2) process them faster, and (3) prune them for brevity.[2]

Beside these specialized departments, many company presidents are trying to cope with the written report problem by hiring technical editors. These editors are being assigned to the president's personal staff. Their task is to summarize and clarify the avalanche of written reports that flow to the modern chief executive's desk.

Analysis

1. Is it the private corporation or the public educational process that is responsible for obtaining acceptable written communication from organizational participants? Explain.

2. What are the advantages and disadvantages of using a middleman, such as the technical editor, in the communication process?

[1] Based on "The Crisis in Corporate Controls," *Dun's Review*, July 1963, pp. 38-39, 61-62.
[2] *Ibid.*, p. 61.

EXECUTIVE VOCABULARY

A recent issue of *Nation's Business* updated the executive vocabulary as follows:

1. *Coordinator*: an executive with a desk between two expediters.
2. *For your approval*: passing the buck to you.
3. *For your comment*: I haven't the faintest idea myself.

4. *For your consideration*: You hold the bag a while.
5. *For your file*: I seem to have an extra copy.
6. *Implement a program*: Hire more people and expand the office.
7. *Orientation*: Move around until we find something for you to do.[1]

Analysis

1. Is this pure humor, or do you think there is something to these definitions?
2. How much "reading between the lines" goes on in executive communication?
3. Can you think of any similar definitions for management terms?

[1] "Executive Trends," *Nation's Business*, March 1968, p. 18.

"READ YOUR WAY OUT OF A PAPER BAG"[1]

The president of a company discussed his reading problem with another executive. "We talked about how we both had a lot of unread materials. I told him about my practice of shoveling all unread materials into paper bags, and bringing them home at night. 'You know,' I said to him, "I think I've got bags at home going back to 1955.' "[2]

The president and his friend soon thereafter enrolled in a speed reading course. In a matter of several weeks, the president boosted his reading rate from a maximum of 150 to 450-500 words per minute. His comprehension remained high or went higher—about 75 per cent. Before the course, the president spent about two or more hours every day with his daily mail. After the speed reading course, he needed only 40 minutes per day.

[1] Based on "Slow Reading's Unprofitable, Can You Afford It?," *Industrial Distribution*, March 1968, p. 55.
[2] *Ibid.*

Analysis

1. Should all managers take a speed reading course? What positive or negative ramifications may this have?

2. Do you have personal examples of speed reading courses?

3. How does reading fit into the communication process?

Chapter Twenty

Specialized Informational Systems

THIS CHAPTER BEGINS by giving comprehensive consideration to budgeting and accounting and to the manner in which they become a part of the managerial process. Specialized informational systems in the various functional areas of management are then discussed. The contribution that can be made by such planning devices as the Gantt Chart and Program Evaluation Review Technique (PERT) is carefully scrutinized. A final section is concerned with the relationship between the planning and control processes.

Section I MAJOR CONCEPTS

Budgeting
Accounting
Gantt Chart
PERT

Quality control
Purchasing
Inventory control
Personnel planning and control

Section II SELF-TEST

True-False

_____ 1. The labor budget specified the amount of direct labor necessary to meet production schedules.

_____ 2. The quantitative information contained in budgets precludes the possibility of deliberate distortion.

_____ 3. A break-even chart shows the relationship between total sales income and costs at outputs ranging from zero to plant capacity.

_____ 4. Time is an important variable in the Gantt Chart, but not in PERT.

_____ 5. Quality is the problem only of production and not of the purchasing department.

Multiple Choice

_____ 1. Budgeting is concerned with the ———— consequences of planning and operations, and accounting with

the ——— consequences measured in monetary and other quantitive terms.
a. Actual—expected
b. Actual—actual
c. Expected—actual
d. Organizational—financial

2. If fixed costs total $10,000 and variables cost $5 per unit, the budget amount for 4000 units would be
a. $50,000
b. $40,000
c. $30,000
d. $20,000

3. The nature and amounts of assets, liabilities, and net worth at a given date are indicated by
a. the balance sheet
b. the income statement
c. the statement of retained earnings
d. the profit and loss statement

4. Which of the following best expresses the nature of "the accepted principles of accounting"?
a. A consensus among accountants about their meaning
b. Considerable differences about how to define them operationally
c. The principles learned by beginning students of accounting
d. A long list of government regulations about accounting practices

5. Which of the following refers to a method for pricing inventories?
a. Straight-line method
b. LIFO
c. Fast write-off provision
d. Mnemonic

6. Which of the following statements about the Gantt Chart is *not* in accord with the facts?
a. Generally assumed to be an important contribution
b. Concerned with planned, rather than actual, performance
c. Presents facts in their relation to time

d. Developed by Henry L. Gantt, a friend of Frederick W. Taylor

7. Which of the following *best* expresses the idea of the critical path in a PERT network?
a. The most slack
b. The least amount of slack
c. Possibility of reducing cost
d. Fewer resources are required

8. Job evaluation is an informational tool of the personnel function. Which of the following best represents job evaluation?
a. The person occupying the job plays the most important role in the evaluation.
b. Job evaluation is a systematic technique for measuring the absolute importance of positions.
c. Each position is rated in terms of common factors and the extent to which factor values apply to it.
d. The absentee record is an example of a variable that is incorporated into the job evaluation.

9. An important planning problem is to determine quality standards for products and services. Which of the following is *not* true of quality planning and control?
a. The purpose of quality planning and control is to achieve the highest possible quality.
b. Quality information should, if possible, be in operational terms.
c. *One* purpose of quality control is to gauge the performance of managerial and operating personnel.
d. The standard of quality will usually be expressed in terms of an acceptable range of variation from norm.

10. Which of the following statements about control is *not* true?
a. The control function is similar to the judicial function in political organizations.

b. Executives should recognize that a comparison of planning norms and performance information may not adequately measure efficiency.

c. The control process generally involves some combination of supervision and indirect techniques.

d. Every deviation from planning norms should be followed by control at any cost.

Essay-Discussion

1. What is the relationship between budgets and efficiency?

2. What was the contribution of the Gantt Chart?

3. How may PERT facilitate the planning process?

Section III ILLUSTRATIVE CASES

ACCOUNTANCY OF OIL DRILLING[1]

The "generally accepted accounting principles" are bitterly criticized and staunchly defended. Most of the criticism centers in the fact that there are too many acceptable ways of doing too many things. The oil industry is a case in point. Accepted accounting principles allow oil companies to handle drilling outlays in one of three basic ways: (1) the company can write them off in the year in which they are incurred; (2) the company can capitalize them and amortize the charges over the life of the well; or (3) the company can capitalize the cost and make an additional charge to income, theorizing that future oil will cost more to find than present production.[2] Many leading oil companies thus treat their drilling costs differently.

Accounting principle defenders, such as the managing partner of a leading accounting firm, say: "We've got to be careful that we don't lose sight of what accounting is attempting to do which is basically to charge each year's operations with the costs of that particular year. It would be nice if everything were simple and uniform, but we have to ask ourselves if it makes sense to give up accuracy for uniformity."[3]

Analysis

1. Who do you agree with, the critics or the defenders? Why?

2. Who determines what the "accepted principles of accounting" are?

3. Relate accounting to the concept of control.

IN THE "RED," BUT DOING WELL

The General Electric nuclear operation presents a paradox for the company. This paradox was recently stated as follows: "While losing money in nuclear power, G. E. is doing well in this field."[1] How can it do both simultaneously? Isn't a measure of success the profit or loss of a project?

One answer suggests that part of the paradox can be explained by the accounting procedure. Unlike Westinghouse which distributes its research and development costs over a number of years, GE posts its development costs as they occur and records its earnings only after the equipment has been installed at the site. Moreover, GE has been losing money on so-called turnkey projects. The

[1] Based on "Accounting—The Other Side of the Ledger," *Dun's Review,* March 1967, pp. 36-37, 89-92.

[2] *Ibid.,* p. 37.

[3] *Ibid.,* pp. 90-91.

[1] "Computer a Bad Word at General Electric," *The Magazine of Wall Street,* April 27, 1968, p. 16.

turnkey procedure supplies complete nuclear plants at a fixed price without cushioning the expense of variable factors.[2]

Analysis

1. Can accounting practices make the difference between profit and loss? How?
2. What implications does the title of the case have for operating policy? For stockholder relations?
3. What role should research and development costs play in the short run? Long run?

_____
[2] _Ibid._

REAL "FIFO"

First In First Out (FIFO) is a theoretical method of inventory costing. Rarely, if ever, does FIFO realistically describe the actual flow of goods and materials through the company's warehouse. A Seattle firm devised a simple system to ensure that FIFO works in theory and practice. All shelving has two signs which remind receivers to store materials on the right side of the shelves and to fill all orders from the left side. To make this system work as easily as possible, the shelves incline slightly from right to left.[1]

Analysis

1. Is this merely an academic exercise of making practice coincide with theory? Explain.
2. To what types of companies would this "real" FIFO seem beneficial? To what types would it not matter?
3. Is the FIFO theory characteristic of other accounting and budgetary control systems?

_____
[1] "How 'FIFO' Works Out in Cambell's Warehouse," _Industrial Distribution_, September 1967, pp. 91-92.

Chapter Twenty-One

Computerized Informational Systems

THIS CHAPTER IS concerned with the contribution that electronic computers have made and will make to the informational process. The first section discusses the capabilities of the digital computer and the nature of the input, storage, arithmetic, logical, output, and control devices. The next section considers some practical problems and possible solutions of installing a computer system in a going concern. The development of computerized informational systems is viewed from two perspectives: (1) the basic processes that begin with computer systems design and end with computer operations and (2) the kinds of computerized informational systems that may be developed in an organization. Finally, attention is given to the impact of the computer on organizing, and conclusions are made about present achievements and future prospects.

Section I   MAJOR CONCEPTS

Digital computer
Input devices
Storage devices
Arithmetic operations
Number system
Output devices

Control devices
Informational systems
Programming
Forecasting and planning systems
Real time systems
Shared time systems

Section II   SELF-TEST

True-False

_____ 1. The fastest input device is the punch card.

_____ 2. Electronic computers are essentially errorproof, as far as the technical aspects of operations are concerned.

_____ 3. The term "real time" means that inputs into the computer occurs much before actual operations occur.

___ 4. Computerized informational systems have been more effective in providing information about the future than about the past.

___ 5. Computer specialists usually have the status of staff and service personnel.

Multiple Choice

___ 1. Computers can do all the following EXCEPT:
   a. Make value judgments
   b. Read and write
   c. Do arithmetic and make logical choices
   d. Remember

___ 2. Input is to reading devices as output is to
   a. arithmetical facilities
   b. memory instruments
   c. control devices
   d. writing devices

___ 3. Computer programming involves all of the following EXCEPT:
   a. Coding problems
   b. Only one way
   c. Sequencing computer operations
   d. Systems analysis

___ 4. An example of an information storage device that is external to the computer would be
   a. magnetic drums
   b. magnetic cores
   c. magnetic tape
   d. a, b, and c

___ 5. A binary number system is
   a. a base-2 system
   b. a base-10 system
   c. neither a nor b
   d. both a and b

___ 6. External control of the computer involves the
   a. sequencing operations
   b. timing operations
   c. human operator
   d. coordination of operations

___ 7. What would probably be the first step in making the decision about installing computers?
   a. "Keep up with the Jones"
   b. Warn all executives that they may be replaced
   c. Hire a computer expert
   d. Determine whether they can be effectively used

___ 8. What is the most accurate statement concerning the design of informational systems?
   a. Computerization can solve all informational problems.
   b. It is more important for the systems designer to know the computer than the specialized field.
   c. The systems function should not be specialized on a functional basis.
   d. The basic problem is to translate informational requirements into computer languages.

___ 9. Computer software refers to
   a. magnetic tape drives
   b. printers
   c. programs
   d. a, b, and c

___ 10. Which of the following is generally *not* considered to be one of the three major kinds of informational systems?
   a. Financial
   b. Advertising
   c. Logistics
   d. Personnel

Essay-Discussion

1. Critically analyze the logical capability of the computer.

2. How would you go about installing a computer system in a company for the first time? How would you approach the expansion of current computer systems?

3. Explain what impact computers will have on management organization.

Section III ILLUSTRATIVE CASES

COMPUTER HYSTERIA[1]

The modern manager seems convinced of the tremendous capabilities of computerized management information systems (MIS). Not so widely publicized are the problems that MIS is developing. Nevertheless, some executives are seriously questioning the value of computerized information systems. As one executive candidly states, "We have seen over the past twelve years some incredible blunders. Twinkling lights, spinning tapes and pastel cabinets seem to have a mesmerizing effect on some managers. In a pell-mell rush to be among the first to play with a new toy, enormous sums have been wasted."[2]

Many computer systems are being installed with very little thought going into the cost, efficiency, or applicability to the job that needed to be done. A major cause of frustration seems to be the mountain of useless data churned out by the 600-line-a-minute computerized information output. As one department head complained, "Before the company started computerizing my department, it took me a month to get a progress report . . . . Now I get a report every other day—but it takes me two months to read it."[3]

Analysis

1. What are some ways of avoiding the problems these companies are encountering with their computer information systems? What are some specific steps you would take before installing the MIS?

2. How would you cope with the very real problem the last-quoted executive states? Is it a problem of useless information or improper interpretation of the output? Explain.

[1] Based on "A Mess in M.I.S.?," *Dun's Review,* January 1968, pp. 26-27, 85-87.
[2] *Ibid.,* p. 26.
[3] *Ibid.,* p. 85.

AUTOMATED HAMBURGERS[1]

A chain of counter-service restaurants in the Southeast is utilizing a computer to give

[1] Based on "Compliments to Chef. He's a Computer," *The Magazine of Wall Street,* April 27, 1968, pp. 28-29.

earnings a boost. The company has been using the computer in the usual ways—cost control, inventory, and so on. In the future, however, the company is literally and figuratively "cooking up" something else for its computer. This is the way the company describes the plan to computerize their operations: "Management's hopes for the longer-term future border on the visionary. An example is the idea of building a series of computer-operated restaurants in which food preparation, customer billing, inventory control and some accounting procedures are automatic."[2] The president says that an experimental unit has been successful, though not necessarily profitable. Its electronic system is capable of broiling 450 hamburgers an hour, frying 174 portions of chicken or shrimp, and preparing 720 frosted drinks and 1140 cups of soda.

Analysis

1. Is it feasible for the computer to replace the chef? Why or why not?

2. Analyze the president's statement that the experimental unit is successful though not profitable.

3. Are there any areas of our economy that the computer will not affect?

[2] *Ibid.,* p. 28.

TALKING COMPUTER[1]

Burroughs Corporation has developed an audio-response data communications system that uses computer-stored information to generate a spoken reply to coded inquiries through a telephone handset. The system can retrieve and play back data, such as a bank account balance, inventory quantity, or stock number, or it can be used to send coded data to computer memory through a Touch Tone telephone keyboard.

[1] Based on "Burroughs Audio Response Data Communications System," *Journal of Data Management,* May 1968, p. 63.

Typically, a bank teller would establish a connection with the computer through a telephone. He would then key in an identification code and a coded inquiry and account number. The request would then be transmitted to the computer over telephone lines. The computer locates the information in its random access files and formulates codes that cause the voice-response generator to produce the proper answer. The voice generator's memory is a rotating, cylindrical, photographic film containing 63 parallel tracks on which numbers, words, and phrases are recorded. The electronic logic of a single system provides for sending out 128 different messages simultaneously. The system leases for $795 a month and sells for $37,200.

Analysis

1. If you were a manager of a bank, what would go into your decision of whether to use this system or not?

2. Discuss technical versus economic feasibility.

3. Relate this talking computer to "real time" computer systems.

COMPUTERIZED FOOTBALL[1]

Electronic data processing is being applied to all areas of the business world. Yet, all

[1] Developed from "Computers & Quarterbacks," *Dun's Review,* September 1967, p. 63.

the creative applications to the business enterprise seem ordinary when compared to EDP's latest convert, professional football. Computer Applications, Inc. has recently developed a Personnel Scouting System, which will enable two scouting groups, representing twelve of the sixteen teams in the NFL, to computerize their scouting reports on 1500 college football players. A scout fills out a form on a prospective player according to variables, such as his name, school, height, weight, position, speed, overall rating, and supplementary comments. This information is then punched onto cards and run through an IBM 7094 to produce reports, which are distributed to the teams. An executive of the company carefully points out that "This is a tool for decision-making. The teams still make their own decisions about whom they want to draft and sign."[2] It is interesting to note that the man in charge of the project's development is a Ph.D. candidate in mathematics and has "no interest in sports whatsoever"!

Analysis

1. How much stock do you suppose the team coaches and managers put in these computer reports?

2. Does it matter that the person who develops a program has no interest in the subject?

3. Do you think the company executive is correct when he cautions that this is only a decision tool?

[2] *Ibid.*

READING: COMMUNICATION IN ORGANIZATIONS: SOME PROBLEMS AND MISCONCEPTIONS

WILLIAM H. READ

The subject of communication in business and industry is the focus of a good deal of current interest and discussion, and like such subjects as education and child-rearing, which have personal relevance for most of us, everyone seems to have a theory. Unfortunately most theories about the complexities of information-exchange in large organizations are sketchy and incomplete. Though much has been written and discussed, none of the assumptions underlying the general thinking in this area have been very systematically examined.

As is so often the case when highly complex aspects of organizational functioning are treated as simple ones, many myths and oversimplifications slowly begin to take hold. The author's current research in management communication in several large organizations has revealed that much of the analyses management makes of its communication problems are colored by several basic notions which may not be false, but do require some further thought and clarification. Three are presented here for examination.

THE FREE FLOW FALLACY

A general notion which has crept into the thinking of executives, not as a logical conclusion drawn from systematic observation, but rather as an unexamined assumption, has to do with the nature of the flow of information in organizations. There seems to be a widely held notion that for organizations to function effectively, information must flow freely and unrestricted upward, downward and across. It is difficult to believe that many executives hold to this idea, and surely if questioned seriously about it, they would not. Yet so often they act as though they do believe it and the idea is given a surprising amount of support by writers in management. It is somewhat like the assumption of a free market—everyone *knows* it is a convenient fiction, yet many *assume* it to be true when they approach certain types of marketing problems.

The simple fact is that effective organizational functioning obviously depends not upon a maximum but on an optimum of information exchange. The communication studies of Kelley,[1] Thibaut,[2] Festinger[3] and many others has amply illustrated that once a power hierarchy of virtually any kind comes into existence, information-exchange is no longer "free" but restricted, shaped and controlled. The very fact of being an administrator means a considerable degree of isolation from what is "going on," and the moment one delegates a task, from that moment on (if the administrator is performing his function at all adequately), he is to some extent insulated from some important aspects of that task. The point is that he not only *is* insulated but he *should be*. In any organization from the smallest to

[1] H. H. Kelley, "Communication in Experimentally Created Hierarchies," *Human Relations*, 1951, 4, pp. 39–56.
[2] J. Thibaut, "An Experimental Study of Cohesiveness in Underprivileged Groups," *Human Relations*, 1950, 3, pp. 251–278.
[3] L. Festinger, "Informal Social Communication," *Psychological Review*, 1950, 57, pp. 217–282.

the largest, tasks appropriate to a particular level must be dealt with at that level and it is a natural phenomenon of organizations that information concerned with tasks be contained, focused and processed at the appropriate level or unit in the organization. It is just such a natural phenomenon of human problem-solving that many executives never fully grasp. Focusing on inter-level communication, except in unusual circumstances a superior-subordinate relationship characterized by a strain to develop free and unrestricted interchange of information is not an adaptive and healthy one, but very likely maladaptive and unhealthy. Elliot Jaques,[4] in his classic study of a British steel plant emphasized that certain barriers to communication are actually necessary if an organization is to get its business done. He refers to "adaptive segregation" as the automatic process by which barriers are set up, more or less by mutual consent between sections or levels of a company to keep channels clear for crucial information. His analysis suggests that no organization can function effectively unless there is at least some "tolerance for uncertainty," that is, the capacity to deal with problems when important information about these problems is missing or scarce.

But what is an optimum in information-exchange? Obviously it is determined in particular cases by the type of function each performs in the organization. Yet often overlooked is the role of personalities and even more centrally, the particular nature of the relationship between a superior and his subordinate. If one really analyses it, this relationship represents not a simple but an exceedingly complex "communication system," and many aspects of it are unique among superior-subordinate pairs despite any similarity of duties and functions they perform.

Emerging out of interaction over time, the superior and his subordinate implicitly, and likely without any concerted plan, work out a pattern or programme of information-exchange based upon mutual expectations about what information should be and must be exchanged

—its content, form and medium. By a process of testing and feedback, of trying and finding out, each learns what is expected in terms of communication with respect to the other. Out of this interaction in their day-to-day work are built relatively stable and consistent systems of expectations which give distinguishable form or pattern to the communication between them. The subordinate comes to know what data about sales figures or customer complaints or scheduling problems are expected of him, in what degree of detail, at what time and in what form. It must be emphasized that the stable systems of expectations, which are the essential ingredients of communication between a man and his incumbent, have a history and are the effects of interaction of the two both as people and as decision-makers in particular jobs. Each time a subordinate hears or reads an item of information and says to himself: "This is interesting (or important), the boss will want to hear about it," that subordinate's anticipation of his boss's interest and concern will likely be based jointly upon the subordinate's knowledge of the boss as a particular kind of personality with particular attitudes, needs and idiosyncrasies, and co-ordinately the boss as a decision-maker who must have immediate access to certain kinds of information in order to function as such irrespective of his particular personality characteristics. Thus, information exchanged between parties in any organization can never be free, but is in fact *programmed* as one programmes statistical information in a particular way so that it can be processed by a computer. Failures in communication can take so many forms that it would be impossible to analyse any significant number of them her in the light of the free flow bias. However, "failure to keep the other person informed" is quite often a symptom rather than a real determinant. Frequently it is the failure, for one or a number of reasons, for these mutual and stable sets of expectations to develop or be maintained between a boss and his underling or, for that matter, between any two organizational members. As an administrator, the boss may fail to clarify plans and objectives which involve the sub-

---

[4] E. Jaques, *The Changing Culture of a Factory* (New York, Dryden, 1952).

ordinate, or may neglect to keep himself posted on changes which inevitably take place in his subordinate's job, so that neither is able to build and maintain an accurate set of expectations about information required by the other.

As individuals, boss and subordinate may be poorly "matched." In terms of personalities—they may "clash," hence the testing and feedback mentioned previously as a necessary means of establishing stable expectations may be impossible because of tension between them. Newcomb,[5] in a classic discussion of this phenomenon, describes in detail how interpersonal tension and hostility act to prevent or destroy any mutual basis for effective communication between two people. Emotionally charged and highly distorted sets of expectations about another's behavior are developed, stabilized and remain uncorrected. Consequently hostility and communication breakdown feed upon each other to render effective co-operation between the two impossible.

Still further, these sets of expectations may become outdated. Superior and subordinate may fail to keep pace with rapid organizational change so that patterns of information interchange between them, which may have worked well in the past, no longer do so because of increased size or complexity of the company. For example, the superior may still expect to be informed by his subordinate of minor emergencies in the subordinate's department even after the greatly increased size and complexity of the department make it cumbersome and time-consuming to do so. Mutual sets of expectations may exist, the selective programming of information may still be a reality, yet a communication breakdown may follow because this programming is not geared for present problems.

"NOISE" AND THE ASSUMPTION OF INADVERTENCE

There is a consistently and widely-held assumption, again quite often implicit, that

members of any organization are the necessary victims of what could be termed "random noise." This latter term, borrowed from the language of information theory, refers to annoying, disturbing or irrelevant messages or signals which occur in any input-output system. Applied to industrial organizations, it would refer to the information waste which inevitably occurs when large numbers of people are required to make large numbers of decisions under pressure of time. In its simplest terms, the general idea is that organizational members are seldom kept as fully informed as they should be, and seldom keep others informed as fully and promptly as possible because of the "busyness" and distractions which are the inevitable features of any enterprise. One makes a procedural change, but neglects to (or forgets to) inform one's subordinates. The engineer makes a slight design change but because of pressure, time and "other things" that flow around him in his job and demand his attention, he neglects to inform the engineering sales department promptly enough. In short, information is withheld, restricted or distorted not through any motive or intention, but because of forgetfulness, thoughtlessness, procrastination or failure to fully realize the importance of certain kinds of information to certain other people in the organization.

There is nothing erroneous or misleading in this kind of explanation for problems and barriers in communication. One *inadvertently* fails to inform others or fails to inform correctly because of the time and pressure of events. But what is too often overlooked and glossed-over in this explanation is the often astounding degree of design and motive which actually can and does take place with respect to the distortion, screening and withholding of information. Too often communication problems are written off as the natural thing, to be expected in any large group of specialized personnel. The myth here is not in the reality of noise and the inadvertent act (the communicator's "sin of omission"), but in the assumption that it is the only factor at work or even that it is the principal cause of problems.

5 T. M. Newcomb, "Autistic Hostility and Social Reality," *Human Relations*, 1947, *1*, pp. 69–86.

The recent study by the author[6] of upward communication in several large corporations showed that managers were considerably less "in the know" about their subordinates' daily work problems when the subordinates were highly ambitious (i.e., placed a high value on promotion and advancement within the organization) than when the subordinates were only moderately ambitious. This and other data clearly demonstrated that subordinates almost invariably screen information which they pass upward (though they seldom realize they are doing so), and the restriction and withholding of any kind of "negative" information (problems and errors) was more strongly pronounced the greater the upward drive of the subordinates. One can easily guess that this screening of information about "what's wrong" is multiplied up the line to the top, hence the often rosy picture top management has of progress in lower ranks.

In a somewhat similar kind of study undertaken currently by the author in several organizations in the northwest, the same type of distortion and restriction of information passed "across" occurs with striking frequency. In many cases of communication breakdown between sections or units, careful analysis reveals the impact of personality idiosyncracies, fear and hostility upon the way in which vital information is withheld or distorted. This conclusion was based not upon ex post facto "psychologizing," but more often than not these interpersonal-emotional factors in communication became readily apparent to the individuals involved during the course of discussion with the interviewer. To illustrate, the following statement was made by one executive during the course of an interview in which he had reported in considerable detail a communication breakdown of quite large proportions with another manager within his own department. The case in question involved the failure on the part of the interviewee, a training director, to get across to his associate the crucial importance of utilizing a training programme in a particular, time-tested way in order to obtain maximum effects.

6 W. H. Read, "Upward Communication in Industrial Hierarchies," *Human Relations*, 1961, *15*, pp. 1–8.

I had thought we had gotten the whole thing straightened out, but I didn't realize until later that he had it all wrong. I know he didn't double-cross me on purpose, but there isn't much love lost between us and I have a strong hunch that he slipped up—"unconsciously on purpose."

Information is, among other things, a weapon and a defense. It can be shaped, changed and in myriad ways utilized by an organization member to achieve his ends, maximize his gain and to weaken the position of his competitors within the same organization. Misunderstandings and problems can be and are created by random noise, administrative oversight, and ignorance of the other person's function. But so long as conflict and competition for limited rewards are intrinsic parts of the psychology of economic enterprises, then "communications training," admonitions to keep channels open, and various formal devices used to facilitate communication can have only limited effect unless equally positive steps are taken to remedy human relations problems.

COMMUNICATION PROBLEMS: CAUSE VS. EFFECT

Like the concept human relations, communication is a difficult one to pin down. Despite the fact that quite frequently "communication problems" are listed along with other types of problems in books on personnel administration or industrial psychology, in point of fact, the two-sided question: "What problems are *not* communication ones, and what problems are *solely* ones involving communication?" is really an unanswerable one. In the broadest sense every difficulty encountered by people in organizations contains some ingredient of distorted, insufficient or poorly-timed information exchange. Very likely even a profound financial problem such as a sudden drop in profits is due in some way to incomplete information about the state of the market or the company's cost position (though the problem would obviously be much more complex than this).

Yet, conversely, few if any problems are solely attributable to inadequate information exchange despite a current tendency for executives to label their problems "communication." Inter-member hostility, inter-departmental cross-purposes, ignorance of the role of other members in the organization, high specialization and other factors interact with communication dysfunction to create organizational problems. Communication problems are thus both cause and effect of major operational and administrative problems in any organization. One interacts with the other.

At the superior-subordinate level, failure of the superior to keep the subordinate informed of plans or impending changes causes apprehension and mistrust in the subordinate, which may in turn cause him to distort or withhold information to his superior. For example, it is difficult for the supervisor to elicit constructive suggestions from a workman whose inadequate knowledge of a pending reorganization causes him to wonder about the permanence of his own future. In terms of communication "across," the production man frequently may fail to inform fully the maintenance man of the problems of time in setting-up and "rolling" after the repair or service of a machine. The maintenance man then reacts with distrust and suspicion when he finds that the production department's figures for machine downtime didn't match his own and are in fact expanded. This mistrust can then adversely affect future relations between these units and make clear and timely information-exchange between them more difficult in future.

In the course of current research in management communication this circular, cause-effect relationship was found by the author to be of striking proportions in a large welfare agency. Here, the welfare claims officers ("middle management" in this organization) complained bitterly about the lack of "feedback" information from the top body of the organization—the claims adjudication board. The consternation stemmed from the fact that the *reasons* for the board's decisions on individual welfare cases sent up were never communicated back down, and frequently the same or similar claims received quite different treatment from the board. Thus the claims officers felt that they were constantly working

in a vacuum and that no clear principle governing the board's decisions could be used as a guide for decisions at lower levels. On checking with members of the board, it was found that they lacked confidence in lower-level personnel because of the bulk of decisions passed upward which could have been handled lower down in the agency! Though this kind of problem undoubtedly has many facets, certainly inadequate communication is both a *cause* of difficulty—adverse effects on middle-management morale, over-centralization of decisions and a "log jam" at the top. This log jam in turn caused loss of confidence, then decreased communication. The cause-effect process here is not one-way, it is circular just as marital discord is at the same time a cause and a result of inadequate interpersonal communication.

This two way interaction between communication and administrative-operational problems suggests that attention to either one can have ameliorative effects on the other. The concerted development of mutual confidence and cooperative attitudes among all segments of the organization can do much to remedy problems of information inter-change, and the reverse is also true.

Certainly, no simple palliatives, administered on a hit-and-miss basis will eliminate the communication problems which beset human organizations. Any organization-business, military or government, is not *just* an economic system, not *just* an arrangement of roles and positions, not *just* a reward and incentive system. It is all of these, but also it is a communication system. As such it merits as much study and research into its functioning as do these other aspects of organization.

Outside Reading: Essay-Discussion Questions

1. According to Dr. Read, what is the optimum in information exchange?

2. Define and discuss "random noise."

3. Analyze Dr. Read's statement that "Information is, among other things, a weapon and a defense."

4. Discuss what organizations are currently doing to overcome some of the communication problems they are facing.

READING: AN APPROACH TO COMPUTER-BASED MANAGEMENT CONTROL SYSTEMS

D. G. MALCOLM AND A. J. ROWE

In an era of automated information technology, the ability to formulate decision criteria precisely and process information electronically should prove valuable in the design of management control systems. One can look forward to organizational structures which more nearly conform to the communication and informational requirements.

In an attempt to explore the problems facing management of large organizations and persons responsible for the design of management controls, the authors have embarked on an intensive research program in this area. Started in April of 1959, the research has been primarily concerned with studying computer-based management control systems.[1] By examining the flow of information and decision processes using computer simulation, insights into the behavior of these complex systems appear possible.

NATURE OF THE PROBLEM

Examining the problems confronting designers of management control systems, one is readily aware of the magnitude of the task. Although management and organizational specialists have been concerned with these same problems for many years, there still remain a large number of questions to be answered. For example:

Reprinted with permission from the *California Management Review*, Vol. 3, No. 2, Spring 1961, pp. 4–15. Copyright 1961 by the Regents of the University of California. Mr. Malcolm was vice-president of the Western Division of Operations Research Inc. and Dr. Rowe was manager of Industrial Dynamics Research for the Hughes Aircraft Company when this article was written.

- To what extent should top management go in developing a philosophy of "management by system"?
- How can top management determine the depth in the organization to which it should extend day-to-day personal influence?
- How can management evaluate proposed computer-based, information-processing, decision-making systems?
- How should management plan the development of an organization to achieve control?

These in turn raise a number of questions for the researcher as follows:

- What is a suitable method for determining the cost and effectiveness of management information or control systems?
- How can appropriate systems be designed prior to their actual installation?
- By what method can various types of information be expressed in terms of a company's over-all objectives?
- What is the best configuration of an integrated management control system?

Specialists have applied a wide variety of answers and approaches to these problems. Examples of traditional methods include: organizational planning, scheduling of operations, inventory control, quality control, and cost control.

It is significant to note that each of these is a component or single aspect of a business and the concept of an integrated total-system control remains practically unexploited. However, it is possible that concise, quantitative, and unequivocal answers to these questions may not be found for a long time.

DEFINING MANAGEMENT CONTROLS

For the purpose of this paper, a management control system is described as a set of policies, procedures, and associated information processing designed to give direction to corporate activities in the following ways:

- By clearly establishing goals;
- By measuring progress in achieving these goals;
- By indicating the need for corrective action.

To achieve an optimal set of management controls, however, it is necessary to "design" a management system in much the same way that equipment itself is designed. As part of this design process, it is a basic requirement that the system designer clearly understand the objectives of the business.

In this regard the traditional statements of maximizing profit or return on investment are not sufficient guides. Modern business is conducted to serve many diverse objectives, making the problem of control more sophisticated than attempting to have each and every action directed toward such goals. Management, therefore, can be considered as the custodians of the resources of an organization with the mission to organize the effort to achieve purposeful objectives and to assure survival of the business.

As part of the control process, a communication network is used to link management with the resources of the business and to provide the information needed for feedback control. The information available to the manager, is therefore used as the basis for control and operating decisions. The core of the design problem, therefore, is in determining which operating decision rules can be reduced to a routine, computerized approach.

The characteristics of information flow and decision rules provide the basic inputs for a study of management controls. It is obvious that the interlinkage between decision points, as well as the density of information flow, has a direct effect on the nature of the organizational structure required for successful opera-

tion. Thus, the constraints of the existing organization must be ignored, and the specifications for an effective organization to make required decisions should be based on the system design activity.

CURRENT APPLICATIONS OF COMPUTERS

Although there is an ever-increasing use of electronic data-processing equipment in the automating of existing information systems, the need to integrate the over-all informational requirements and to redesign a given system is often overlooked.

More generally, applications are made in one area of the business, such as finance or manufacturing, and little more than checks for compatibility are made with respect to the total system problem.

This piecemeal approach is most frequently justified on the grounds that one must build gradually in developing a total system. However, there is a growing recognition that this approach leads to suboptimal results.

In current applications, the use of electronic computers does not tap one-tenth of their ultimate potential. Although this condition is particularly true of industrial, as contrasted with military, applications, it is a situation that will become a matter of increasing concern to those who use computers, especially as they realize the nature of this potential. The situation, conceivably, could become worse before effective long-range programs are designed and in use.

APPLICATIONS IN MILITARY SYSTEMS

If one examines the Air Defense Command, it is readily apparent that the prototypes of highly automated information systems are currently being established for management use. Examples of such systems which operate with extremely short feedback time, often referred to as operating in real-time, can be seen in SAGE[2] (Semi-Automatic Ground Environment) and SACCS (Strategic Air Command Control System). Both of these systems are computer-based, command-control systems.

In the course of the design and implementation of these Systems, a number of changes were made in the Air Defense Command structure. The computer control system itself was used as the basis for organizational changes which led to the centralization of many activities.

A further development which was necessitated by the requirement for design and implementation was the concept of a system manager. The ESSPO (Electronic Support Systems Project Office), was given the mission of properly managing the joint efforts of system analysis, system design, computer manufacturing, computer programming and system training.

REAL-TIME CONTROL

In military applications, the computer has been used as an integral, on-line controlling device. In this context, the terms, "real-time control," "communication," and "information system," emerge as system design concepts.

"Real-time" is used to mean that the desired information is transmitted into a centralized computer instantaneously and without conversion. The significance of "real-time" control lies in the fact that information is used as it is developed and that elements in the system are controlled by the processed information immediately, not after the fact, or by making periodic forecasts of the expected future state of the system.

To achieve "real-time" control, the computer processes information, compares it with predetermined decision criteria and issues instructions to men or machines, or both, for corrective or purposeful action. Further, the computer, by means of direct outputs, informs affected parties of this information as it is developed. This is "real-time management information."

By examining the best known examples of systems of this type currently found in the

military, one may find some guidance in design approaches that may be useful in evolving better on-line management control systems for industry.

MILITARY SYSTEMS

The experience gained in the development of military command control systems can be summarized under the following topics:

- Use of the Systems Analysis Approach,
- Problem Formulation for Computer Programming,
- Use of New Computer Applications, and
- Use of Formalized System Training.

While the following are broad generalizations, it would appear that the quickest route to effective development of a truly integrated management control system involves a proper point of view on the part of management in regard to the possible effects of information flow on the organization structure. That is, the possibility of recentralizing and the eliminating of certain functions must be within the system designer's scope.

Further, to perform a system analysis there must be proper organizational status for the design function and top management must plan for the necessary lead time to perform its activities. Finally, while it should be evident, it is worth emphasizing that top management participation and support is vital to obtain desired results.

SYSTEMS ANALYSIS APPROACH

In reviewing the development of a system such as SAGE, one is impressed with the magnitude of the design process. The design of this system necessitated spelling out precise system requirements. This, in turn, provided the basis for more effectively meeting the needs of the air defense system.

In contrast to the systems approach, the question that is often asked is "What can be done to improve or automate existing practices?" In looking over the process of creating new management control systems, it becomes obvious that this latter approach is often the easiest to justify and, thus, has been the route traditionally followed.

In essence, the design process is based on answering the question "What is the best system?" and is generally called the systems analysis, or systems engineering, approach. Thus, one principle in creating a new system involves a careful look at the requirements of the system via the systems engineering approach. A brief description of the steps generally involved is as follows:

1. *Establish criteria for management information needs:* (a) Establish the objectives or mission of the system. (b) Determine current information, decision, display, and report practices, by use of graphical flow analyses.

2. *Develop the preliminary design:* (a) A preliminary statement of system requirements; i.e., specific reporting frequencies, types, and routings of reports, type of equipments, displays, etc., should be established. (b) Determine what can be automated using computer programming and what to leave as currently performed. We must remember here that technology is changing rapidly. Simon[3] predicts that by 1984 it will be technically possible to automate any and all functions in an organization. (c) Balance current requirements with growth considerations.

3. *Evaluate the preliminary design:* (a) Determine the cost of hardware and applicable costs. (b) Assess training implications and requirements. (c) Establish the nature of the improvements to be gained.

4. *Develop a revised model of the proposed system:* (a) Use of systems analysis or an experimental approach involving simulation or gaming, to test the design. (b) Obtain the participation of the ultimate users.

5. *Determine system specifications:* (a) Evaluate alternative means of achieving the proposed design. (b) Consider the relationship to other system requirements.

6. *Install, de-bug, modify, extend the system:* (a) Provide for maintenance and updating. (b) Allow for flexibility in operating and modifying the system.

COMPUTER PROBLEM FORMULATION

In the application of computer-based systems, it has become evident that there is a need for precise formulation of the computer program. Descriptive statements are not sufficient, rather quantitative or analytic formulation of problems is required.

Furthermore, factors such as kind and size of memory, speed of computation, manner of indexing, and rounding must all be taken into account in computer programming. Methods of filing information, data accumulation, and reporting requirements are also significant aspects of program design.

It is often necessary to reformulate a problem to conform to the computer requirements; although this consideration is becoming less important with the availability of large-scale digital computers.

At the outset of a given computer program, a decision must be made whether to have a flexible, general purpose program or one designed for the immediate specific use. Modular programming which treats each section of a program separately provides considerable flexibility at only a small cost in computation time and storage.

COMPUTER "LANGUAGE"

Probably the most difficult aspect of the problem is the actual coding or programming language. Not only is the coding a time-consuming and difficult process, but the system designer must convey the intent of his work to programmers, thus compounding the problem.

Considerable effort is currently being expended in the development of computer languages which can be used more readily by system designers. This, in part, recognizes the fact that as much time is often spent in coding a problem as in the formulation. In this regard, then, considerable work remains to be done to develop computer languages which will simplify the operational instructions for the computer programming task.

USE OF NEW COMPUTER APPLICATIONS

The capability of the computer to process information rapidly, store information conveniently and provide accuracy has made significant inroads on long-standing problems. Some of these computer applications are:

1. *On-line control:* As has been mentioned previously, on-line, direct read-in and read-out, integrated computer operation has been used in military systems. The importance of this technical achievement should not be underestimated. However, the feasibility of utilizing this on-line control feature for industrial application requires research and analysis to determine the cost and effectiveness of a given application.

2. *Management-by-exception.*[4] The data processing capability of high-speed computers, as used in the military, has made possible centralized operations using large masses of data which have been carefully sorted by built-in criteria. Only exceptions requiring attention are presented to decision makers by the computer. This feature could be extended to provide centralized control in management systems. PERT (Navy Polaris program) is an example.

3. *Interrogation, or fast-simulation possibilities:* Using a computer-based system, the human monitor can, in a sense, ask "What would happen if I issued this command?" This interrogation feature, often called "fast-simulation" requires the building of analytic models which incorporate desired predictive capabilities. Appropriate computer models for business situations may eventually provide the potentiality of on-line management control systems.

USE OF FORMALIZED SYSTEM TRAINING

In the course of developing major new military systems, it has been found that provision for training people in the on-going operations of the new systems is needed. The training in a system such as SAGE involves elaborate simulations of a predicted attack environment.

This represents a new concept to the management world. The justification for this elaborate training stems from the fact that there is no other way to adequately train the people to perform under an attack situation.

However, a significant additional value in this approach should be pointed out. The proficiency of a system is determined by its operation as a whole, involving the communications and interrelations of many people and machines. Therefore, the proficiency of individual acts must be judged by measures appropriate to the system context.

It would hardly be desirable to emphasize performance at one part of the system that would be detrimental to the total system performance. In short, each person should be trained to act in an optimal way from the total system point of view.

Therefore, to adequately provide for proper performance in such broad systems, a comprehensive means of training using simulated exercises is required. Furthermore, the need for this training is not dependent on whether the environment is real or hypothetical.

SIMULATION MODELS ESSENTIAL

It appears that when radically new concepts in management control are installed, quite likely simulation models will be required. The installation time, the acceptance, and therefore even the ultimate efficiency attainable by the control systems will be considerably enhanced by appropriately designed simulation exercises along with proper criteria for measuring performance in relation to the total system.

Using a systematic design approach, as shown in the preceding discussion, it is possible to develop improved, total, computer-based management control systems. In view of the requirements of current air defense systems, the need for computer-based systems was readily justified. However, industrial systems have not reached the point where objectives can be set forth in clear and unequivocal terms and thus it is difficult to evaluate a given system design.

In short, the only feasible means for meeting

the military requirements for rapid, high volume, and accurate data handling was the use of computer systems. Given these requirements, one could systematically design a feasible system. On the other hand, the capability of rigorous evaluation of a number of alternative designs has generally been considered too costly. However, the acceptability of the military approach for the business world will undoubtedly be predicated on the ability to evaluate control concepts prior to actually installing new systems.

If the advantages of information recentralization are to be achieved in practice, they must first be proved beneficial to the organization; and secondly, they must be both desired by and acceptable to management.

In practice, however, these two requirements are often in conflict. Although it is difficult to assess the value of a new system, it appears desirable to develop a design approach that is both evaluative and instructive. Such an approach can be instrumental in the realization of promised benefits of an integrated management information system. An approach which appears to be the most suitable, and perhaps the most effective in the long range, is the use of computer simulation.

COMPUTER SIMULATION

As a problem-solving tool, computer simulation has been used for a number of years. It has enabled management to experiment with and test certain types of policies, procedures and organizational changes in much the same way an engineer tests new designs. With the use of computers and the development of probability methods, computer simulation can also be applied to complex operating plans or management controlling systems in addition to day-to-day operating problems. The method is similar to war gaming techniques used by the military and the paper and pencil techniques used by systems and procedure specialists.

In a sense, simulation is a synthetic means used to imitate the behavior of a system for the purpose of studying the response to specific changes. Where the problem is entirely physical in nature, such as in testing aircraft, a physical model can be used. However, in studying management control systems, which deal with the flow of information and decision networks, an exact analogue of the problem may not be possible.

An approximation, usually in the form of a mathematical or symbolic model, is used which describes the elements and properties of the system under study. Thus, a model for a management control system is a means for providing a formalized statement of system behavior rather than a physical analogue of the system.

A DESIGN TOOL

Simulation has only recently been considered as a useful tool for the design of management control systems.[5] A similar approach has been taken in the research program conducted by the authors,[6] where computer simulation is used as a laboratory for examining system behavior. To conduct such experimentation, an analytic model of a total business system has been developed which explicitly characterizes the information flow, decision rules and physical processes of a business system.

To the extent that this model describes the behavior of the elements of the system in a realistic manner, the conclusions drawn should prove useful in the design of management controls as applied to large-scale, complex organizations and their associated information processing.

However, in view of the intricately complex nature of a total business system, intuition alone cannot be considered sufficient to evaluate new concepts or designs. While on the other hand, extensive experimentation directly in an actual plant to evaluate alternate designs poses almost insurmountable problems.

Aside from the inevitable disruptions and possibly unrealistic results, valuable time would be lost in gathering performance data. In addition, costly mistakes might result if the consequences of actually carrying out a given experiment cannot be predicted in advance, and there is no control. These considerations, therefore, strongly support the use of computer simulation both as a research and design vehicle.

EXPERIMENTS WITH MODELS

Research in Management Controls implies experimentation; however, the manner of experimenting is dependent upon the results desired. An exploratory type of experimentation is possible by simply changing parameters of the simulation model and observing the resultant system behavior.

Thus, insights into the response characteristics of the system are obtained by examining the results shown in the computer output. Another manner of experimentation is to specify given system designs and subject these to many conditions and observe the effects. This latter method is principally used to test the significant differences among alternative designs.

"POLICY LABORATORY"

Since the computer output provides a summarization of information reflecting system behavior generated during simulation, it is possible to obtain a continuous time trace of the changes in system performance and the interdependencies among the elements of the system. It is this capability of being able to examine, in considerable detail, the changes which result from alternate system designs that has led to the term "policy laboratory" being applied to computer simulation.

THE MODEL AND ITS ROLE

To simulate management controls, then, it is necessary to have a model which provides a formal statement of the business system's behavior. Computer simulation, however, is seldom an exact analogue of the operation of an actual system. Rather, simulation performed on a digital computer can only approximate continuous, simultaneous activity. If the elements and properties of the system have been properly defined, then the parameters and variables can be readily controlled and measured.

The model may be symbolic, mathematical, or descriptive; however, it should be constructed so as to include properties which are sufficient to define the behavior of the system.

FORCING FUNCTION

The variables describe behavior for a given set of parameters. The forcing functions provide the external stimuli which cause the system to react—for example, orders which enter a system cause men to work, machines to run, and so on. In this way, orders become a forcing function for the system. Whatever particular form is used, a model provides the frame of reference within which the problem is considered.

A model often indicates relationships which are not otherwise obvious. However, it should be noted that a model need not duplicate actual conditions to be useful. A model should be designed to predict actual behavior resulting from changes in the system design or application of new decision rules. Such prediction implies an understanding of the manner in which the system reacts; that is, being able to specify the outputs for a given set of inputs. This approach differs from the conventional concept of treating the system as a "black box."

Since a simulation model is merely a means for testing new ideas, the simpler the model, the more effective for research or design purposes. It is not necessary to incorporate all possible aspects of system behavior in the model; rather, only those variables which contribute substantially to system response characteristics need be incorporated.

To this end, a model can be considered as an initial experiment to determine what factors are most significant in a business system. The model can be refined or expanded as experimental data describing the system performance and sensitivity to various factors become available.

DEVELOPING A BUSINESS MODEL

For the purpose of studying management controls, modeling should be centered about the information, decision-making and control aspects of the business. The majority of simulations to date, however, have been concerned with the physical activities within a business such as scheduling of products,[7] control of inventory, movement of vehicles, and maintenance of aircraft, to name a few.[8]

On the other hand, since management control is concerned with the more intangible aspects of the business, modeling is a far more difficult problem.[9] Reviewing some of these modeling considerations in detail indicates the task involved.

DECISION-MAKING PROCESS

If the decisions in an organization are associated with the physical points where they occur, then the decision-making process can be characterized by the decision rules and associated information. Interlinkages among the decision points represent the communication channels.

To simulate an organization with an appropriate degree of reality, it is necessary to establish a suitable communication network. In addition, the many decision criteria and decision rules have to be stated analytically to be amenable to computer programming.

QUEUING EFFECTS

If a decision maker is viewed as a processor of information, the rate of arrival of information and the time taken to process decisions will result in an average delay or queuing effect. Analysis of such delays will provide one important measure of system effectiveness.

The speed of information transmission, as well as the number of decision points, however, must be closely coupled with the capability of the system to respond to varying inputs. By assigning costs to alternate means of information transmittal, the cost of on-line controls can be assessed.

ORGANIZATIONAL CONSIDERATIONS

Since delays in decisions are a function of information flow and queuing, they have a direct effect on the organization structure. For example, introducing alternate decision channels to permit more effective information flow might lead to radical changes in an organization. A simulation model could thus examine different forms of organization structure and evaluate the effect of changes on the system performance.

Decentralization in an organization leads to the possibility of distortion in information due to the number of levels through which the information must pass; whereas this effect may be avoided in a more centralized organization. Therefore, the modeling must treat with this consideration in order to provide a suitable basis for studying management control systems.

USES OF THE COMPUTER MODEL

Up to this point, the discussion has been primarily concerned with the modeling process itself. Let us now turn to some of the specific problems which can be studied using such a simulation model.

PRINCIPLES OF SYSTEM DESIGN

An important consideration in management control is the relationship of the total business system to the control methodology employed. In a sense, management controls are embedded in the broader consideration of total system design.

In view of the sparsity of knowledge in this area, computer simulation provides a means for examining a multitude of alternate designs with the possibility of developing basic design principles.

TESTING SYSTEM OBJECTIVES

As has already been discussed, the formalizing of business objectives is probably one of the most difficult aspects in establishing useful management controls. This aspect of the problem is particularly important since there are a number of competing objectives in any system which must be taken into account to avoid suboptimization.

Using a computer model, the possible consequences of different combinations of objectives can be examined. It is evident that there may not be a set of universal objectives which apply to all businesses; rather, actual objectives are generally dependent upon the willingness of managers to take action in the face of uncertainty and with inadequate information.

MEASURING SYSTEM PERFORMANCE

During the course of running a computer model, a means for explicit measurement of system performance must be provided. In actual practice, methods of measurement have involved long delays from occurrence to reporting of events due to the lack of high-speed data-processing equipment. However, with the increased use of computers, processing and summarizing data will prove a less formidable task, and measures of system performance can be based on actual operations.

Using fast simulation as discussed for the SAGE system, managers will have the option of periodically introducing real-time control. In addition, using a simulation model new measures of performance can be developed and tested.

DESIGN OF MANAGEMENT CONTROLS

A number of design concepts that should be explored in the development of new management control systems are:

- The use of information feedback loops, providing on-line control;
- The use of variable control limits in place of arbitrary standards as the basis for corrective action;
- Inclusion of formalized decision rules in the control system to (a) provide for optimization of the business system, (b) provide for improved response characteristics of the system;
- Use of a sampled-data approach for providing information on system performance. This is similar to the "exception principle."

Although these four items do not constitute an exhaustive list of all considerations, they do provide some idea of the complexity of designing management control systems.

All too often, management controls are treated as ends in themselves rather than as the means of improving total system performance. In the case of corporate budgeting, for example, funds may be spent unnecessarily to forestall budget cuts at a later date.

Another illustration of the misuse of the control concept is traditional costing practices that force the business to conform to arbitrary standards. As stated by Warren Alberts of United Airlines,[10] controls should be considered as guides for obtaining improved performance and not as a means of restricting performance.

If the design process, as discussed here, is at the system level, there is greater assurance that management controls will truly be integrated. The process of modeling and formalizing the structure of the business system should itself bring clarity to the inter-dependency of management control with planning, policies, objectives, and decision rules. As our understanding of the behavior of business systems improves, we should be in a position to develop effective design principles for management control systems.

REFERENCES

1. A. J. Rowe, "A Research Approach in Management Controls," *Journal of Industrial Engineering*, May–June 1960, Vol. XI, pp. 251–258.

2. A computerized air defense system using data automatically correlated with known flight plans to detect presence of unknown aircraft. Also provides automatic guidance of interceptors.

3. H. Simon, "The Corporation: Will It Be Managed by Machines?" *Management Review*, Nov., 1960.

4. D. G. Malcolm, J. H. Roseboom, C. E.

Clark, W. Fazar, "Application of a Technique for Research and Development Program Evaluation," *Operations Research*, Vol. 7, September-October 1959, pp. 646–669.

5. D. G. Malcolm, "A Bibliography on the Use of Simulation in Management Analysis," *Operations Research*, March-April 1960, Vol. 8, pp. 169–177.

6. *System Simulation Symposium Proceedings*, American Institute of Industrial Engineers, New York, May 16–17, 1957.

7. D. G. Malcolm and A. J. Rowe, *Management Control Systems*, the proceedings of a symposium held at System Development Corporation, John Wiley, 1960.

8. A. J. Rowe, "Toward a Theory of Scheduling," *Journal of Industrial Engineering*, March-April 1960, Vol. II, pp. 125–136.

9. C. W. Cragin, et al., "Simulation: Management's Laboratory," Simulation Associates, Bradford, Mass., April 1959.

10. W. E. Alberts, "The Concepts of Management Control," *Management Control Systems*, New York, Wiley, 1960, p. 14.

Outside Reading: Essay-Discussion Questions

1. How do the authors define a management control system and in what three ways will it give direction to corporate activities?

2. Explain the "management-by-exception" computer application.

3. What role does the "forcing function" play in systems management?

4. How will the computer affect the traditional (budgetory, accounting, inventory, etc.) control systems?

PART VI

LEADERSHIP AND MOTIVATION

Chapter Twenty-Two

The Problem of Motivation

T HE FIRST PART of this chapter is concerned with the problem of organizational survival. The problem of motivation is reviewed and related to organizational dynamics. The discussion then turns to the nature of the burdens and benefits of organized endeavor and the manner in which they affect cooperative behavior.

Section I MAJOR CONCEPTS

Motivation
Physiological drives
Cultural norms
Theory X and Theory Y

Burdens and benefits of organized endeavor
Groups
Status
Hierarchy of needs

Section II SELF-TEST

True-False

_____ 1. Frederick W. Taylor would be more inclined to accept Theory X than Theory Y.

_____ 2. In Professor William F. Whyte's study of human relations in restaurants, different kinds of food had different status values.

_____ 3. Productivity is obviously lower in an office with a great deal of socializing.

_____ 4. Status has little or no relationship to motivation.

_____ 5. Team craftsmanship has reference to pride in the objectives of a group.

Multiple Choice

_____ 1. Which of the following terms best describes an aspect of Theory Y?
   a. Must constantly use sanctions
   b. Dislike for work inherent in man
   c. Self-direction and self-control
   d. Will play or rest rather than work

_____ 2. All of the following are aspects of the dynamics of "primary groups" EXCEPT:
   a. Face-to-face association

b. Norms of behavior

c. Identify with the group

d. Wide geographical dispersion

____ 3. Which of the following does *not* express the conclusions of Army and Air Force research during World War II on the role of the primary group in combat?

a. Significantly reduced combat effectiveness

b. Set and enforced group standards of behavior

c. Supported and sustained the individual soldier

d. A primary motivating force among Air Force combat personnel

____ 4. A Chicago waitress, named Jo, decided to quit her job. Her sister Ellen told the supervisor she was also leaving, but she later changed her mind. Why?

a. The supervisor gave Ellen a raise in pay.

b. Ellen's sister Jo decided not to quit.

c. The "girls" convinced Ellen that she should stay.

d. Ellen could not find another job in the Chicago area.

____ 5. The brief sketch of "Who else calls him Tony?" points out what aspect of status?

a. Status is a problem of deadwood.

b. Status is a relative problem.

c. Status must confer formal titles.

d. Status should be closely related to abilities and aspirations.

____ 6. The mode of dress in a small group studied by Miller and Form was primarily enforced by

a. management planning

b. control decisions of the owner

c. functional needs

d. social sanctions of group

____ 7. Which of the following situations would tend to create less conflict than the other three?

a. A woman "foreman" giving orders to skilled lathe operators

b. Waitresses giving orders to highly skilled cooks

c. A teenager giving orders to middle-aged construction workers

d. A bartender calling on waitresses to pick up their orders

____ 8. Probably the best incentive in motivating cooperative behavior is

a. monetary and material

b. social satisfactions

c. status

d. a combination of a, b, and c

____ 9. What is *not* true of the concept of culture?

a. It may be roughly defined as the totality of norms that govern behavior in a society.

b. It assumes that man must constantly begin anew; he has nothing to fall back on.

c. It can be transmitted from one generation to the next through informal means.

d. It can be transmitted from one generation to the next through formal means.

____ 10. Which of the following is *not* one of Maslow's hierarchy of needs?

a. Economic

b. Esteem

c. Safety

d. Physiological

Essay-Discussion

1. What is the nature of human motives?

2. How does Theory *X* differ from Theory *Y*?

3. How do primary groups influence organizational behavior?

Section III ILLUSTRATIVE CASES

"POOR RICHARD'S" INCENTIVES

Benjamin Franklin wrote the following: "I have not yet, indeed, thought of a remedy for luxury. I am not sure that in a great state it is capable of a remedy; nor that the evil is in itself so great as it is represented.

"Suppose we include in the definition of luxury all unnecessary expense, and then let us consider whether laws to prevent such expense are possible to be executed in a great country, and whether, if they could be executed, our people generally would be happier, or even richer.

"Is not the hope of being one day able to purchase and enjoy luxuries, a great spur to labour and industry?

"May not luxury, therefore, produce more than it consumes, if, without such a spur, people would be, as they are naturally enough inclined to be, lazy and indolent?"

Analysis

1. Do you agree with Franklin that the ability to purchase and enjoy luxuries is a great incentive for labor and management? Why?

2. Do you agree with Franklin that people are naturally inclined to be lazy and indolent? Relate to Theory *X* and Theory *Y*.

3. How would you relate "Poor Richard's" incentives with modern motivational theory?

"PLAYBOY OF THE YEAR"[1]

A supply company in California annually awards the title, "Salesman of the Year." The president of the company explained the significance of the award and how the judging works: "Each year we ask each of the factory men who work with us regularly to fill out a ballot rating each of our eight salesmen on six factors which we feel are important to selling success. To prevent the balloting from becoming a popularity contest, we ask that each salesman be given a numerical rating (1 to 5) for each salesmanship factor."[2] The winner receives an engraved trophy, and his business cards are engraved in gold with the notation "Salesman of the Year 19___." The trophy is presented at the Los Angeles Playboy Club by a very shapely "Bunny." "In the three years we have had this program," says the president, "we have found a very high correlation between an individual's rating and his sales volume."[3]

Analysis

1. Do you think that titles, trophies, and gold-engraved cards serve as incentives?

2. Do you think the "Bunny" added another incentive for the company's salesman?

3. Can you think of any other "gimmicks" or status symbols that may motivate salesmen and/or managers?

[2] *Ibid.*
[3] *Ibid.*

YOUNG MAVERICKS[1]

A recent magazine article points out the increasing turnover of young executives. Anywhere from one-third to one-half of all college graduates move to different jobs within the first five years of employment. Money, of course, is a factor but often is not as important as psychic satisfaction in the job and gaining experience that is necessary for making top management later on. One cocky, aggressive young executive, who is now on his third job in a little over six years, comments: "The important thing is to get experience you can build on. You have to keep on learning. The money comes later."[2] Another young refugee from a large bank's special development train-

[1] Reported in "Success at Metro is a Gold Card and a Trophy from Bunny Sam," *Industrial Distribution,* September 1967, p. 90.

[1] Based on "Those Restless Young Executives," *Dun's Review,* July 1968, pp. 37-39.
[2] *Ibid.,* p. 37.

ing program left after a couple of months (although he thought it was "a great place to work") for a "small, swinging" export-import firm where he could do "creative and individual things over a much broader field at a much earlier age."[3]

---

[3] *Ibid.*

Analysis

1. Based on this illustrative case, what would you say is the prime factor that motivates young executives? Why?

2. What would you do to retain your young talent? What about their initial training programs?

Chapter Twenty-Three

Dynamic Leadership

THIS CHAPTER DEALS with the dynamics of leadership in formal organizations. Leadership is viewed from a number of perspectives. First, leadership is approached from the vantage point of techniques that may be used to enhance cooperative endeavor. Second, a number of specific actions that may be taken by a leader to enforce and reinforce authority are considered. A final section is devoted to governing through law and the importance of differentiating legislative, executive, and judicial functions.

Section I MAJOR CONCEPTS

Leadership
Authority of position
Participation
Styles of leadership

Organizational versus personal goals
Reinforcing authority
Legislative, executive, and judicial functions

Section II SELF-TEST

True-False

_____ 1. A managerial position is an important source of authority.

_____ 2. An open challenge to authority should not frequently be permitted.

_____ 3. The human relations approach has eliminated the need for imposing sanctions to enforce authority.

_____ 4. The lenient superior tends to create a sense of obligation on the part of the subordinate.

_____ 5. Business organizations have generally segregated legislative, executive, and judicial functions in the manner of the United States federal government.

Multiple Choice

_____ 1. All of the following would tend to maintain the authority of position EXCEPT:

a. An executive in a hierarchical system should help maintain the authority of executives in other positions.

b. A superior should generally communicate decisions involving matters that have been delegated to subordinate executives.

c. The superior may consult subordinates about possible alternatives but should make the final decision on matters that fall within his jurisdiction.

d. Proper performance of the decisional responsibilities of the position is important in maintaining authority.

2. General Billy Mitchell was judged to be *wrong* in

a. his forecast of the future significance of air power

b. the way in which he planned the Battle of Bull Run

c. publicly challenging the authority of his superiors

d. his behavior toward subordinate personnel under his command

3. In the Lewin, Lippitt, and White study of leadership types, "democratic" was defined as

a. complete freedom for group or individual decision

b. all policy matters of group discussion and decision, encouraged and assisted by the leader

c. all determination of policy by the leader

d. nonparticipation by the leader

4. According to research by Lewin, Lippitt, and White at the University of Iowa, which of the following leadership techniques was most acceptable to the boys involved?

a. Laissez faire

b. Democratic

c. Authoritarian

d. Dictatorship

5. Specific sanctions tend to be most effective under which of the following conditions?

a. Many specific sanctions are needed to maintain authority.

b. People are generally satisfied with their jobs.

c. Morale is low.

d. A complete breakdown in authority is evident.

6. Which of the following words best describes the extent to which severe, specific sanctions are normally used to enforce decisions?

a. Never

b. Always

c. Often

d. Rarely

7. Leniency in supervision is viewed by Professor Blau as

a. Psychological weakness

b. A frequently effective strategy

c. A reliance on sanctions

d. All of the above

8. Which of the following is most similar to "planning decisions"?

a. Legislative function

b. Leadership function

c. Judicial function

d. Control function

9. What is the most accurate statement about leadership and authority?

a. An executive is never a leader by virtue of the position he occupies in the hierarchy.

b. Authority accorded an executive is not necessarily related to any personal leadership abilities he may possess.

c. Position plays no part in the authority relationship.

d. Proper performance in a given position plays no part in maintaining authority.

10. The grievance procedure in collective bargaining would be most closely associated with which of the folowing?

a. The executive process

b. The management process

c. The legislative process

d. The judicial process

Essay-Discussion

1. How does position influence authority?
2. What is the strategy of the lenient superior?

3. To what extent have business organizations segregated the legislative, executive, and judicial functions?

Section III ILLUSTRATIVE CASES

A HAPPY BIRTHDAY

A supervisor in a power plant keeps an up-to-date personal history on each of his twenty-five employees. He records such things as the subordinate's birthday, wedding anniversary, hobbies, something about the man's children, and last, but by no means least, the name of his dog. These bits of information are filed on a chronological basis. Every day he checks the file to see which employees should receive special consideration and to refresh his memory about them. For example, in the case of a birthday, the supervisor would stop and wish the man a happy birthday. He would ask how Johnny was getting along at Fort Benning and whether Mary likes State College.

Analysis

1. Do you think that this is a good leadership technique? Why?
2. How can techniques such as this backfire on the user?

THE DEATH PENALTY

Several states recently abolished the death penalty. There were many arguments both for and against this action. Some legislators referred to the Bible in support of the death penalty: "He that smiteth a man, so that he die shall be surely put to death . . . eye for eye, tooth for tooth, hand for hand, foot for foot. . . ." Others opposed the death penalty with: "Blessed are the merciful: for they shall obtain mercy." One state representative contended that "we're feeling sorry for the wrong people. . . what happens to families of murder victims?" Another asserted that he was not

against the death penalty, but against the inhumane way in which it is carried out. There was sentiment for the use of gas chambers as opposed to "hanging by the neck until dead." A major argument against the death penalty was the possibility of errors in conviction. Examples of confessions by another person after the innocent party had been duly executed were used to support this idea. But there are others who contend that such examples are rare and that the processes of the law afford sufficient protection. Many questions were asked about the effectiveness of the death penalty in reducing crimes of violence. One state with the death penalty has the highest murder rate, but another also with the death penalty has the lowest murder rate. One legislator, who opposed the death penalty, suggested that "if we really believe in the exemplary value of the death penalty, we would hold hangings in stadiums with a great deal of publicity." Another thought that severe penalties were necessary to mold people's character.

Analysis

1. Do severe sanctions, such as capital punishment, uphold and reinforce authority?
2. What do you think is the major issue when analyzing the death penalty?

LONG-DISTANCE PARTICIPATION[1]

Every month the president of an insurance company, via a telephone hookup to loud-

---

[1] Developed from "The Whole Staff Has a Voice in Running Sentry," *Business Week,* July 30, 1966, pp. 112-114.

speakers, reports to everyone in the various branches. Then comments, suggestions, and questions are directed to the president by salesmen, underwriters, and secretaries. There are also weekly telephone conferences between the home office executives and the eight regional vice-presidents, as well as many nonscheduled conferences.

Company personnel give arguments on both sides of this participative style of management. On the positive side are examples such as the marketing department's request from field personnel on improving cost controls. The response from underwriters, office managers, and salesmen yielded many good suggestions. The head of marketing said; "The program was sold before it was published, and the regional offices knew it wasn't dreamed up in an ivory tower."[2] Another vice-president, however, warned that the new participative system will not work "unless you have a compatible group. You can't have political climbing. The danger in the old system was its inflexibility. The danger in the new is busybodiness."[3]

Analysis

1. How would you weigh the advantages versus the disadvantages of participative techniques?

2. Could this system of participation work without the technological advances made in communication?

---

[2] *Ibid.*, p. 114.
[3] *Ibid.*

Chapter Twenty-Four

The Responsibility of Management

THERE ARE MANY conceptions of managerial responsibility. The question of "To whom is management responsible?" can be answered from a legal, economic, or labor viewpoint. The modern tendency seems to be a broader view of responsibility to stockholders, employees, customers, and creditors. Although managers assume a responsibility to all of these interest groups, they can and should develop strategies pertaining to each. If managers are to meet the challenges of functional and professional obligations, they will have to incorporate a moral responsibility to the organization.

Section I MAJOR CONCEPTS

Executive responsibility
Legal responsibility
Labor responsibility
Moral responsibility

Economic responsibility
Employee strategy
Stockholder strategy
Organizational conflicts

Section II SELF-TEST

True-False

_____ 1. Most stockholders in large corporations take an active part in management.

_____ 2. Barnard includes customers in his scheme of organization and places them on a par with employees, stockholders, and creditors.

_____ 3. There is objective evidence that the salaries of most top executives are too high.

_____ 4. There is at present no unified theory of social welfare to determine what kind of decision will best serve the society.

_____ 5. The people who make up management can be considered to be an interest group.

Multiple Choice

_____ 1. Classical economic theory was philosophically oriented toward

a. the consumer
b. the executive
c. labor unions
d. the corporation

_____ 2. Under a strict interpretation of corporation law, management is required to manage in the best interest of
a. creditors
b. customers
c. stockholders
d. suppliers

_____ 3. Which of the following would be most inclined to assume that the traditional market does *not* give the worker his proper share in the distribution of income?
a. Labor leader
b. Classical economist
c. Majority stockholder
d. Corporation lawyer

_____ 4. In recent years, executives in large corporations (like Jersey Standard) have tended to support which of the following conceptions of managerial responsibility?
a. A narrow legal conception
b. The public be damned, but only in the short run
c. Stockholder interests are primary
d. Responsibility to many interests

_____ 5. Executives are given an opportunity to take advantage of lower capital gains rates through
a. deferred income plans
b. higher salaries
c. stock options
d. reduced salary levels

_____ 6. Deferred executive income plans tend to have which of the following consequences?
a. They increase the total tax burden.
b. They reduce total take-home pay.
c. They increase gross salary paid per year.
d. They increase total net salary.

_____ 7. Chester I. Barnard told of a telephone operator on duty at a lonely place from which she could see the house in which her mother lay bedridden. The house caught fire; the operator
a. ran to help her mother who was barely able to get out
b. stayed at the switchboard while the house burned down
c. violated no moral codes
d. filled many buckets of water to help firemen

_____ 8. Which of the following best describes the moral problems of executives?
a. Codes pronounced by preachers in the pulpit
b. The norms of governmental legislation
c. Morality is no problem to the business executive
d. There are many moral codes to which executives respond

_____ 9. What is the best statement concerning stockholder relations?
a. The best way to keep happy stockholders who are interested in income in the short run is to retain most of the earnings.
b. Management should ignore stockholders because they can cause a lot of trouble if they are not satisfied.
c. Management often disregards the potential political support stockholders may give.
d. Stockholders should be ignored because by law they cannot purchase new issues of securities.

_____ 10. What is most closely related to moral responsibility?
a. Cooperation induced by wages
b. The organizational purpose has become a personal purpose
c. Cooperation induced by craftsmanship
d. Cooperation induced by social satisfactions

Essay-Discussion

1. In economic theory, what is the responsibility of management?

2. What strategies can management develop toward its employees?

3. To whom do you think management should be responsible? Why?

Section III ILLUSTRATIVE CASES

IT BEATS A BOX LUNCH[1]

The Chesapeake and Ohio Railroad utilizes stockholder parties to create a sense of loyalty to the company and add a significant amount of revenue to the company as well. Over a million dollars have been spent by stockholders who travel to the parties' site, the C & O owned Greenbier Hotel, by the company's railroad. Although the stockholders receive reduced rates, they more than make up for it by taking out the slack during the railroad's and the hotel's off season. The parties have created such an interest that many people have purchased C & O's stock primarily to attend the parties. As one stockholder aptly put it, "It certainly beats the box lunch other companies give their stockholders."[2]

Analysis

1. Why don't more companies do this?

2. Are there any disadvantages to management of active stockholder interest and participation?

3. Can you think of other ways of stimulating stockholder interest?

[1] "The C & O's Happy Holders," *Business Week*, December 7, 1963, pp. 96–98.
[2] *Ibid.*, p. 98.

DISCRIMINATORY APTITUDE TESTS[1]

In March 1964 an Illinois Fair Employment Practices Commission examiner ruled that an employment aptitude test administered by Motorola Corporation unfairly discriminated against a Negro job applicant. He reported that in light of current circumstances and the objectives of the law, the test did not lend itself to equal opportunity for culturally deprived and disadvantaged groups. The designer of the aptitude test stated that the objective of the test was not to exclude Negroes but to help evaluate the trainability of a prospective employee. In November 1964 the Illinois FEPC concurred with its examiner's finding that Motorola had discriminated against the job applicant in the case. However, the Commission did not agree with the examiner that the company must give him a job. They decided that a payment of $1,000 by the company to the job seeker would constitute an adequate remedy. An executive made the following comment on this decision:

> We feel that the recent Illinois Fair Employment Commission ruling is completely ridiculous. It would be chaotic if this ruling is allowed to stand. There should be no discrimination because of race, religion, national origin, or color. The employer must be allowed to choose the quality of employees that suits his needs.

Analysis

1. In terms of management responsibility, comment on the FEPC ruling in the case.

2. Comment on the executive's statement quoted above in terms of management responsibility.

3. Does the large corporation have any responsibility to alleviate the race and unemployment problems facing the United States today? Explain and relate to current events.

[1] Based on Max S. Wortman and Fred Luthans, "The Incidence of Antidiscrimination Clauses in Union Contracts," *Labor Law Journal*, Vol. 16, No. 9, September 1965, pp. 523–532.

"A FAIR DAY'S WAGE FOR A FAIR DAY'S WORK"

Business Week annually reports executive salaries. For 1967 the highest-paid executive was Frederic G. Donner who retired November 1, 1967, as chairman of General Motors. He received a straight salary of $169,617 plus a bonus of $460,000 for a total compensation of $629,617 for 1967. This represented a drop in salary for Mr. Donner, who received $790,-000 the previous year.[1]

Although Donner is the highest-paid executive, other top executives are making almost as much. International Telephone and Telegraph Chairman Harold Geneen earned $485,000 and Johnson and Johnson Chairman P. B. Hofmann was compensated $486,000.[2]

When Robert McNamara was chief executive for Ford Motor Company, he was in the $400,000 salary range. As Secretary of Defense he was paid $34,000.

Analysis

1. How would you justify executive salaries?

2. Who essentially decides whether to give the top executive $300,000 or $400,000?

3. In light of managerial responsibility, discuss executive compensation.

[1] See "What's a Good Man Worth?", *Business Week*, June 1, 1968, pp. 56–57.
[2] *Ibid.*

NAPALM MANUFACTURER[1]

Dow Chemical is the producer of napalm used extensively by United States forces in Vietnam. The picketing of Dow recruiters on college campuses throughout the nation has received much publicity and controversy.

The president of Dow stated the company's position in the controversy as follows: "We intend to continue making napalm because we feel that as long as the United States is sending men to war, it is unthinkable that we should not supply the materials they need."[2] Napalm represents about one half of one percent of Dow's sales. The company is involved in many lifesaving ventures, such as health research and clean water and makes large contributions to the hospital ship, S. S. Hope.

Those who picket Dow charge that the company is a war profiteer and/or accuse it of complicity in an allegedly immoral government policy in Vietnam.

At this writing, the company has reviewed its position, and, although they feel that the demonstrations may be damaging in the years to come, they have made the decision to continue supplying the government with napalm.

Analysis

1. Would you make the same decision? Why? Why not?

2. What responsibility does the corporate entity have in this case? Individual managers?

[1] Based on "How Dow Saves Lives," *Nation's Business*, February 1968, p. 56.
[2] *Ibid.*, p. 56.

READING: THE ANATOMY OF LEADERSHIP

EUGENE E. JENNINGS

We often hear that ours is an age without heroes and that business is without leaders. The towering personalities of the past seem, to some, to have considerably more specific gravity than their successors of today.

This indictment, while containing some truth—more, in fact, than should leave us feeling comfortable—overlooks the rugged individualists still on the business stage; more than a handful of flamboyant entrepreneurs and, throughout the ranks of business, aggressive, assertive individuals who openly or secretly hunger for leadership roles.

Nonetheless, the charge that we have allowed leadership to lapse as a necessary executive art deserves close examination. In too many companies the careful man has replaced the tycoon who was willing, in an earlier time, to take uncommon risks by boldly seizing initiative. Decision making has become diffused, decentralized and impersonal in many organizations.

Why this has happened is, to some extent, an inevitable result of social and economic change. The unrestrained, owner-managed enterprises of the late 19th and 20th centuries are no more. Ownership of our largest and even many of our smallest organizations is today dispersed, and direction flows not from an ownership caste but from cadres of professional managers who are responsible to boards of directors, to government regulators, to organized workers and to a fickle consuming public.

Reprinted by permission of the publisher from *Management of Personnel Quarterly*, Vol. 1, No. 1, Autumn 1961, Bureau of Industrial Relations, Graduate School of Business Administration, University of Michigan, pp. 2-9. Dr. Jennings was Associate Professor of Business Administration at Michigan State University when he wrote this paper.

But more important than why the climate of leadership has changed is that today's business organization, and tomorrow's, will require a new breed of restless men with imagination— men perhaps not cut from the same cloth as the old titans but nonetheless ready and able to break free of conventional procedure and move into untried fields. The problem, therefore, is: How can business encourage its managers and managerial aspirants to assume a more vigorous leadership role?

TODAY'S APPROACH TO LEADERSHIP

The term "leadership" is indiscriminately applied to such varied activities as playground supervisor, committee chairman, club president, business executive, and politician. Furthermore, research has produced such a variegated list of traits presumably to describe leadership that, for all practical purposes, it describes nothing. Fifty years of study have failed to produce one personality trait or set of qualities that can be used to discriminate between leaders and non-leaders.

This failure to identify leadership traits in individuals has led us to look elsewhere for the keys to leadership. If a person does not become a leader because he possesses a particular pattern of personality characteristics, maybe he becomes a leader because of something outside of him; that is, the situation determines which men will rise and be chosen to leadership.

The transfer from the personality to the situation has altered our whole approach to leadership. The situational approach appealed to our ideal of democracy, our belief in the impact of the environment on the individual and our need to do something quickly about our shortage of leaders. Because it denied that leaders are born and affirmed that leaders are made, this approach stimulated a deluge of executive training and leadership development programs.

No doubt leaders often need propitious moments to rise. Without such occasions they might remain unknown. In this sense, the situation is indeed influential, but need not be determining. *First,* aggressive action can sometimes overcome a difficult situation. *Second,* initiative often helps determine what the situation actually is. The individual manager can never know the exact situation unless he pits himself vigorously against it. It is in striving to overcome adversity that he finds his full capacity for leadership. This is a fact too often forgotten today.

Admittedly, great events in history are always a marriage between the man and the circumstances, but what is crucial is which predominates. The fact is that the situation holds within it the distinct possibility of several different leaders rising to power. The "right man for the right situation" is a subtle but lethal kind of fatalistic thinking that must not be cultivated if business is to mtaintain its necessarily dynamic and creative nature.

What Leaders Do

Where modern measurement fails to define leadership, history offers some suggestions. Plato, for example, conceived his ideal society as having three occupational classes—workers and slaves, guardians, and philosophers. In this society the king would draw up the plans and the philosophers would carry them out with the aid of the civil service and military officers comprising the guardian class. Here we have a specific distinction between leadership and execution. Leadership determines the overall plan and infuses the system with a character and direction that could not come by keeping close to the day-to-day stream of problems.

Hence the leader is a beginner of plans carried out by an executive. Machiavelli, Carlyle, Nietzsche, William James, Woodrow Wilson, John Dewey, Lenin, Franklin D. Roosevelt and Churchill all made similar distinctions. Few who have given thought to this distinction have failed to find merit in it. The leader's role is initiating, beginning. It is born of imagination and a sense of mission. It involves great personal risk.

The executive may bring about changes too, but they are of the type warranted by the situation and appropriate to the organization. He operates more in terms of active needs than can be handled by immediate supervision. Consequently, he does not substantially change the character or direction of his organization.

Although both types are needed, few leaders make good executives and few executives make good leaders. It is the rare man who excels at both.

Who Are Today's Leaders?

If, in today's society, we are replacing dynamic men with efficient men, the next question is: What causes this imbalance? The answer may be provided by a closer look at the qualities of leaders. They are found in the sense of purpose, power and self-confidence. In numerous studies of both contemporary and historical figures, these three qualities stand out as essential to fulfilling the role of leadership. When any one of these qualities is lacking, leadership suffers.

BUREAUCRACY LIMITS LEADERSHIP

Men who lead must have vision of real possibilities of the future and must articulate them to the people. This ability to raise one's sights, to get above the struggle, to see beyond triviality, is becoming increasingly rare. We may disparage the men who today see only dimly what tomorrow will clearly need to be done, but there is a condition which subsumes all of us. This condition is one of bureaucratic stagnation. In a society such as ours, there is the strong tendency to develop a civil-service mentality. Our whole society is developing this bureaucratic mind in business, unions, church, school and government.

The individual's role is largely identified by the position he occupies, and these positions, in turn, are systematically integrated to provide the highest degree of coordination and efficiency possible. Public distrust of the bureaucracy is not a reaction against inefficiency, however. The bureaucracy is quite efficient in most cases, due to its emphasis on coordination and efficiency to the exclusion of all other goals. It is a common characteristic of the bureaucratic individual that, while his single-mindedness brings specific events into sharper focus, he is blind to the periphery beyond which lies a different world.

Bureaucratic society assigns each individual his functions, the area of his authority and the standards of proficiency. The worker is harnessed in to ensure the exact performance essential to keep the huge system under control. If any sort of decision is assigned to him or demanded of him, it is duly taken within the limited province of his function without his having to delve to the bottom of things. Duties and regulations laid down to guide him are applied meticulously in such a manner that risk is avoided. There is no semblance of a genuinely creative community of action, let alone sensitive insight into things above and beyond. Initiative is not possible to any great degree or the whole system would fall apart. Risk is eliminated by the sacred adoption of the system's rational rules and regulations, even though they appear irrational to the individual.

Greatness or Efficiency?

In a society becoming heavily bureaucratic, as we are, great men are subordinated to efficient men. The executive type has dethroned the leader. Plato's "achievement" is without its antecedent "beginner." No one person really "begins." Man is enmeshed at all times in an intricate set of relationships that prohibits his seizing the helm and steering a course of his own choosing. Our community "leaders" of today rarely want to shoulder responsibility. They seldom want to decide anything without endorsement. Some committee, group or precedent must be represented in everything

they do and upon which they can shift the onus if things go wrong. In the bureaucratic society, the ultimate court of appeals is a previous set of actions that have become a method or system held consecrate because at one time, when things were less complex, it more visibly promoted the general interest. The ends were more within assessment. Upon this method or system, in one of its multifarious forms, accrues the individual's final responsibility. Each individual is a tiny wheel with a fractional share in the decision, but no one effectively decides.

But all of this is consciously realized by many people; many rebel, some silently and some openly. They feel so intimately interlocked in social processes that they do not know how much they rely upon others and their system. Leadership is not a conscious problem to people today because they are not conscious of themselves as leaders. They wonder curiously about what people mean who refer to them as leaders.

The bureaucratic mode of human existence destroys heroic vision. We are today a relatively unpurposeful society. So much is this the concern today that Eisenhower ordered a commission to look into national goals. Luce of Time-Life, Inc., ordered a series of articles on "What Is Our National Purpose?" It is interesting that neither endeavor created much of a national reaction. No great movements for change and reform have emerged. But yet, to speak intelligently today of our national purpose is beyond our ability, so long have we become accustomed to seeing the parts, not the whole, immediate aims rather than long-range goals.

Bureaucracy and the civil-service mentality have contributed in the past to the destruction of the Roman and British empires. They are presently engulfing the individual in America, his ability to see and feel beyond his role or commitment.

Organizations Demand Conservatism

This lack of heroic vision makes individuals "all too executive." Today all too many executives merely add their dots to a series of dots reflecting the evolving histories of their organizations. Under the ethic of finishing the unfinished task started by his great predecessors, this type of executive receives the advantages and benefits of power-seeking without incurring the risk of the leader's attempt at major innovation. In short, he seeks success and personal advantage but does not have a sense of purpose or historical opportunity.

The illusive and masquerading feature of all of this is that the organization typically continues to get bigger. Someone usually gets credit for the growth partly because giving credit is a strong habit carried over from our heroic past. The mania for bigness is, however, a perfect example of how many executives today fit into the on-going direction and character of their organizations in such a manner that they merely mid-wife the enterprises through what are actually predetermined courses. There is no change from the normal or expected pattern of growth as a consequence of his personal efforts, but rather only a continued increase in size and complexity under the illusion of heroic leadership. It simply is not fair for the executive under these circumstances to be given the title of a leader since change is really not change after all.

THE POWER STRUGGLE

In other words, power is a disruptive and reformative—a creative—tool in the care of a leader. The power of one who acts as an executive is a sustaining and maintaining—a conservative—tool. Many executives today do not have a strong creative opportunity or sense of purpose but have the same drive for power as their predecessors. An individual who has a strong drive for power, but who does not have a strong purpose to which he can attach that drive, would, necessarily appear more power-seeking than he might actually be. There is, of course, a lot to be said for the argument that his power drive may tend to increase in the absence of an objective goal that will give it form and sanction. But in either case, the very "nakedness" of his power-seeking would seem to prompt him to inhibit it, which in turn

brings on a psychological condition whereby it becomes even more difficult to develop heroic thrust. If we keep in mind, then, that the problem of many executives today is that they must appear to be thrusting and aggressive while at the same time not appear to be too power-seeking, we have in capsule the essence of what they are trying to do. In other words, how to extricate themselves from these paradoxical demands is indeed the key to their success today.

One reason why all too few executives wish to have power to accomplish great and noble things is that the power struggle involves considerable personal risk. To remove the risk one must, of course, make his power permanent. But in making his power permanent the executive cannot make it apparent, for in doing so he necessarily makes enemies of both those who are equally driven by the same urge and those who abhor the evil effects that power brings to both the organization and the personality of the individual. Implementing the power drive subtly and silently is a delicate skill that separates the power élite from the more common contenders. It is extremely difficult to learn the rules of acquiring through subtle means the necessary power with which to control others. It is for this reason that many executives fail to achieve the power necessary to effect major changes.

We might note that the price of failure is, often more than not, forfeiture of the gains won by the attempt at leadership. This penalty often includes the loss of executive position. So the accepted pattern of many executives has become to gain power and make it permanent by not personally causing or sponsoring major innovations. For them it is safer to use power as a conservative force than as a creative force. Consequently, this kind of executive is not only as interested in gaining power as was his predecessor, but he is today incomparably more skilled in gaining and maintaining his power than in knowing and using his power for creative purposes.

The executive who makes the mistake of emerging into the fierce light of daring leadership is apt to become caught in dilemmas his talents are inadequate for resolving. Furthermore, a major innovation is something that requires time to work itself out. Even if the program goes on to achieve success in heroic proportions, the executive could be knocked off because of an errant move in the interim. Anyone who takes long chances will find that the averages are against him. This we found to be an axiom of political experience. Major changes set loose unknown forces that gather a momentum of their own and smash through to results unwanted by anyone, including the executive. Consequently, it is far wiser to sponsor many minor changes that only appear to be tests of ability although they must, of course, be beneficial to the organization, and many executives are becoming aware of this fact.

Using Group Responsibility

One favorite technique of many executives today is to place the responsibility for major changes in the hands of groups and thus shield themselves from the responsibility of complete failure. The idea here is to delegate to the "responsible group" those problems that are of major significance. By this means, the executive assumes more "individual responsibility" for the more numerous minor innovations with the thought that many minor innovations will give heroic stature more easily than one major change, especially one that hazards failure or is cushioned by group responsibility. In effect, the strategy is to become cumulatively heroic through acts that are so integrated as to compound themselves.

It may be argued that this new conservatism is made possible partly by large bureaucratic organizations wherein decisions must be increasingly made by the group method. Since the group is generally more conservative than the individual, the executive naturally becomes less radical and creative. Then too, the increasing use of group meetings, both formal and informal, has forced out into the open the good intentions of the executive. As long as the executive could personally and privately deal with his superiors, subordinates and peers, he did not have to reveal or fear to reveal his intentions toward power. He received ethical justification under the code of enlightened self-interest.

But the convening of a group makes it imperative for the ambitious executive to manifest the most noble intentions simply because a group has a moral quality that is not found in the members taken separately. All good princes today know that in such quasipublic gatherings as conferences, committees and even informal meetings, one must never be anything less than noble and moral and, above all, never appear too eager or overtly ambitious. The revealed ambition of an executive is grossly magnified by the ratio of the number of group members who witness the accidental dropping of his disguise. This means that in group meetings the executive today must hide his apparent need and drive for power by not being radically different, or at least not standing pat on a radical program. He knows that sponsoring a terribly different idea automatically forces him to draw upon the total power resources available to him. This is never done today.

Taking the Limited Offensive

The third characteristic of a leader is his strong inner will to resist forces that might move him away from his mission or purpose. He must be strong in character and use the full force of his personality. There is a growing tendency today in our society to assume a limited offensive. For many, the mark of the successful individual is that he never uses the full potential of his personality. Of course, no one ever uses the full potential of his personality, but we are concerned here that many an executive uses increasingly less. This lack of self-directedness shows up in his interpersonal relations. He is calm but engaging, argumentative at times but not disagreeable, alert but not too trusting. He approaches people easily but also he is able to move out when he gets involved. The word is "heavy" when he talks about the conversations he seeks to avoid. When caught unavoidably in a "heavy," he has the skill to work problems through to a convenient and acceptable solution, but in those cases his personality is invariably engaged on behalf of calming the disturbances, restoring the equilibrium and thwarting accusations of being "difficult."

In all cases, blows of lethal and total effectiveness must never be swung, even in the form of words. It is far better to succeed a little bit than to destroy the opposition completely, which always brings trouble later because of bitterness and recrimination. Pleasantries can never remove the pain of a grievous offense. This kind of individual believes strictly in a limited offensive with maximum opportunity for numerous engage-disengage sequences that will persuade but not offend. Above all, he must not make apparent his resources as an individual apart from his position, because of the tendency to impute ambition to the individual who shows personal talents that are not directly identified with the accepted norms and practices of his function and position. In other words, there is a tendency to confuse the individual with his formal rank and function in the hierarchy.

NO SENSE OF MISSION

Many individuals generally have no grand design, no mission, no great plan calling for change and progress. It is the true leader who has a grand design, which is reflected by a chain-like sequence of relevant and integrated events that serve as stepping stones. Of course, the grand design may not be easily deciphered until it is completed. Contrariwise, the individual lets each situation dictate to him his special set of techniques and plans of action. He sees no overall strategy except that which reflects the on-going and established interests of the various claimant groups involved in his organization. This allows him maximum flexibility without the personal risk of long-range programs.

It is difficult for the typical individual to have a deep and disturbing sense of mission when he is so specialized and boxed in by bureaucratic formulas that he cannot rise above the trivia to see what is ahead, above and behind. But if he suffers from "administrivia," he more importantly suffers from annihilation of all privacy.

Escape from Thinking

Heroic leadership requires not so much a determination to outmaneuver the other fellow, but an ability to anticipate the effects of action now in progress and to devise plans that will be essentially preventive rather than remedial. But who is doing the thinking? Telephone any executive during business hours and you will probably be told he is "at a meeting," for he spends most of his time "in conference." The executive has a genius for cluttering up his day, and many have somehow managed to persuade themselves that they are too busy to think, to read, to look back and to see into the future. Being busy is more than a national passion, as some believe, and it is more than an excuse—it is a means of escape. The real question concerning the opportunity for leadership is not the time or lack of it that is provided for thought, but the value that is placed on thought. Our society has always been action oriented, but lately what little thought has existed has been largely sacrificed to meetings where thinking is done in haste and geared to specific problems at hand, to say nothing of the power tactics that consume vast amounts of intellectual and emotional energy.

The individual today has a passion for discussion. He may use grave and decisive words, may even adopt divergent attitudes at strategic moments, but never stands his ground, especially for a radical idea or program. The stance that he takes is commonly referred to as "a convenient point of reference," but this reference is subject to shifting. By this means he is able to transfer the discussion to a new plane, insisting upon complete objectivity when it is necessary to ensure avoiding any subjective or emotional involvement. The individual's true home is a kind of superficial intellectualism in which his thoughts appear to have a logical coherence, his word choices are for maximum effect. He oozes with intuitions and hunches, or he reports on the latest research findings from scientific studies of elaborate detail, rigorous methodology and unimpeachable authorship. The use of anonymous authorities is itself an indication of how he has become abstracted from the reality about him.

Executives Fight a Phantom Battle

Now what all of this amounts to is that the power struggle going on within these vast human systems found in business, government, education and union organization is without a fighting front. It is a phantom battle. The clever use of the "littles" of sophistry, the impersonalization of arguments, the resorting to anonymous authorities, and the appeal to the "powers that be" (which somehow always remain nameless), make the development of a purposive life futile. The executive fights among the shadows and the noble myths are subject to momentary change. What appears at first to be a united front becomes later divided against itself, where adversaries join forces and the man on the right or left of the large oval conference table stands ready to pose as a friendly "devil's advocate" or "his majesty's loyal supporter," depending upon what the situation warrants. The attempt to discover the true fighting front and unveil the nameless powers for even a brief moment is to destroy ambiguity and oddly enough to promote general resistance and unrest. Apparently a modern truth today is that to be safe one must never feel secure.

Executives Lack Creativity

In summary, and in preparation for the challenge and conclusion, the individual is rapidly becoming a kind of power-seeker who appears to be a leader because he is skillful in getting support, popularity and rapport with a minimum of "heavy" involvement. He is trying hard to become skillful at working with people and using resources of committees and decision-making groups. He appears to be a good human relations practitioner or social engineer, but actually considers these human relations principles as means by which he may intelligently and subtly play the power game. But in playing this game he does not cause major innovation.

This is the new rule which makes the power game drastically different from that of his predecessors such as Carnegie and Rockefeller, Senior. Seeking only to fulfill the expectations of others and to live within the established imperatives of his organization, the executive finds it unnecessary to the pursuit of self-interest to champion radically new and great programs and to risk willingly the greater inner resources available to him as a unique individual. What at first glance appears to be a lack of self-direction due to a kind of cunning or strategy turns out, after a second look, to be a result of inner weakness. The executive today is not to be seen as a malicious power-seeker; he is not to be morally castigated. His problem is not completely his fault. He is to be understood as one who lives in a high pressure system in which there are few opportunities available to him whereby he can attach his ambition and desire to succeed to the top to a great and noble purpose. In short, it is not out of choice that the executive wears the face that he does. Unfortunately this feature makes his problem incomparably more difficult.

Although we do not know how many have taken to the anonymity of large-scale organization as their avenue of escape from the responsibilities of leadership, it seems plausible that this picture represents many of the top executives in our major large institutions, including business and government. We might further believe that as the scale and complexity of these institutions increase, and the pressures they necessarily generate become more imperative and inhibiting, even the strongest-willed executive will find it necessary to operate without greatly engaging his unique and effective personality. The increasing pattern of half-hearted attempts at leadership is tending toward drastic consequences of which the annihilation of the individual's productive or creative resources is one of the more imminent possibilities.

WHAT IS THE IDEAL LEADER?

With these possibilities besetting the aspiring leader today, what are the conditions of ideal? What is an ideal type of leader? Our superior man is necessarily a "free man," but not free in the sense that he exists outside of an organizational system. Our ideal is not a hermit because a hermit is still a prey to the world.

While fighting against his world, a hermit only escapes it in order to continue to exist as a human being. He thus takes on a kind of sincere falseness wheich negates his virtuous intentions. It is simply foolhardy, in a society as heavily populated and as massively organized as ours is today, to believe that one can escape physically. And it is unheroic.

The fact that the individual cannot escape places limitations on Clark Kerr's recommendation for coping with organizational society. Mr. Kerr rebelled at the current practice of human relations and recommended that the individual should give himself to many organizations rather than to one and reserve for himself the aspiration of limitlessness rather than project this quality into the character of organization. This is precisely what the contemporary person is doing to-day, but he does not get in return this feeling of limitlessness.

Only becoming half-involved in any one organization prevents the individual from realizing his true and full powers within. He cannot come into meaningful grips with his huge organization unless he firmly resolves that he is going to play an active aggressive role in it. It is only through active participation in molding events with a sense of direct responsibility for their consequences that one can achieve the personal strength necessary to live in harmony with the pressures of the organization without being absorbed by them. And this is what the executive needs today. Rather than a social ethic with which to justify and give sanction to the enormous power of the organization over him, the individual needs a stronger will with which to put his total productive resources to work for him and his organization.

The concept of our ideal shows us that only through struggle, through meeting directly the harshness and tyranny of the real world, can a man come to his own self. Until then he feels extremely abstracted from the stream of life, and he consumes vast amounts of physical and psychological energy trying to overcome his feelings of powerlessness.

But more importantly, he can never really get the feel of the true character and direction of the organization if he does not become totally involved in it. Without this feeling and grasping kind of intellect, it is difficult to become intimately involved in a creative plan to make over the character or re-chart the direction of the enterprise or some part thereof. One can only fall back on the drive for power —the common denominator among the alienated—when he does not have the inspiration to lead and accomplish a great and noble life purpose. But this purpose must of necessity be intimately tied to the character and direction of the organization in which the individual seeks his principal source of livelihood. No amount of leading and accomplishing great and noble purposes in extra-organizational endeavors, as seen in the current rage for charity, community and recreational activities, will overcome the psychological vacuity brought on by the lack of purposeful involvement in an individual's major activity throughout the day. This fad of finding purpose in life outside of the business or government or union organization is a prime example of the modern individual's tendency today to distribute himself among too many organizations. While the organization balloons to gigantic proportions and the executive comes to find less and less personal involvement in it, he is, so to speak, busily passing the charity hat around in his community to help the needy and the suffering. It is not fanciful to suggest that this extra-organizational effort is the executive's way of escaping from his primary leadership responsibilities. Nor is it disrespectful to suggest that this escape mechanism is a desperate attempt to recapture his lost sense of personal worth.

For some executives, however, the extra-organizational activity is done merely because this is what a successful and well-adjusted executive should do today. In this case he cannot be classed as a leader for he is not really sincere. But we must reaffirm that in many cases the executive becomes an extraorganizational man not because of choice but rather because of a compulsive need to escape from an environment that offers less and less opportunity for personal thrust. The extraorganizational pattern is an important means whereby the executive who has a strong drive for power can more fully satisfy this need. It is not possible to relate this type of activity to virtue because it results from compulsiveness, from inner weakness, rather than from inner strength. That is to say, the executive becomes an extraorganizational man not because he is a superior person whose vast reserve of energy cannot be adequately used by any one organization, but rather because he has a low reserve of energy owing to a lack of both power and opportunity to use whatever productive resources he has within his principal organization.

We now arrive at the heart of the matter. The leader of the future will be that individual with the great mission to overcome the mass feeling of alienation and self-inadequacy. He will recognize that this struggle starts not with his community, not even with his principal organization, but rather it starts with *himself.* He puts his own house in order; he gradually and diligently develops the necessary values, courage, and self-control whereby he can successfully become identified with, but not absorbed by, his organization. He disciplines himself to wholeness, and from this newly acquired inner strength he dominates the pressures of his organization and leads the people about him. In this way power over others comes to him because he is inwardly a superior person. The emergence of this hero, who is admittedly a rare gift to any organization or society, will by the changes he helps bring about prepare the way for other executives to become better leaders.

There are many executives today who are on "crusades" to restore the uncommon man, bring back the independent spirit, destroy the organization man and revive the Titan's inner-directed conscience. They write books, give speeches, appear in only the most proper public gatherings and social circles, associate with the elites of their choice, buy and in some cases read the best literature, and identify with the most sophisticated authors. If it were not for the fact that they are so noisy and public about this build-up we would actually think of them as somewhat sincere. Contrarily, we cannot help but believe that this eagerness to appear to be something akin to our superior person is really the attempt to assure themselves that they are what they are not. It fol-

lows that only a few will be able to recapture the will to lead. Of course, it never has been absolutely extinct, but the point is that these few promising executives need to be encouraged or they will find that their way back to conspicuous leadership will be too strenuous for them. Some may believe that everything must be done, every available resource must be used to help develop the promising executive into a superior type of person. The danger of this advice is that the appearance of a leader with the hero's sense of historical purpose cannot be well planned and predicted. This, however, makes it all the more imperative that we should do certain things that are within our power to create a conducive atmosphere for the reappearance of the man of exceptional talent.

How Today's Organizations Kill Leadership

To this end there are certain specific practices within our society that warrant special criticism at this time. To begin with, the organization today has achieved a life of its own. It goes rambling on seemingly immune to the personal advances of any one executive. It has created a kind of social or impersonal system of leadership which is the product of many individuals acting expertly at their chosen tasks. Then, too, the reduction of competition allows the oligopolistic or monopolistic firm to ramble on without apparent need for the great and personal mastery of the heroic monarch of the past. As Crawford Greenewalt has said, the "responsible group" has replaced the "responsible individual" and the corporation's health and future is that much more assured. This, however, is questionable.

But with the replacement of the responsible individual by the responsible group, the executive is merely given a more concrete and convenient unit whereby he can advance his own individual interests without any more opportunity for heroic thrust when the responsible group has replaced the responsible individual. The last thing that the executive needs today is to have this additional obstacle placed before him which he must hurdle in his attempt to be aggressive and creative. One does not place another obstacle before an individual who already feels alienated and powerless. Nothing has caused as much arrestment of his leadership opportunity as the responsible-group concept. We have previously suggested that it will make all the more the power artist and that much less the purposeful leader.

There are few features of our society that show less faith in personal, conspicuous leadership than in this growing concept of the responsible group. It may be suggested at this time that the growth in acceptance and use of the responsible group portrays, in dramatic form, our growing loss of faith in conspicuous leadership and our feelings of inadequacy. The group might very well be used to keep the individual informed of what is going on, but he should not be allowed to use it as a chief tool for power-seeking. Executives should be encouraged to seek power that comes from a superior inner awareness and sensitivity to what the future character and direction of the firm should be, not power that comes from an ability to manipulate people and to use social techniques.

The need for inner strength may indicate that the executive should be protected from groups by having conferences formally scheduled. At present many committees are called on an informal basis which often amounts to calling a conference whenever someone pushes the panic button. Since the panic button is pushed often in an alienated society, the executive is always in conference. By having conferences as infrequently as possible, the executive will not be at the mercy of the panic-button pusher. At least this might be tried until the promising executive has developed sufficient inner reserve to restrain from pushing the panic button or jumping mechanically to the alarm whenever he or some other executive gets into a little difficulty. He will then have to look within for the resources with which to work himself out of difficulty—an almost unheard of practice today in many organizations. This too may be too much of a struggle for him today so that care must be taken that he is not given too much freedom from the group without an adequate recovery of his individual resources.

Who Will Be Our Leaders?

It is impossible to determine who the future leaders will be. Any attempt at scientific selection will produce a contemptible arrogance resulting from a lack of awareness of the limitations of technical kinds of identification and selection. Attempts to determine exactly the traits of a leader have resulted in complete failure. In spite of this we all have a crude but amazingly efficient sensitivity to the essence of leadership and to the existence of great leaders. We can recognize them even though their characteristics cannot be scientifically measured. The tendency today is to deny these rare men any psychological room, let alone social status and organizational prestige. We have tried to present some of the characteristics by which we can identify leaders, but these traits were only roughly described because words can only approximate the emotional quality with which we identify our heroes. To be sure the actual worship of heroes today has acquired a grotesque posture as seen in current biographical literature. But the essential spark is still there in the minds and hearts of many people and needs only to be rekindled.

In other words, it is not that we cannot recognize our leaders, but rather that we no longer value them as highly as we once did. Therefore, scientific tests should definitely be discouraged so that our eminently more superior powers of observation and intuition can once again help us to find and to raise to our highest positions men of rare and exceptional leadership potential. In this way talent and ability will be brought into line with position, all of which will help, but of course not guarantee, a return to heroic leadership.

Recommendations as to how to structure and reorganize for the rebirth of leadership could become so demanding and pervasive that the tendency to rely too heavily upon organization to eliminate the organization man could move us one notch back rather than one notch forward. All suggestions to help bring about a superior man in our organization should be tempered by judicious concern for the extreme fallacy of organizing to return to independence. We must be careful to place our reliance upon the individual to find his way to psychological recovery and not upon the forces inherent in the group and organization.

Time Out to Think

With this due caution, there is still another recommendation reflected in our concept of the superman. This recommendation concerns the value we place upon thought that is private deliberation resulting from a well-disciplined use of one's intellectual reserves. Each executive who shows promise of heroic leadership should be allowed ample opportunity to think. Perhaps once every five or seven years he should be given a year off with pay so that he can read and study and perhaps even write. When it is possible to organize his time and responsibilities, he should be given time off to think—to get away from his office, and become aware of the broader possibilities found in studying literature, philosophy, art and the social sciences. Under proper and well-conceived circumstances this effort will not be an escape from leadership responsibilities, although this is a distinct danger. However, this program can be effective only with men who are willing and able to make major innovations and assume great responsibility and risks and who will profit from getting out and seeing a broader or higher purpose to which their organizations and they may become devoted. A vigorous emphasis on the value of the thoughtful man will allow a leadership to come forth that will be devoted to great and noble missions not out of compulsive needs but out of choice that comes from inner wisdom.

Of course, finding ways to give the promising executive this opportunity to develop his intellectual resources will require a change in present-day values. The direction and character of the typical business organization will have to be changed since the man of action has theretofore been its standard breed. While we wait for some great innovator to show us the way toward the major innovation, there are some small things we can do ourselves. Most important among these is to reverse our tendency to walk into offices and homes, and

backyards for that matter, because of an overpowering need to have friends and acquaintances. We can afford to be hard on ourselves and others who want not privacy but companionship. A good brother's keeper is one who helps the other person to suffer a little by leaving him alone and unengaged because this will in the long run help him to struggle and perhaps find himself.

THE CHALLENGE

Human progress occurs to a great extent through the intellectual efforts of its great men. Leadership might well be viewed as thought in command, while action and implementation might be the limitations imposed upon the individual who does not have or cannot use superior intellectual resources. Displacing or eliminating this great resource will assuredly reduce our opportunity and potentiality for change and progress.

In conclusion ours is a society whose chief characteristic is a lost sense of self-direction as seen in the tendency to escape from leadership responsibility. The challenge is to revive the individual's unique powers of purposive striving and his courage to assume and sustain great risks. To be sure, there are many recommendations that could be made to this end, but because the purpose of this article is to diagnose our problem today, we have highlighted only a few. They include denial of the value of extraorganizational effort, resistance to the responsible-group trend, respect for a man's privacy, faith in men of rare ability and giving highest value to that talent reflected in thought deliberation.

Outside Reading: Essay-Discussion Questions

1. Analyze Dr. Jennings' statement that "few leaders make good executives and few executives make good leaders."

2. What is a technique that executives may use to shift responsibility for major changes?

3. Who does Dr. Jennings feel will be the future leaders?

4. Discuss the requirements you think will be necessary for future business leadership.

PART VII

EXECUTIVE DEVELOPMENT

Chapter Twenty-Five

Executive Qualities and Executive Education

THE PROBLEM OF leadership succession is given comprehensive consideration in the first part of this chapter. Attention is then given to the nature of the qualities that make for success in executive work. The remainder of the chapter is concerned with educational programs for executive development and the use of simulation techniques to develop decisional and other skills.

Section I MAJOR CONCEPTS

Leadership succession
Executive success
Qualities of successful executives

Executive education
Simulation techniques

Section II SELF-TEST

True-False

_____ 1. The rights of private property have precluded leadership succession based on ability to manage.

_____ 2. Executives make few decisions without comprehensive scientific research.

_____ 3. The large majority of business and industrial positions are filled by non-specialists from liberal arts colleges.

_____ 4. The advantage of the case method in training executives is that it provides objective answers to decisional problems.

_____ 5. A review of an individual manager's

career pattern will give the least objective information of success in his managerial capacities.

Multiple Choice

_____ 1. Which of the following best expresses leadership succession in twentieth-century United States?
   a. Instability
   b. Superhierarchy
   c. Revolutionary
   d. Decentralized

_____ 2. Which of the following has been *least* important in determining leadership succession in American business enterprises?
   a. Property rights
   b. Professional training
   c. Political parties
   d. Executive experience

_____ 3. William E. Henry noted that a successful executive views authority as
   a. something that must be overcome
   b. a controlling but helpful relationship
   c. detrimental to his successful career pattern
   d. none of the above

_____ 4. According to William E. Henry, successful executives seem generally to have
   a. greater feelings of personal attachment toward subordinates than superiors
   b. a feeling that subordinates portray the things representing the past rather than the future
   c. identification with subordinates and thus are effective in gaining their acceptance
   d. all of the above

_____ 5. Data on the educational background of top executives indicates that
   a. top executives are not so well educated as the general population
   b. less than 5 per cent possessed college degrees

   c. top executives studied in 1952 were better educated than those studied in 1928
   d. a liberal arts education is almost useless in executive work

_____ 6. The Pierson and the Gordon-Howell reports on business education make the following conclusions EXCEPT:
   a. Business education should avoid too much emphasis on vocationalism.
   b. Business education should avoid the extremes of specialization.
   c. Business education should give emphasis to the development of professional business leaders.
   d. Business education should be financed through private rather than public auspices, except where extreme hardship can be proved.

_____ 7. Professors John D. Glover and Ralph M. Hower of the Harvard Graduate School of Business Administration make the following conclusions about their cases EXCEPT:
   a. There are no "answers" in this casebook.
   b. Instructors will have *the* answer *after* the student has attempted a solution.
   c. Students are always welcomed to the opinions of the authors.
   d. The authors have *an* answer but not *the* answer.

_____ 8. How do business games differ from the case method?
   a. They are concerned with decisional problems.
   b. Their purpose is to train executives.
   c. There is no difference worth noting.
   d. Participants are required to live with their decisions.

_____ 9. When players "compete" in terms of the best results rather than with one another, the game is
   a. a nonbusiness game
   b. a purely competitive game

c.   a noninteracting game
d.   a nongame
_____ 10.   Role playing generally involves the following EXCEPT:
a.   Acting
b.   Emotions
c.   Listening
d.   Photography

Essay-Discussion

1.   What is the relationship between private property and leadership succession?

2.   What are some of the difficulties in measuring successful executive performance.

3.   How do scientific methods relate to the decision-making problem?

Section III   ILLUSTRATIVE CASES

"MARRY THE COMPANY"[1]

The chief executive of one of the largest firms in America gave a lecture on how to be a success in the modern corporation. He stated that if young managers want to get to the top of their companies, they must be willing "to get completely involved" in the organization and "to invest themselves wholeheartedly in the enterprise." He went on to say that only those men who are willing "to marry the company, never divorce it" can succeed. The chairman also mentioned that individual responsibility, hard work, and self-discipline are necessary.[2]

These prescriptions coincide with the traditional virtues and attitudes of the early entrepreneurs and empire builders. He says that shortcuts popularized in current fiction, such as "How to Succeed in Business Without Really Trying," never work.

Analysis

1.   Do you agree or disagree with the chief executive's analysis of executive success in the modern corporation? Why?

2.   How does his analysis fit with such comments as "It's not what you know but who you know"?

3.   Evaluate performance versus personality as successful qualities in corporate management.

THE GENERATION GAP[1]

A recent article probed the phenomena of the young corporate president (under 40 years of age). The keys to success seemed to revolve around the following two themes. First, do not let yourself get into a rut; continually adjust your aspirations for yourself and the company. A boyish chief executive says: "The most important thing for a president to keep asking himself is 'Where do I go from here?' I have found that established checkpoints for myself helps."[2] The second requirement for success seems to be the proper technique of delegation. A young president emphatically states: "By luck, ambition, aggressiveness or what have you, I was thrust into the role of company president. It has been difficult at times because basically I am a doer, and authority has been the hardest thing for me to give up. But I'm learning."[3]

Although it is not pointed out in the article, it is interesting to note that most of the young presidents who were interviewed had the same last name as the company they worked for.

Analysis

1.   Do you agree with the advice given by the young presidents?

---

[1] Based on "It's Men Up Front That Count," *Business Week*, May 1, 1965, pp. 73-74.
[2] *Ibid.*, p. 74.

[1] Based on "Dilemma of the Young Presidents," *Dun's Review*, August 1967, pp. 41, 56-59.
[2] *Ibid.*, p. 56.
[3] *Ibid.*

2. What are the implications of the last sentence as far as executive success is concerned?

3. If you decided to enter the world of big business, would you have the goal to be president? How would you achieve your goal?

"THE M.B.A."[1]

A recent *Fortune* article depicted the modern Master of Business Administration as M.B.A.—the Man, the Myth, and the Method. The author contrasts the old with the new M.B.A. The old M.B.A. usually came from Harvard with a lot of self-confidence gained not from book learning, but from analyzing and debating business decisions through the time-tested "case method." The new M.B.A. is characterized as coming from Harvard plus many other recognized business schools

[1] Based on Sheldon Zalaznick, "The M.B.A.—The Man, the Myth, and the Method," *Fortune,* May 1968, pp. 168-171, 200-206.

equipped with not only the case background, but also some understanding of the behavioral sciences, humanities and a cool confidence in quantitative analysis and decision making. His education is geared to general management rather than functional specialization. The author states: "His mind is keen, his ambition is endless, and his guru is Robert McNamara."[2] Most employers in industry, commerce, and government seem awed by the M.B.A. and are willing to pay the $12,000 starting salary demanded by M.B.A.s from the prestigious business schools.

Analysis

1. Why are companies after M.B.A.s?

2. What is there about the M.B.A.'s education that differentiates him from one holding a Bachelor's degree in business? Law degree?

3. What do you think would be the optimum educational background for obtaining desired executive qualities? What part should the case method play in the education process?

[2] *Ibid.,* p. 169.

Chapter Twenty-Six

Company Executive Development Programs

MANAGERIAL POSITION DESCRIPTIONS are related to executive qualities in the first part of this chapter. Attention is then given to the subjects of executive recruitment and promo-

tion. Company educational and training programs are scrutinized in the last section of the chapter.

Section I   MAJOR CONCEPTS

Position descriptions
Recruitment
Testing

Executive development
Promotion
Training programs

Section II   SELF-TEST

True-False

_____ 1. Position responsibilities should generally be expressed in operational terms.

_____ 2. There is a great deal of evidence that "C" students have "better" personalities for executive work than "B" and "A" students.

_____ 3. The results obtained in intelligence tests are influenced by acquired knowledge and skills.

_____ 4. University-sponsored training pro-

grams are limited to a broad executive development approach.

_____ 5. The need for "hard-knocks" type of experience has been eliminated by coaching and related training techniques.

Multiple Choice

_____ 1. Which of the following was more closely related to salary progress in the Bell Telephone study than the other three?

a. Quality of college
b. Self-support in college
c. Rank in graduating class
d. Substantial extracurricular achievement

____ 2. Which of the following statements about company executive development is *not* valid?

a. There has been a large growth in company executive development programs since World War II.
b. Some companies maintain their own educational facilities and faculties.
c. Most recently developed programs are in the area of foremanship training.
d. Instructional techniques are similar to those used by universities.

____ 3. Which of the following best describes the instructional techniques used in management training programs?

a. Case method
b. Business games
c. Lectures
d. All of the above

____ 4. All of the following involve simulation EXCEPT:

a. "Hard-knocks" type of experience
b. Computer-umpired business games
c. Role playing
d. The case method

____ 5. All of the following are aspects of "coaching" EXCEPT:

a. The conscious creation of a learning environment
b. Intruding and interfering in the affairs of the subordinate
c. Subordinates should have the "opportunity" to make mistakes
d. Interest in the future of subordinates

____ 6. According to the Bell Telephone study on the relationship between class rank and salary progress, which of the following best describes the importance of self-support in college?

a. No appreciable effect
b. Highly important variable
c. As important as high grades
d. More important than high grades

____ 7. This self-test is an example of an

a. Aptitude test
b. Interest test
c. Intelligence test
d. Achievement test

____ 8. What is probably *not* a classification for executive qualifications on position descriptions?

a. References
b. Experience
c. Education
d. Personal characteristics

____ 9. What is the most accurate statement concerning test validity?

a. Refers to consistency of results
b. Refers to whether the test measures its intended purpose
c. If high, eliminates the need for executive judgement
d. If high for one purpose, will be high for another purpose as well

____ 10. What may management training be used for?

a. Increase competency in a present position
b. Provide opportunities for self-development
c. Prepare people for promotion
d. All the above

Essay-Discussion

1. What factors are important in forecasting future executive needs?

2. How important are interviews in the recruiting process?

3. What is the basic difference between "directed" and actual experience?

Section III   ILLUSTRATIVE CASES

RECRUITING "BONUS-BABIES"[1]

The new Master of Business Administration (M.B.A.) graduate is a prize most companies are after today. The M.B.A. is so sought after that a group of placement directors recently aired their complaints about "high-handed," "unethical," and even "stupid" recruiting tactics. A spokesman for the placement directors claimed that recruiters were offering U. S. Savings Bonds to faculty members for recommending student talent. He said that the faculty members "angrily refused" such offers. Some companies were also charged with pressuring M.B.A. candidates to change their minds after they had committed themselves to work for other firms. The spokesman concluded that "business-school placement may be headed for something close to the 'bonus-baby' system of organized ball."[2]

Analysis

1. Should recruiters be concerned with ethical standards? Why?

2. What part does the recruitment function play in a company's executive development program?

[1] Reported in Sheldon Zalaznick, "The M.B.A.— The Man, the Myth, and the Method," *Fortune,* May 1968, p. 169.
[2] *Ibid.*

"INSULT TRAINING"[1]

The *Wall Street Journal* recently reported that many companies are using "insult training." The sessions encourage the participants to criticize one another very harshly. The purpose is to allow the trainees, who act out realistic sales situations, to see themselves as their customers do and then adjust their pitch. Sample insults are the following: "Listening to you talk is like reading a bad book. . . . Take your thumbs out of your vest. You look like

[1] Reported in "Labor Letter," *Wall Street Journal,* May 21, 1968, p. 1.

a Las Vegas gambler."[2] One company claims the insult experience was so beneficial that it boosted a group's monthly commissions 41 per cent above the office average. However, some participants balk at publicly laying bare their faults and claim that the ego-bruising is demoralizing rather than helpful.

Analysis

1. What type of executive training is this insult course similar to?

2. Would you recommend such training for your staff? Why? Why not?

[2] *Ibid.*

"CHARM SCHOOL"[1]

The president of a small company became concerned over the social mannerisms of his management team. Most of his managers were homegrown, moving up from the production line without the experience of college. He stated: "They were doing a fine job but, frankly, the table manners of our men needed polish." The men's "awareness of [social] shortcomings impaired their self-confidence."[2]

To handle this problem, the president placed a copy of Amy Vanderbilt's *Etiquette* in the company library and introduced an "executive charm school" to the management development program. A woman from a business institute was put in charge of the program. He conducted monthly dinner meetings discussing pointers on dress and grooming, table manners, and the management of elbows and napkins.

The president notes the effect of the $500 annual cost per man of the program as follows: "Our men now participate in a wide range of outside activities—giving talks at trade meet-

[1] Reported in "The Brass Gets a Quick Polish," *Business Week,* June 18, 1966, pp. 182-184.
[2] *Ibid.,* p. 182.

ings, serving as officers in trade associations, etc. The program has not only improved them as individuals, it has brought in new business to the company."[3]

Analysis

1. Do you think that this program was justified?

2. Can you see any negative effects of this program?

[3] *Ibid.*, p. 184.

"SEMINARMANIA"

Executive seminars ranging from two-day meetings on sales techniques to ten-day sensitivity training sessions are very much in vogue. As the title of a recent magazine article suggests, "There's No Business Like Seminar Business."[1] The American Management Association makes its $10 million annual income principally from some 1500 seminar-type meetings. An estimated 18,000 trade associations and consultants and more than 2000 private and public educational institutions run business seminars.[2]

Some executives are beginning to question the tangible benefits of these seminars. For example, a president who attended numerous executive seminars states: "Many are a waste of time, too academic and unrealistic in what they teach. Some merely set up rules as they go along. As a matter of fact it's hard to tell whether any have been effective."[3] Other critics claim that the seminar often becomes an unrealistic platform for academic "experts."

Analysis

1. Are these criticisms justified?

2. What are some advantages of executive seminar meetings?

3. Who should attend these types of seminars?

[1] "There's No Business Like Seminar Business," *Dun's Review*, September 1967, pp. 36-37, 93-98.

[2] *Ibid.*, p. 36.
[3] *Ibid.*, p. 37.

READING: MANAGEMENT GAMING: A PRACTICAL EXERCISE

RICHARD M. HODGETTS

For hundreds of years people have been intrigued by the game of chess. The large number of combinations that can be employed with the pieces presents a dynamic challenge to both participants. Thus, a good player, while developing his strategy, is constantly aware of his opponent's moves. Playing chess has often been felt to be analogous to waging war. The pawns can be envisioned as troops, the knights as artillery, and the bishops as aircraft. The king is, of course, the people and must be protected at all costs. Thus, chess provides a simulated, or make-believe, war game.

Today, of course, generals rely little on chessboards to provide them with experience in protecting their countries and waging war against an enemy. We are all familiar with the war games conducted by the military. These are very complex undertakings. The general remains in his headquarters and, with his staff, he carries out a mock or make-believe attack. The experience attained by the general puts him in a good position to handle a real attack by a foreign power, as he has been practicing what to do should just such an attack come.

Virtually every American child has had a very similar experience, except that he has practiced being a manager. How many children have not passed countless hours playing Monopoly? Memories of building hotels on Boardwalk and Park Place undoubtedly spring immediately to mind. Believe it or not, that game has probably done more to make Americans business-minded than any textbook or newspaper.

Monopoly will not make a manager of you

any more than playing chess will make you a general. But it is a beginning! However, you need a more realistic environment. The general has his war games. Does management have anything similar? Indeed it does! There is such a thing as a management game. Its purpose is to acquaint the participants with managing. All participants are divided into teams. Each team represents a company, and all teams compete against each other. The game permits each team to make decisions and see how well it has done. Other decisions can then be made. "Learning by doing" is stressed. If you had to explain to someone how Monopoly is played, you might find it easier to abandon a depth explanation and rather let him learn by playing. Your understanding of how a management game works can also be best explained by having you play it. The game that has been written in this article is very simple, yet it contains the essence of what the most sophisticated management games have. Here is a chance for you to practice being a top level manager.

UR OWN COMPANY
(Management Simulation)

Rules for Playing the Game

1. There should be 5 to 8 members per team. One should be elected president and the others should be assigned roles in the areas of advertising, salesman, R&D, and the purchase of market information. The president's responsibility is to see that there is coordination in the firm and ensure that the form is filled out and submitted to the umpire.

This paper was specially prepared for this book. Dr. Hodgetts is an Assistant Professor of Management at the University of Nebraska.

2. All teams start with the same amount of money—$200,000.

3. Each team is competing with the others for sales.

4. Each team is selling heavy equipment within three geographic areas of the United States—West, Central, and East.

5. Each team has one plant which produces 10 machines per quarter. (Each decision period constitutes a quarter.) Production cannot be increased or decreased.

6. These 10 machines are sold throughout the three geographic areas. The gross profit from each machine is $12,000. Cost of goods and salesmen's salaries have already been deducted.

7. In order to sell these machines, it is necessary to use salesmen and advertising.

8. Each team has 12 salesmen. This number remains constant throughout the game.

9. Each team divides its salesmen within the three areas. (Naturally, the greater the number of salesmen, the greater the opportunity of making a sale.)

10. The cost of each page of advertising is $5000. Each page affects only the area in which it is purchased. Hence, if a team places five pages of advertising in the Central area, this expenditure does not help its sales in the Eastern or Western area.

11. Each team decides if it wishes to invest any money in research and development (R&D). R&D improves the quality of the machine and thereby increase the demand for it. By investing money in R&D a "product improvement" can be obtained. This is merely a patent that will lead to an increased demand. If one team obtains a product improvement, all other teams are informed of it, so that they can take some action if they wish. R&D must be invested in blocks of $10,000.

12. There are a given number of machines being demanded throughout the entire three areas. This total figure can be obtained by purchasing market information for $10,000. Although it does not tell the team the number of machines demanded *per area*, if purchased on a regular basis it gives a trend on the total sales picture. This information should be purchased before filling out the form.

Decision Making

From the above rules, the team must make four decisions:

1. Determine whether to purchase the total sales potential for the three areas (cost of $10,000).

2. Distribute the 12 salesmen in the three areas.

3. Decide how much advertising to do in each area (each page of advertising costs $5000).

4. Decide how much will be invested in R&D this quarter (R&D is invested in blocks of $10,000).

Example

Let us run through a practice quarter (Quarter 1, Year 1) with an imaginary team. First, it must make the four decisions. Then the team fills out the following form and gives it to an umpire. The umpire computes the sales and returns the form. The team finishes filling it out. This constitutes a quarter of play.

For example, let us assume that a team made the following four decisions:

1. The team decided to purchase market information. The president tells the umpire, and he informs them that the total sales potential is 90 machines.

2. The team placed four salesmen in each area.

3. The team decided on three pages of advertising in each area.

4. The team feels that $40,000 in R&D is needed.

These four decisions are then filled in on the form as in Fig. 1.

EXAMPLE DECISION FORM

_1_ Quarter
_1_ Year

	West	Central	East
Number of Salesmen Assigned	*4*	*4*	*4*
Dollar Amount of Advertising Spent in Area	*$ 15,000*	*$ 15,000*	*$15,000*
Sales (Filled in by Umpire)			

Amount Invested in R&D $ *40,000*

Product Improvement
This Quarter
(Filled in by Umpire)

_____Yes _____No

Profit and Loss
   Sales $_____
   Expenses $_____
   Profit $_____

Balance Sheet
   Beginning Cash $_____
   Profit(+) or Loss(−) $_____
   Ending Cash $_____

Figure 1

This form is picked up by the umpire who then indicates that four machines have been sold in areas 1 and 2, and two machines in area 3. The form, as it would be returned by the umpire, is shown in Fig. 2.

EXAMPLE DECISION FORM

_1_ Quarter
_1_ Year

	West	Central	East
Number of Salesmen Assigned	*4*	*4*	*4*
Dollar Amount of Advertising Spent in Area	*$ 15,000*	*$ 15,000*	*$15,000*
Sales (Filled in by Umpire)	*4*	*4*	*2*

Amount Invested in R&D $ *40,000*

Product Improvement
This Quarter
(Filled in by Umpire)

_✔_ Yes _____No

Figure 2

Upon receiving the information from the umpire the team merely has to fill in the Profit and Loss statement and the Balance Sheet. They would be completed as shown in Fig. 3.

Profit and Loss
   Sales $ *120,000*
   Expenses $ *95,000*
   Profit $ *25,000*

Balance Sheet
   Beginning Cash $ *200,000*
   Profit(+) or Loss(−) $ *25,000*
   Ending Cash $ *225,000*

Figure 3

Since 10 units were sold at $12,000 each, sales are $120,000. Advertising cost $45,000 (3 x $15,000) and R&D $40,000. Market information cost $10,000. Thus, expenses are $95,000 and profit would be $25,000. By adding this profit to the beginning cash with which the team started the game, $200,000, the ending cash balance of $225,000 is arrived at. The latter figure then becomes beginning cash in Quarter 2, Year 1. You should now be ready to play "Ur Own Company" game. Good Luck!

DECISION FORM

_____Quarter
_____Year

	West	Central	East
Number of Salesmen Assigned			
Dollar Amount of Advertising Spent in Area			
Sales (Filled in by Umpire)			

Amount Invested in R&D $_____

Product Improvement
This Quarter
(Filled in by Umpire)

_____Yes   _____No

Profit and Loss
    Sales $_____
    Expenses $_____
    Profit $_____

Balance Sheet
    Beginning Cash $_____
    Profit(+) or Loss(−) $_____
    Ending Cash $_____

Figure 4

READING: COMPUTERIZED MANAGEMENT GAMING

LESTER A. DIGMAN

Over the past few years, management games have come to be an important addition to the "tool kit" of the management development specialist. Even though games have been shown to be complementary to, rather than substitutes for, other managerial training tools, they do have certain rather unique advantages. For example, games, especially computerized games, can inject an element of realism into a training situation that the more conventional techniques are hard-pressed to duplicate. The gaming session gives the participant involvement—he is "living the situation," hence he has to "live with" both his decisions and those of his competitors. Thus, the gaming session can become a "dynamic case study," providing the participant with rapid feedback of the results of his decisions, rather than conjectural analysis by his instructor.

Games do have their disadvantages, however; they are only as "good" as the underlying model. In addition, games cannot provide the equivalent of experience in business, but they can provide one of the most important components thereof, "experience in learning from experience." It is this ability, the ability to adapt, that is of critical importance in today's rapidly changing world of management.

Although games can vary in complexity from those requiring only one or two decisions per period of play to complex, computerized simulations requiring hundreds of decisions, complexity alone does not indicate quality. The worth of a game can better be judged by the *kinds* of decisions a team must make, rather than by the number of total decisions.

This paper was specially written for this book. Mr. Digman is an Instructor of Management at the University of Iowa.

The more complex games, however, are generally more realistic—more like the real world than their less sophisticated counterparts. The choice of the game, then, depends upon the administrator's goals for his training session. The following section describes a relatively complex, computerized game designed to teach general management relationships.

EXECUTIVE MANAGEMENT GAME[1]

Introduction

The business simulation exercise is introduced to help you learn more about business in particular and management in general. The more specific objectives are to (1) increase your abilities to solve problems, (2) improve your decision-making processes, and (3) illustrate the complex relationships that exist among the major decision areas of business.

You have been assigned to individual companies, with each company responsible for determining its own objectives, goals, and organizational structure. Each company is in competition with all other companies and interacts with them; that is, the firm's decisions influence and are influenced by all other decisions made in all of the competitive companies, as well as by the economic environment.

Participants in the Executive Management

[1] This management game is a multifirm, two-product, deterministic, computerized top management game developed by the author at the University of Iowa under the guidance of Professor J. M. Liittschwager. The underlying model is essentially an extensive modification of the UCLA Executive Decision Game No. 2, a multifirm, one-product game developed by James R. Jackson and others at the University of California at Los Angeles.

Game act as top-management teams representing firms competing in a manufacturing industry. The "firms" may organize the responsibilities within the group as the members desire, but the following decisions are required each quarter:

1. For the firm:
   (*a*) Additional Investment in Plant
   (*b*) Additions or Payoffs on Bonds and Bank Loans
   (*c*) Payment of Dividends to stockholders, and
   (*d*) Whether or not to split the common stock
2. For each product:
   (*a*) Unit sales price
   (*b*) Advertising Budget, in $
   (*c*) Research and Development Budget, in $, and
   (*d*) Production Volume

The teams, acting as top-management, control their firms by entering the above decisions for the quarter on their Decision Forms.

On the basis of these decisions an Operating Statement (Fig. 1) is calculated and printed by the computer and presented to the firm in question. On the basis of this "feedback information" of the previous quarter's results, the teams arrive at decisions for the subsequent quarter.

It is important for each firm to realize that the industry in question is unique in that specific experiences from the game may not apply to a particular real world industry. That is, the assumptions governing the mathematical model of the game are designed to resemble a representative, rather than specific, manufacturing industry.

Market Information

Each participating firm may manufacture and sell up to two individual products. The products may be considered to be noncompetitive lines or models of the same type of product. One of the products has been considered as a quality line (Product Q), and the other may be considered as its lower-priced, economy counterpart (Product E).

The potential market for each of the two products is determined by similar, but distinct, relationships depending primarily upon product price, research effort, selling effort, and the general economic level of the industry.

PRICE. Demand for each of the products varies inversely with price, with the Product E demand curve being slightly more elastic than Product Q's. The market overreacts somewhat to any change in price from that of the previous quarter.

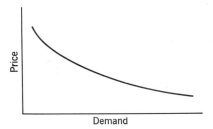

R&D. The effective research effort, which determines the relative quality of the product within its category of Q or E, depends to a large extent on the level of research expenditures in the previous several quarters (this effect is more pronounced in the case of Q than for E). In addition, the effect of R&D expenditures is subject to the "law of diminishing returns."

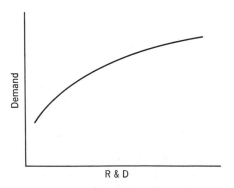

ADVERTISING. The effective advertising effort, like R&D, depends upon past advertising expenditures, but the effects of current advertising expenditures are felt much more quickly than R&D. Advertising is also subject to the law of diminishing returns and, like R&D, is independent between the two products.

ECONOMIC INDEX. The Economic Index for

the industry has a direct effect upon the potential market for each firm. In general, product demand increases with an increase in this index, but the increase is more pronounced for Q than for E; that is, the market shifts somewhat toward Q as the Economic Index is raised.

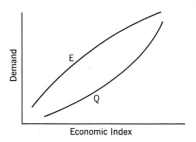

Plant and Equipment

The Plant and Equipment is valued at $20 per unit of total capacity, and replacement costs are equal to this figure. The capacity is interchangeable between Q and E, valued at $20 for each. The depreciation rate (capacity and valuation) is 2.5% per quarter. Excess plant and equipment cannot be sold; depreciation is the only means available to reduce plant capacity. If you wish plant capacity to remain the same you must allocate 2½% of present plant value to *Plant Investment*. If you wish to increase plant capacity, you must allocate at $20 per additional unit of capacity desired to *Plant Investment*. This allocation is in addition to 2½% allocated to maintain present capacity.

Manufacturing Costs

The manufacturing costs are roughly doubled for each unit that is produced (Production Volume Decision) in excess of the available plant capacity, due to added costs from overtime and purchasing from other manufacturers. Inventory is valued on the basis of manufacturing costs per unit.

Administration and Selling

The Administration and Selling Expense reflects expenses in the following areas: supporting departments, such as Personnel, Administrative Services, and other staff functions; and sales force salary and expenses. Therefore, this expense includes variable and fixed factors, and may be expected to vary with the available plant capacity.

Miscellaneous Expense

The Miscellaneous Expenses can be expected to include the indirect costs of production, inventory carrying charges, and additional expenses due to "crash programs" for plant expansion and sudden capacity increases. As a guideline, Plant Investment should not exceed $2,000,000 for any quarter.

Liabilities

Two types of liabilities are present for each firm. Bank loans are available with an interest and carrying charge of 6% per annum. Bonds may be purchased at 4% per annum, and may not be reduced for a specified period following issuance. Both loans may be increased at any time, and no borrowing costs are incurred.

Stock Market

Each firm is issued 400,000 shares of common stock at $20 per share. Due to economic growth the market value is $40 for each firm at the start of the game. The following factors influence the market value of the firm's stock; dividend policy, company growth and sales factors, and industry factors, such as the Economic Index and growth in total industry market. The firms may effect a two-for-one stock split at any time, but this should not be done if the current market quotation is at a "low level."

Tax Fund

The income tax fund is calculated on the basis of 48% of the net income, and allows tax credits for periods of negative profits.

Operating Statements

The Operating Statements (Fig. 1) are calculated in accordance with generally accepted

```
OPERATING STATEMENT
FIRM      6    PERIOD        0

                        PRODUCT Q        PRODUCT E
SALES VOLUME              214127.          558047.
PCT OF INDUSTRY SALES       11.11            11.11
UNITS OF INVENTORY        110873.          171953.
MANUFACTURING COSTS   $   780882.     $  1395323.
CAPACITY NEXT QUARTER                               770000.

                PROFIT AND LOSS STATEMENT

INCOME
   NET SALES REVENUE                           $  4675215.
EXPENSES
      MANUFACTURING COSTS           $  2176205.
      REDUCTION IN INVENTORY VALUE  $  -141454.
      DEPRECIATION                  $   385000.
      ADMINISTRATION AND SELLING    $   442500.
      ADVERTISING                   $   404000.
      RESEARCH AND DEVELOPMENT      $   569000.
      MISCELLANEOUS EXPENSES        $   285013.
TOTAL EXPENSES                                 $  4120264.
   INTEREST AND CARRYING CHARGES               $     6500.
NET INCOME                                     $   548451.
ADDITION TO FEDERAL INCOME TAX FUND            $   263256.
PROFIT FOR THE PERIOD                          $   285194.
DIVIDENDS PAID                                 $   100000.
   ADDITION TO OWNERS EQUITY                   $   185194.


SHARES OF COMMON STOCK OUTSTANDING              400000.
EARNINGS/SHARE OF COMMON STOCK         $            0.71
STOCK MARKET QUOTATION                 $           40.00
AVERAGE STOCK MARKET QUOTATION         $           40.00


                    BALANCE SHEET

            ASSETS                   LIABILITIES AND OWNERS EQUITY

CURRENT ASSETS                   CURRENT LIABILITIES
   CASH               $  3043741.     BANK LOAN          $   100000.
   INVENTORY                     LONG TERM LIABILITIES
   PRODUCT  Q $  384794.            BONDS              $   500000.
   PRODUCT  E $  413671.  $  798465.   TOTAL LIABILITIES           $   600000.
                                 OWNERS EQUITY
FIXED ASSETS                        CAPITAL STOCK               $  8000000.
   PLANT AND EQUIPMENT  $ 15400000.   SURPLUS                   $ 10642206.
TOTAL ASSETS           $ 19242206. TOTAL LIABILITIES AND OWNERS EQUITY $ 19242206.
```

DECISION FORM #1
Firm No. _____

Quarter No.	Stock Split	Selling Price		Advertising Expenditure		R & D Expenditure	
		Q	E	Q	E	Q	E
Trial							
1							
2							
3							
4							
5							
6							
7							
8							
9							
10							
11							
12							

DECISION FORM #2
Firm No. _____

Quarter No.	Production Volume		Plant Investment	Dividends Paid	Liability Reduction	
	Q	E			Bank Loans	Bonds
Trial						
1						
2						
3						
4						
5						
6						
7						
8						
9						
10						
11						
12						

accounting procedures and should be self-explanatory. If not, you may wish to review the pamphlet, *How to Read a Financial Report*.

Company Objectives

The first thing you should do, as a part of a management team, is to get together and determine your corporate objectives. Objectives may vary widely from one group to another and there is no one "correct" set of objectives. Your management team will be evaluated based on the reasonableness of its objectives and the degree to which the objectives are met. The objectives should be written out in detail and if the objectives are later found to be lacking in terms of coverage and/or specifics, they can be amended in writing. These objectives are to be turned in with the second-quarter decisions.